PROCEDURAL JUSTICE

LAW AND PHILOSOPHY LIBRARY

VOLUME 10

MICHAEL D. BAYLES
Department of Philosophy,
Florida State University

PROCEDURAL JUSTICE

Allocating to Individuals

KLUWER ACADEMIC PUBLISHERS
DORDRECHT / BOSTON / LONDON

Library of Congress Cataloging in Publication Data

Bayles, Michael D.
Procedural justice : allocating to individuals / Michael D. Bayles.
p. cm. -- (Law and philosophy library)
Includes bibliographical references.
ISBN 0-7923-0567-1
1. Law--Methodology. 2. Judicial process. 3. Law--Philosophy. I. Title. II. Series.
K212.B39 1990
340'.1--dc20 89-24643

ISBN 0–7923–0567–1

Published by Kluwer Academic Publishers,
P.O. Box 17, 3300 AA Dordrecht, The Netherlands.

Kluwer Academic Publishers incorporates
the publishing programmes of
D. Reidel, Martinus Nijhoff, Dr W. Junk and MTP Press.

Sold and distributed in the U.S.A. and Canada
by Kluwer Academic Publishers,
101 Philip Drive, Norwell, MA 02061, U.S.A.

In all other countries, sold and distributed
by Kluwer Academic Publishers Group,
P.O. Box 322, 3300 AH Dordrecht, The Netherlands.

Printed on acid-free paper

Printed in the Netherlands

CONTENTS

EDITORIAL PREFACE

During the last half of the twentieth century, legal philosophy (or legal theory or jurisprudence) has grown significantly. It is no longer the domain of a few isolated scholars in law and philosophy. Hundreds of scholars from diverse fields attend international meetings on the subject. In some universities, large lecture courses of five hundred students or more study it.

The primary aim of the Law and Philosophy Library is to present some of the best original work on legal philosophy from both the Anglo-American and European traditions. Not only does it help make some of the best work available to an international audience, but it also encourages increased awareness of, and interaction between, the two major traditions. The primary focus is on full-length scholary monographs, although some edited volumes of original papers are also included. The Library editors are assisted by an Editorial Advisory Board of internationally renowned scholars.

Legal philosophy should not be considered a narrowly circumscribed field. Insights into law and legal institutions can come from diverse disciplines on a wide range of topics. Among the relevant disciplines or perspectives contributing to legal philosophy, besides law and philosophy, are anthropology, economics, political science, and sociology. Among the topics included in legal philosophy are theories of law; the concepts of law and legal institutions; legal reasoning and adjudication; epistemological issues of evidence and procedure; law and justice, economics, politics, or morality; legal ethics; and theories of legal fields such as criminal law, contracts, and property.

MANAGING EDITORS

ACKNOWLEDGMENTS

This book grew out of my work on procedural law for a previous book. I became convinced that philosophers had ignored issues of procedural justice and that often proper procedures were more important than substantive principles for the practical achievement of aims. Thus, I set out to write a book exploring the philosophical and ethical basis of procedural justice. However, as it developed the book became more one of legal philosophy than ethics. Philosophers have written little on procedural justice, so most research materials were in law. There seemed no point in trying to develop a strictly ethical theory until I had a firm grasp of the legal matters. Moreover, like myself in the beginning, most philosophers are unaware of the legal analyses. Consequently, Part I of the book largely elucidates current legal principles. Part II develops a theoretical framework for law and ethics. Part III then illustrates how that framework applies to two important areas.

As usual, my thoughts on the subject were greatly clarified in teaching two courses related to it, one at the University of Western Ontario in 1984 and the other at the University of Florida in 1986. I wish to thank the students in those courses. Eric Baker, my research assistant at the University of Florida during the Spring 1986, performed invaluable library research. Joseph Grcic read a draft of the entire manuscript and gave some general comments. Work on the manuscript was partially supported by a Research Development Award and a Graduate Research Assistantship from the Division of Sponsored Research, University of Florida. Two until recently anonymous referees—Carl Wellman and Timothy Terrell—provided helpful comments on the penultimate draft, although I am confident they will think it could still have been improved.

For preparation of camera-ready copy, I thank Florene Ball, and especially Donald Herget for much work on the tables and diagrams and final printing.

Parts of the manuscript are significantly revised versions of previously published material. Four paragraphs in section two of chapter 1 and the first six of section two of chapter 7 are taken from "Procedural Due Process," in *Philosophical Foundations of the Constitution*, edited by Diana T. Meyers and Kenneth Kipnis (Boulder, Colo: Westview Press, 1989), pp. 207 and 210-12, copyright © 1988 by Westview Press, Inc. Finally, two paragraphs of the third section of chapter 1, a paragraph in chapter 5, the first three sections of chapter 6, and the first section of chapter 8 are drawn from *Principles of Law* (Dordrecht: D. Reidel Publishing Co., 1987), §§ 1.2, 2.3.9, 2.1.1-2.1.3, and 2.2.

LIST OF ABBREVIATIONS

ABA	American Bar Association
APA	Administrative Procedure Act, 5 U.S.C. (1978)
Cdn. Charter	Canadian Charter of Rights and Freedoms, Constitution Act, 1981
CE	Council of Europe
IEEE	Institute for Electrical & Electronics Engineers
LRCC	Law Reform Commission of Canada
MSA	National Conference of Commissioners on Uniform State Laws, Model State Administrative Procedure Act (1981)
OAS	Organization of American States
RSA	National Conference of Commissioners on Uniform State Laws, Revised Model State Administrative Procedure Act (1961)
UN	United Nations

CHAPTER 1

INTRODUCTION

Issues of procedural justice pervade modern society. They arise within families in making collective decisions, allocating household chores, and disciplining children. Education is replete with procedural justice issues, from student admissions through grading to certification for graduation. The justice of procedures for making employment decisions—hiring, firing, promotions, and awarding merit pay—are often challenged. Questions of procedural justice also arise in various other areas of daily life—methods for determining the credit rating of individuals and allocating scarce resources such as donated organs. Even minor everyday activities such as checking out at a grocery store can involve procedural justice, as when people enter line ahead of others. When government interacts with citizens, procedural justice is almost always relevant; methods for determining eligibility for benefits such as social security and welfare, awarding contracts, appraising property for taxes, granting and revoking drivers' licenses, and imposing criminal sanctions can all be just or unjust. Issues of procedural justice also pertain to elections and methods of legislative decision making.

Lawyers are more aware of procedural justice issues than any other group in society, because procedure plays a central role in the law. Justice Felix Frankfurter remarked that "[t]he history of liberty has largely been the history of procedural safeguards" (*McNabb v. United States*, 318 U.S. 332, 347 (1943)). Justice Douglas commented, "It is not without significance that most of the provisions of the Bill of Rights are procedural. It is procedure that spells much of the difference between rule by law and rule by whim or caprice" (*Joint Anti-Fascist Refugee Comm. v. McGrath*, 341 U.S. 123, 179 (1951)). Kenneth Culp Davis's claim that "the essence of justice is largely procedural" is an exaggeration, but it is not as far off the mark as one might suppose (Davis 1972, 192). Despite the pervasiveness and importance of procedural justice, philosophers have largely ignored the topic. The philosophical literature since Aristotle has divided justice into distributive and rectificatory (or retributive) justice. Procedural justice is not even accorded a place in the classificatory scheme! The vast bulk of philosophical literature on justice, especially during the latter half of this century, has focused on distributive justice (see also Davis

1977, 444). Most of the legal literature focuses on the justice of particular procedures without articulating a general theory to support the claims made. General considerations of procedural justice have centered on procedural law, natural justice in administration, and the "due process" clauses of the U.S. Constitution (amends. V, XIV(1)). This book is a modest attempt to redress the balance by considering principles of procedural justice for one type of decision.

Procedural Contexts

Issues of procedural justice arise in at least three different contexts which might require different analyses. One context is that of group decision making. One subdivision of this context concerns deciding issues. *Robert's Rules of Order* and other rules for conducting meetings constitute procedures that can be just or unjust. Another subdivision concerns choosing officers or representatives. Procedures for electing legislators are not the same as those for legislative debates and actions, yet both involve collective or group decision making. Although a completely general theory of procedural justice would encompass procedures for collective decision making, they are not considered here. One reason for omitting them is simply that the issues of procedural justice are too many to be considered in one book. Another reason is that decision theorists and others have examined many of the problems that arise in group decision making, such as weighted voting and the effect of the order in which issues are presented.

A second context of procedural justice issues is resolving conflicts between two or more parties. Conflicts are typically settled by appeals to strength (fighting or coercion), negotiation, mediation, counseling, arbitration, or adjudication. Many of these issues arise in legal procedure. Although there is considerable discussion of adjudication, conflict resolution procedures are not the focus of this book. I have addressed justifiable procedures for legal adjudication elsewhere (Bayles 1987, chap. 2). A vast legal literature also exists about particular problems in these areas.

This book focuses on procedural justice in the context of decisions to impose burdens or to confer benefits on individuals—burden/benefit decisions. The individuals can be either natural persons or organizations such as corporations. Benefit-conferring decisions encompass such matters as entitlement to social security or welfare, awarding grants or merit pay, admission to college or an intensive care unit, and hiring. Sometimes these decisions involve evaluating individuals against a standard or norm, for example, has an individual met the conditions for receiving social security disability payments. Other burden/benefit decisions involve comparing individuals against one another on the basis of some standard or norm. For example, merit pay is usually competitive. Individuals are judged by some standard, then compared with one another, and the benefit conferred depends on one's comparative ranking. These latter decisions will be called 'competitive', and the former 'noncompetitive' decisions. When no modifier is used, both types are included.

Burden/benefit decisions are often presented as conflict resolution ones. For example, if two companies are competing for a television station license, the Federal Communications Commission may hold a hearing in which each side presents its case. Noncompetitive decisions are also sometimes formulated as conflict resolution ones. The most obvious example is the Anglo-American criminal trial. A criminal trial involves a noncompetitive evaluation of an individual against substantive criminal law standards, yet it poses the issue as a conflict between two parties—the prosecution and defendant. Indeed, a major legal trend, at least in the United States, has been to convert burden/benefit decisions into conflict resolution ones. This has contributed to principles for adjudication being the dominant legal conception of procedural justice in this context. However, in many situations the full adversary adjudication model is inappropriate. One of the main questions to be considered is when it or another model is appropriate.

Some Distinctions

Procedure and substance Procedural justice is contrasted with substantive justice. Most people have a common-sense grasp of the difference. Procedure concerns the process or steps taken in arriving at a decision; substance concerns the content of the decision. The two are conceptually distinct, for one can use different procedures for the same substantive issue and the same procedure for different substantive issues. Hence, a substantive topic cannot imply a procedure, nor a given procedure imply a particular substantive topic.

Recently, in the context of U.S. constitutional law, some people have denied that substance and procedure can or should be distinguished. Suppose Aileen has a right to continued employment except when dismissed for good cause.

One argument is that the existence of good cause, and thus the extent of the right, depends on the procedure provided for determining its existence (*Arnett v. Kennedy*, 416 U.S. 134, 152–54 (1973)). This argument, however, confuses the truth of a proposition (that good cause exists) with a method for determining its truth.

Another argument is that one can convert a substantive matter into a procedural one. For example, Aileen's right could be stated as a procedural right to appeal dismissal and to be reinstated if it was shown to have occurred without good cause (Mashaw 1987, 436). The very posing of this claim, however, presupposes the distinction. The right to appeal is taken as procedural rather than substantive. Moreover, one can distinguish a substantive element, namely, whether good cause existed, from the procedure. One might generally classify the right as a procedural one because that is dominant in the description, but the two elements can be distinguished.

A third argument is that in evaluating a substantive rule one must consider the procedures by which it is applied (Alexander 1987, esp. 325, 328). The procedures used to apply it will affect the consequences of adopting the rule and thus its merits. Although much can be said for this claim as a normative view, it does not imply that one cannot separately evaluate the substance of rules and procedures for their application or that it is never useful to do so. Aileen's right not to be dismissed except for good cause is preferable to a right not to be dismissed except for religious or political deviation, regardless of the procedures used to implement either. Moreover, onc can plausibly claim that a hearing before an impartial decisionmaker is a better procedure for either right than trial by ordeal.

This is not to deny that substance can be significant for what procedure is appropriate. But usually a procedure is good or bad for a broad range of subjects. Thus, criminal procedure is thought appropriate for all crimes; few distinctions are made in the appropriateness of procedure depending on the crime. Civil procedure is virtually the same whether the subject be property, contract, or other civil matters. Even the old procedural distinctions between law and equity have largely vanished. Hence, whatever the merits of merging procedure and substance in constitutional law (which I think are none; see Bayles 1988), it can be useful to consider procedures by themselves.

Pure, perfect, and imperfect procedural justice Perhaps the major exception to the claim that recent philosophers have neglected procedural justice is the contribution of John Rawls (1971, 85–86). He distinguishes between pure, perfect, and imperfect procedural justice. Pure procedural justice occurs when whatever the outcome of a procedure, it is just. No independent standard of a just outcome exists, and its justice is determined by the procedure. For example, in a fair game of chance, such as roulette or the toss of a die, any outcome in a particular case is just. Of course, the roulette wheel or die must be fair, and the determination of a fair die or wheel is dependent on the outcomes in a series of cases. That is, a fair die is one that in a infinite series of tosses would turn up one number as frequently as another. In a particular toss, however, any actual outcome is just.

Perfect and imperfect procedural justice differ from pure procedural justice in that independent criteria of the justice of particular outcomes exist. Procedures are evaluated by their producing just outcomes in particular cases. Perfect procedural justice characterizes those procedures, if any, that always give just outcomes. Assuming an equal desire for some good to be distributed among a number of persons, say, a pie, if one person divides the good (cuts the pie into pieces) and chooses last, then everyone will get an equal-sized piece. Imperfect procedural justice characterizes procedures that are not guaranteed to produce a just outcome in each case. One is thus led to evaluate such procedures instrumentally by their likelihood of producing just results.

Rawls's conception of pure procedural justice has been challenged (Nelson 1980; see also Davis 1982, 100–01). Although such situations certainly exist, the explanation, it is claimed, is not that some characteristic of the procedures transfers to the justice of the outcome. Instead, all such examples, like betting on a roulette wheel or a bargained-for sale of property, can be explained (and justified?) by people's entitlement to the money or property involved and their voluntarily exercising their rights. Indeed, even gambling on a game of chance in which one's mathematical expectation of gain is less than zero can be justified by entitlement and voluntary agreement.

This argument is not completely persuasive. One can distinguish between 'justice' as meaning 'justifiable everything considered' and as 'justifiable in a particular respect' (having a just-making feature). The above argument at best shows that entitlement and voluntary exercise of rights are sufficient to establish the moral permissibility of an action or interaction. Yet, there might still be features that are unjust or unfair even if outweighed by other considerations. For example, if the betting odds in a lottery favor the state, even if a person knowingly and voluntarily plays, there is an unjust aspect. One could credibly claim that a lottery that did not favor the state as much would be more fair or just. Similarly, people often think that a contract is unfair or unjust if one party has great bargaining power over another, even if the weaker party knowingly and voluntarily agrees to it.

The conditions of voluntariness and entitlement collapse into a procedural requirement of voluntariness. The requirement of voluntary participation imposes procedural restrictions—no use of force or fraud. Voluntariness is not a substantive matter; it is a procedural one. It has to do with how the participation came about or how a decision was made. One can voluntarily decide to do or not to do something, so voluntariness is independent of the outcome (participating or not participating). Not being entitled to property gambled or exchanged amounts to fraud, for one's conduct implies that one has the right to transfer it. Thus, if a person was not entitled to the property used and the other person was not aware of this, that person would not voluntarily participate. If the other person was aware, then he or she voluntarily agreed. Of course, gambling with another's property can be unjust to that person, but it does not make the gambling transaction itself unjust. Consequently, this condition of entitlement reduces to voluntary participation.

Voluntary agreement to a procedure cannot be the fundamental basis for the justice of procedures. First, the unfairness or injustice of a procedure can be given as a reason for not voluntarily participating in an activity. If voluntary participation made the procedure just, then this reasoning would be circular. The procedure could not be unjust if one voluntarily participated, so one cannot give its injustice as a reason for not voluntarily participating. Second, voluntary agreement cannot justify itself as a just procedure. The principle that voluntarily agreed to procedures are just cannot be justified by being voluntarily accepted.

Because voluntary participation is itself a procedural principle, albeit a subordinate one, it supports the claim that justice in procedures can transfer to the justice of outcomes. If just procedures could not (at least partially) justify outcomes, then only perfect or imperfect procedural justice would be possible. More importantly, procedural justice would have to be a solely instrumental value—procedures would be just insofar, and only insofar, as they produced correct or just outcomes.

A central issue, discussed in chapter 6, is whether procedural justice for burden/benefit decisions is a purely instrumental value. It readily appears to be a form of imperfect procedural justice. Standards by which individuals are to be evaluated provide independent criteria for evaluating just outcomes. The outcomes are just when they are a correct application of substantively just standards. So, as long as such standards are available, burden/benefit decisions cannot be pure procedural justice. Rarely if ever can procedures be devised that always yield just outcomes as determined by an independent standard, so perfect procedural justice is irrelevant. However, it does not follow that the only grounds for procedural justice are instrumental. Some features of procedures might contribute to their justice but not to the correctness of outcomes.

Burden imposing, benefit conferring, benefit terminating, and burden relieving Thus far burden and benefit decisions have been mentioned as though there were no difficulty distinguishing them. Unfortunately, matters are otherwise. Imposition of a burden makes a person worse off. A typical uncontroversially burden-imposing decision is one to punish an individual for commission of a crime. Conferral of a benefit makes a person better off. A typical benefit-conferring decision is the award of a grant or promotion. However, some decisions might be viewed as either the refusal to confer a benefit or the imposition of a burden.

Consider a decision to cease providing a person unemployment insurance payments. As something is being taken away, namely, payments, one might view the decision as imposing a burden. Alternatively, as providing unemployment insurance payments is conferring a benefit, one might view the decision as a refusal to confer future benefits. The difference between these two views is what is taken as the baseline. If the baseline is the person receiving payments, then cessation of payments makes the person worse off and imposes a burden. If the baseline is the person's situation before receiving payments, then cessation of payments leaves the person in the baseline condition and is therefore a refusal to provide a benefit. Some of the more controversial issues of procedural justice arise in such ambiguous cases.

Benefit-terminating decisions are those to cease providing benefits that the decisionmaker or organization the decisionmaker represents previously decided to provide. A decision to cease social security disability payments is a benefit-terminating decision. The agency previously decided to make the payments and is now changing its decision. Deprivation of liberty for commission of a crime is not a benefit-terminating decision, because the criminal justice system did not previously grant freedom. If liberty is generally granted at all (which is unlikely), it is by the constitution or an act of the legislature for all citizens and not the result of a determination about the individual in question.

Burden-relieving decisions correspond to benefit-terminating decisions. The former cease imposing a burden that was previously imposed on the individual. The decision to impose the burden must have been made by the person making the decision, by an organization that person represents, or by a person or organization with the task of imposing such burdens. The burden-relieving decisionmaker has the task of determining when it should cease. This complicated set of conditions regarding the imposition of the burden is needed to distinguish certain types of cases. For example, if my daughter is being charged interest on her unpaid credit card balance and I pay off her debt so that the interest is no longer charged, my decision or action is a benefit-conferring one, not a burden-relieving one. The credit card company, not I, decided (with her advance consent) to impose the interest. In contrast, the decision of a parole board to grant parole is normally a burden-relieving decision. Although a court, not the parole board, imposed the burden, the task of deciding to relieve that burden is assigned to the parole board. (The preceding four paragraphs are from Bayles 1988, 210–11.)

Justice and morality On various grounds, some philosophers distinguish between principles of justice and other moral principles. Principles of justice might be said to be those based on rights or those that can be enforced by coercion. No such distinction is made here. All normative principles about procedures for burden/benefit decisions are here included in procedural justice.

One might, then, challenge the use of 'justice' for these principles, or at least all of them. Some principles or parts of them will be based on efficiency or other considerations, such as minimizing disputes. Surely efficiency is to be contrasted with justice.

Two responses are possible. First, all of the various principles can be used to justify procedural requirements. One could, then, contend that the subjects of procedures have rights to the required procedures. They can justifiably claim that the procedures be followed and have grievances if they are not. As thus generating claim-rights, the principles establish justice (as rights). However, we will not consider whether the particular requirements should be treated as claim-rights. One might still complain that this does not make the principles themselves principles of justice.

Second, there are reasons for using 'justice' in a broad sense to cover all the justifiable principles of procedure. One reason for the broader use here is the straightforward connection to issues of justice. Substantive justice (distributive and rectificatory) concerns the allocation of burdens and benefits among individuals and groups. Burden/benefit decisions make such allocations and thus fall within the domain of justice. The procedures then concern the just allocations of burdens and benefits. This argument does not work for the procedural context of group decision making. This argument does not assume that an independent standard of substantive justice exists (but see Davis 1982, 100–01). To do so would beg the question about instrumental analyses of procedural justice. Another simple reason is that 'procedural justice' is the common expression for this topic. Some theories are based solely on efficiency considerations, and it would be odd and misleading to say they contained no account of procedural justice. One could, of course, simply talk of the morality of procedures, and the reader can view this work as concerned with that rather than procedural justice in some narrow sense.

A Normative Method

The major aim of this book is to justify normative principles for procedures in making burden/benefit decisions. Consequently, they need to be distinguished from standards and rules. Both principles and rules are norms for human conduct. Principles can be distinguished from rules in various ways (see Raz 1972; Dworkin 1977, 22–28; Bayles 1978, 42–44). Two features are here taken to characterize principles. First, principles do not necessarily determine an evaluation and must be weighed or balanced against one another. For example, it may be a principle that people should expeditiously bring legal cases. It does not necessarily follow that a dilatory action should be barred, because a contrary principle might also apply, for example, that courts should not permit injustice. Because principles do not necessarily determine an evaluation and can conflict, principles have 'weight'. Some have more weight than others. Second, principles are usually more general and vaguer than rules. The greater generality of principles than rules pertains only when they concern the same topic. Rules are relatively clear-cut (see MacCormick 1981, 41–42, 85). In contrast to a principle that legal cases should be brought expeditiously, a rule might simply prohibit bringing an action more than two years after breach of a contract. Being clear-cut, rules are not usually weighed and balanced against one another; however, they can conflict and then one must choose which rule, if either, to follow.

Standards present criteria for evaluating things, persons, or conduct as good or bad, better or worse, and so on (see Bayles 1989, 25–26; Bayles 1978, 42–44). Unlike principles and rules, they are not limited to human conduct. Some criteria admit of degrees, for example, the amount of liquor a person is bringing into the country. Others do not, for example, whether a welfare applicant is married.

Standards can be in two different relations to principles and rules. First, standards can be incorporated into principles or rules. For example, both the principle about bringing legal cases expeditiously and the rule requiring cases to be brought within two years use the standard of time since the cause of action accrued. However, the principle picks out a vague range on the standard while the rule picks out a cut-off point (see also MacCormick 1981, 64).

Second, principles and rules can present criteria of standards. Consider the criminal law murder rule. For ordinary citizens, it functions as a rule prohibiting specific conduct. For judges and juries in murder trials, it functions as one of several criteria for a decision whether to impose a burden—punishment. If the person did not intend to kill, then he or she is not guilty of murder and so punishment for that is inappropriate. However, there are various other criteria that need to be used—justifications and excuses. One might include all the defenses as part of a rule about homicide, but it would not be perspicuous to do so. Moreover, other criteria are relevant to determining the type or amount of punishment appropriate, such as previous record, remorse, and so forth. The crucial point is that the rule about murder functions as a norm prohibiting the act of murder in the first instance. Jurors and judges use it as a criterion of a complex standard for evaluating a person and deciding whether to impose punishment and, if so, how much.

Procedural justice is not limited to legal requirements, so principles are needed for both legal and nonlegal requirements. Moral principles include both legal and ethical ones. Chapter 7 considers the extent to which procedural principles or rules should be legally required. A central claim in this book is that while the general principles of procedural justice are the same in law and ethics, enforcement costs and other considerations limit the extent to which the law should impose them.

Moral principles are justified if rational persons would accept them for use in a society in which they expected to live (Brandt 1985, 169; Brandt 1979, 10–16; Bayles 1987, 4–7; Bayles, 1978, 51–54). A rational person uses logical reasoning and all relevant available information in acquiring desires and values, deciding what to do, and accepting moral principles. Logical reasoning is not restricted to deductive logic but also includes inductive logic or scientific method. A rational person considers arguments for and against principles, accepting those for which there are sound arguments and rejecting those supported only by unsound arguments or against which there are stronger sound arguments.

All relevant available information is all pertinent information that a person in the situation can obtain. First, it is information, not necessarily knowledge, that a rational person has. Information includes more than just knowledge construed as justified true belief. Information can include false beliefs if those beliefs are the best supportable ones at the time. People are rational if they use the best information available, even if it later turns out to be incorrect. Second, information is available if it is publicly ascertainable. Available information includes publicly available scientific information as well as factual information justified by evidence accessible to the public. The information available thus varies over time.

Information is relevant to the acceptability of a moral principle if it indicates that the principle's use would advance or retard the realization of some value, disvalue, desire, or aversion. The advancing or retarding of values and disvalues is perhaps usually a consequence of a decision made in accordance with a principle. That is, conformity to the principle produces a decision that has good or bad consequences. However, the advancing or retarding of values can also be inherent in acting on a principle; acting on a procedural principle might advance or retard values independent of affecting the outcome. For example, the legal principle of harmless procedural error is that a procedural error is not a basis for overturning a decision if it did not affect the outcome in the case. Nevertheless, such an error might have adversely affected some value such as fairness. Indeed, if it did not, it is unclear why it is an error. Contrarily, conformity to the principle might have advanced fairness, but its doing so could not be the result of the particular outcome, because the same outcome occurred when it was not followed. Of course, the effect on fairness is a consequence of acting on the principle, but it is not a consequence of the particular substantive outcome. To this extent, nonconsequentialist considerations are incorporated into the method.

Although a normative basis is needed for determining the acceptability of moral principles, it need not be a moral one. It can also include ordinary desires or aversions, for example, to achieve wealth or to avoid punishment. These cannot be irrational desires or aversions, those that one would not acquire if one had all relevant available information and used logic, because rational persons would not have them. However, rational persons might have different desires, for example, some like pudding and others not.

An example might clarify the method. Consider a rule permitting slim but not fat applicants for research grants an opportunity to present more than cursory information to support their applications. A rational person would not accept such a rule for several reasons. First, as information from the applicant is likely to be useful in determining the merits of a grant, the outcomes would more likely be incorrect than with a rule permitting both types of persons to provide information (a consequentialist consideration). Second, providing some persons but not others a greater opportunity to be heard based on considerations irrelevant to their desert is unfair whether or not outcomes would be better with an alternative rule (a nonconsequentialist consideration). Third, if one did not know whether one was fat or slim, such a rule could adversely affect one's chances of obtaining wealth (fulfilling desires).

Differences in people's circumstances can make it rational to accept different principles. Thus, in the previous example, if one knew one was slim (or fat), it would be rational (not) to accept the rule. Specifying people's circumstances includes specifying the type of society in which they expect to live. The analysis here assumes that the society is an industrialized Western one. Indeed, the usual background assumption is North American society—the United States and Canada.

When ordinary people justify conduct and principles, they are trying to decide what is rational—what a fully rational person would want, accept, or do. They also recognize that no one is perfectly rational; we all have irrational desires and accept principles that fully rational persons would not. Nonetheless, if a large number of ordinary people have examined and tried to live with principles, those that survive are likely to be rationally acceptable for people in their situation. This establishes a presumption in favor of such principles; the presumption can be rebutted by sound argument.

Consequently, it is reasonable to examine those procedural principles that have been consciously examined and accepted by thoughtful persons in the appropriate conditions. This has primarily occurred in the law and declarations of human rights. Thus, four primary sources for procedural principles are human rights statements, constitutional law, criminal law, and administrative law. These are the legal fields that have primarily focussed on burden/benefit decisions. The law of civil procedure, although concerned with conflict resolution, is relevant as a model and source of principles in constitutional and administrative law.

The Adversary Adjudication Model

Not surprisingly, at least in the United States, the dominant legal model of a just decision-making procedure is an adjudicatory trial-type hearing (see also Galligan 1986, 355). One reason for this model's dominance is simply that lawyers are trained in it and thus disposed to believe that it is just and accurate (Macdonald 1981, 12). However, they probably use negotiation or mediation to resolve most actual disputes that they handle. Another likely reason is that many early Supreme Court cases interpreting due process in the administrative area involved regulatory agencies. Activities of regulatory agencies are closer to the criminal model than those of benefactory agencies (those distributing benefits such as social security). Consequently, people naturally tend to apply criminal law principles to them. Finally, burden/benefit decisions affecting particular individuals are closer to adjudication than legislation.

Two features are often used to distinguish rule making or legislation from adjudication, although probably no set of necessary and sufficient conditions can be given. One feature is that adjudication is retrospective and based on past or present facts, whereas legislation is prospective—changing legal statuses and relations in the future (see *Prentis v. Atlantic Coast Line Co.*, 211 U.S. 210, 226 (1908)). The second feature is that legislation is usually general, concerning classes of people and actions, whereas adjudication is particular concerning specific individuals (see *Bi-Metallic Investment Co. v. Colorado*, 239 U.S. 441 (1915); Pierce, Shapiro, and Verkuil 1985, 248–52). However, sometimes rule making can affect only one or a couple of identifiable individuals and thus constitute a burden/benefit decision. Moreover, some court decisions are primarily prospective, and some legislation is retrospective. The federal Administrative Procedure Act (APA) generally uses the prospective/retrospective distinction but includes licensing, which is prospective, under adjudication (5 U.S.C. § 551(4)–(7)). The Model State Administrative Procedure Act (MSA) primarily uses the general/particular distinction (MSA §§ 1-102(5) and (10)).

Adjudication also needs to be distinguished from other forms of decision making. The following features generally do so (see Golding 1975, 108–12; Golding 1978, 101–02). (1) There is a particular dispute. (2) Particular parties are involved; the dispute is not between large, amorphous groups such as environmentalists and industry. (3) A third party is involved. (4) A hearing is held in which information concerning the dispute is presented. (5) The third party "settles" the controversy by rendering a decision. (6) This decision is based on principles and rules—those of the substantive law—with reference to the information presented at the hearing.

This concept of adjudication applies to dispute resolution. Most burden/benefit decisions need not involve a dispute, at least in the first instance. A teacher determining a student's grade is making a burden/benefit decision, but no dispute or controversy is involved, at least in the first instance and usually not even after the decision has been made. An adjudication model tends to structure burden/benefit decisions as dispute resolution ones.

The second element of the dominant model is that adjudication is adversarial. Various bases have been offered to distinguish adversarial procedure from inquisitorial or investigatory procedures. One basis is the use of precedent and the roles of the decisionmaker and parties. In continental inquisitorial systems, judges are active in acquiring information and decisions in particular cases supposedly do not set precedents for future ones which are decided independently by applying a rule. Another basis is whether a hierarchical or decentralized model is used. For present purposes, 'adversarial' or 'adversary' is used to designate situations with conflicting interests of two or more parties who have primary responsibility for the gathering and presentation of information at a hearing (Frankel 1980, 13; Golding 1978, 106; Simon 1978, 36). This distinguishes the adversarial setting from settings in which only one party is involved or the decisionmaker has primary responsibility for obtaining and presenting information.

Part I primarily examines the procedural principles of this model. They are not taken as necessarily determinative of acceptable moral procedural principles for burden/benefit decision making. Many of the principles are drawn from human rights statements, constitutions, common law, and model statutory law. As indicated above, such recognition establishes a presumption, but only a presumption, of their justifiability. Critical arguments are sometimes deployed to modify or add to the principles or to choose among alternative interpretations. Although these arguments primarily operate at a common-sense level, they implicitly appeal to the method of rational persons accepting rules for a society in which they expect to live. In effect, the reader is appealed to as such a person. Chapter 2 examines the principle that a decisionmaker should be impartial. Chapter 3 considers the principle that a person affected by a decision should have an opportunity to be heard. Principles concerning the grounds for decisions are considered in chapter 4. Chapter 5 examines the principles of consistency, adherence to precedent, and following rules, often called formal justice.

Part II presents a theory of procedural justice for burden/benefit decisions based on the principles rational persons would accept. Chapter 6 argues for a fundamental norm for justifying and evaluating principles of the sort analyzed in Chapters 2–5. Chapter 7 analyzes the limits to legally requiring just procedures. It assumes that if principles should not be legally required, they are still ethically binding. Chapter 8 analyzes the limits of the adversary adjudication model, presents alternative decision-making models, and indicates what procedural principles they involve and when they are most appropriate.

In Part III, the theory and principles are applied to two types of situations that frequently involve the borders of law and ethics. Chapter 9 assesses procedures for the discipline of professionals. These decisions are usually burden-imposing or benefit-terminating ones. The last chapter then applies the theory to various employment decisions—hiring, promoting and awarding merit pay, demoting and disciplining, and dismissal. Between them, professional discipline and employment involve almost all the various combinations of burden-imposing, benefit-conferring, benefit-terminating, and burden-relieving decisions governed by law or ethics. They thus provide a realistic range of situations for evaluating the theory.

PART I

TRADITIONAL PRINCIPLES

CHAPTER 2

IMPARTIALITY

That procedural justice requires an impartial decisionmaker is almost universally recognized. Yet, complete impartiality is not always attainable, and sometimes what it involves is unclear. In the criminal and civil law context, a person has a recognized human right to have his or her case heard by an impartial tribunal. The International Covenant on Civil and Political Rights (UN 1966, art. 14(1)) and the American Convention on Human Rights (OAS 1969, art. 8.1) both recognize the right to trial by "a competent, independent, and impartial tribunal" for criminal and most civil cases. The European Convention for the Protection of Human Rights and Fundamental Freedoms also requires that the tribunal be independent and impartial, but it omits the requirement of competence (CE 1950, art. 6(1)).

To be competent, a decisionmaker should be legally authorized, know the standards or norms by which the decision is to be made, and have the intellectual ability to evaluate evidence in light of the standards. Judges' competence (as opposed to jurisdiction) is rarely legally in issue, because judges usually meet the legally established criteria for appointment and parties are reluctant to challenge judicial competence, say, for alcoholism, for fear of provoking antagonism. Outside the judicial context, the competence of various persons to make burden/benefit decisions can be a more important consideration. For example, most academics would object were promotion and tenure decisions made by nonacademics. We shall not consider further the qualifications for a competent decisionmaker which are highly dependent on the subject matter.

The right to an impartial tribunal is also recognized in many constitutions. The U.S. Constitution guarantees of due process (amends. V and XIV(1)) require an impartial tribunal. The Canadian Charter of Rights and Freedoms recognizes a right to a hearing by "an independent and impartial tribunal" for all criminal offenses (art. 11(d)). Its requirement of "fundamental justice" also probably incorporates at least the requirement of impartiality in other contexts (Cdn. Charter § 7).

The right to an impartial tribunal is also recognized in law. For centuries, the requirement of an impartial tribunal has been one of the two common-law principles of natural justice (Schauer 1976, 48). The fundamental notion is that no one should be judge in his or her own case. This principle is commonly taken to include that a decisionmaker (1) not have a particular interest in the outcome, (2) not demonstrate prejudicial conduct at a hearing, (3) not be sitting in appeal of his or her prior decision, (4) not be both prosecutor and judge, and (5) not exhibit bias (Macdonald 1987, 237 n. 37).

The APA now provides for a significant independence and impartiality of administrative law judges. It prohibits their being assigned "duties inconsistent with their duties and responsibilities as administrative law judges." For purposes of actions against them, as for improper or inefficient job performance, administrative law judges are under the Merit Systems Protection Board rather than specific agencies (5 U.S.C. §§ 3105 and 7521). Finally, the MSA provides for disqualifying presiding officers "for bias, prejudice, [and] interest" (MSA § 4-202(b)).

Rational persons would accept a principle of impartial and independent decisionmakers for a society in which they expected to live. Although each person would be better off with a decisionmaker favorable to him or her, permitting partiality would not be an acceptable principle. The central problem with partiality is ensuring that it is exercised for rather than against one. Many people might be able to be reasonably confident of that in a few situations, and a few people might have reason to expect that in many situations. But we are here considering a very general principle for all situations in the whole society. Most people will thus be best off with a principle of impartiality. Only such a principle could be publicly acknowledged and accepted by most persons, which is necessary for principles for a whole society to operate. Of course, this principle needs to be balanced against others and can be outweighed by them in certain contexts.

Thus, a fundamental principle of procedural justice in burden/benefit decisions is that decisionmakers be independent and impartial. In the criminal law context, both independence and impartiality are strongly supported. Independence is a weaker requirement in the administrative law context, especially for informal decision making. Outside the legal context, it might be exceedingly difficult and sometimes undesirable to require independent decisionmakers.

Three main types of factors can prevent decisionmakers being independent and impartial. First, they might lack impartiality due to a conflict of interest or bias. Second, they might be under the control of an interested person or organization or have functions incompatible with independence and impartiality. Third, they might receive information from an interested person in a manner that at least suggests partiality.

Interest, Bias, and Necessity

Decisionmakers lack impartiality if they have a personal interest in the outcome or are biased. A personal interest is involved if the person benefits, usually financially, by one outcome more than another. Personal benefit should not be restricted to narrow self-interest; it should include benefit to a decisionmaker's near relatives in whose well-being he or she is presumably interested (but see Flick 1984, 150 (includes under personal involvement not automatically disqualifying)). The benefit must be greater than what any citizen could expect from an appropriate decision. Members of the Environmental Protection Agency do not have a personal interest preventing impartiality simply because they will benefit from clean air and water.

Interest The clearest form of partiality due to personal interest is bribery. The Model Penal Code makes it a criminal offense to offer, confer, agree to confer, solicit, accept, or agree to accept any pecuniary benefit or other benefit as consideration for a decision as a public servant (§ 240.1 (Proposed Official Draft 1962)). The harm involved is not necessarily to another party, for that can occur only when burdens or benefits are distributed on a competitive basis. It would not occur, for example, in bribing an official to grant social security disability benefits. The harm is to governmental interests, not those of specific individuals, and thus indirectly to average citizens (Feinberg 1984, 63). Either burdens will not be imposed as the law prescribes, or benefits will be improperly awarded at taxpayer expense. In some cases, perhaps no one is worse off or harmed, but the objection remains. Law enforcement penalizes only a minor percentage of violators, and the failure to punish a given violator might not have any effect on crime rates. A strong retributive principle of punishment would be violated, but few scholars support strong retributivism. Governments around the world function fairly effectively with graft. Indeed, in some countries, graft and bribery are a recognized method of doing business. Bribery might even be the most efficient system for some decisions, because those persons most willing to pay for decisions would receive them. The objection to bribery goes deeper than inefficiency due to incorrect outcomes. There is an intentional unfairness in the application of the law. This seems morally objectionable even if no one is harmed.

Lack of impartiality can also be due to mere personal interest. Unlike bribery, no one has intentionally made it in the personal interest of the decisionmaker to reach a particular outcome. Instead, a preexisting relationship makes an outcome to the personal benefit of the decisionmaker. The classic English case is *Dimes v. Grand Junction Canal* (10 Eng. Rep. 301 (H.L. 1852)). The Lord Chancellor was a substantial stockholder in a corporation that brought a suit in equity, and at one point he affirmed relief to the corporation. Even though the House of Lords did not contend that the Lord Chancellor was influenced by his interest in the corporation, it reversed the action. Decisionmakers must avoid even the appearance of influence due to personal interest (Flick 1984, 155).

The prohibition of the appearance of impropriety is common in the law. The Code of Judicial Conduct specifies that a judge should avoid the appearance of impropriety in all activities (ABA 1972, Canon 2). It is not immediately clear why the mere appearance of impropriety or partialilty should be condemned. For example, if in *Dimes* the Lord Chancellor's decision was indeed correct, then the outcome was substantively just. If one evaluates procedures by their producing correct outcomes, then the mere appearance of impropriety is not necessarily a defect. Personal interest is bad only if it actually operates to produce an unjust outcome.

Four relations are logically possible when a decisionmaker appears to have a personal interest. This interest does not influence the outcome, and the outcome is (1) just or (2) unjust. Personal interest influences the outcome, and the outcome is (3) just or (4) unjust. For practical purposes, (1) and (2) can be treated together, because the personal interest does not affect the decision and thus does not explain the outcome.

If one is solely concerned with the justice of outcomes, that is, evaluates procedure instrumentally, only the fourth situation need be avoided. Only in it is personal interest operative and the outcome unjust. Removing the personal interest in situations (1) through (3) will not improve the justice of outcomes. In short, imperfect procedural justice provides no direct argument against the appearance of impropriety.

If one lacks a standard of just outcomes or is unable to apply it independently to determine which outcome is just, situations (3) and (4) cannot be distinguished. Practically, although perhaps not theoretically, one is operating with pure procedural justice. Both situations should be avoided, because one does not know whether the personal interest did contribute to an unjust outcome. Nonetheless, this argument does not provide a reason for prohibiting the mere appearance of impropriety—situations of types (1) and (2) where personal interest does not influence the outcome.

Two reasons can be given for prohibiting even the appearance of impropriety (personal interest). First, establishing whether personal interest influenced a person's decision is often difficult. This point differs from that above. There the difficulty was knowing whether the decision was just or unjust; here, the difficulty is knowing whether personal interest was operative. It does not operate merely by being another factor put into some equation, for example, a judge considering precedents, facts, and personal interest. It usually works more subtly by affecting the perception of facts and the weight given to various considerations. Consequently, to guard against personal interest incorrectly influencing a decision, one must prohibit all situations in which a decisionmaker appears to have a personal interest in an outcome, where it might be operative.

Second, to avoid demoralization, one should ensure confidence in decisionmakers. This concern is with the consequences of the appearance of impropriety beyond the justice of particular decisions. Rules and regulations primarily operate without direct sanctioning or enforcement. That is, voluntary compliance is necessary for the effectiveness of most rules. If people believe that decisions are not made in accordance with rules, they have less reason to comply voluntarily. People often stand to gain personally from noncompliance, and a rule's expected benefits are less likely to occur if it is not properly applied. Consequently, compliance might involve a useless sacrifice; immediate personal gain is sacrificed with no compensating general benefit from the rule's observance. In effect, rules create a public good depending on compliance by others, and without assurance of such compliance or proper remedy for noncompliance, one has no reason to comply oneself. This can produce demoralization.

Three distinct points or stages are involved in demoralization. The first is the simple loss of confidence in the appropriateness of decisions and fairness of decisionmakers. Second, a loss of confidence can lead to a perception of foolishness, pointlessness, or sacrifice in complying with rules, regulations, and principles (acting morally) when others are not and are getting away with it. Third, the belief that compliance is pointless can lead to noncompliance.

This reasoning applies beyond the law and government rules. Suppose corporate purchasing managers accept dinners and ball game tickets from suppliers, although in fact their decisions are not influenced by the gratuities. Still, other potential suppliers might think that the system is corrupt. If so, they will focus less on the quality of their products or bids and more on providing benefits to purchasing managers. Company personnel in other departments might come to believe that purchasing managers decide on the basis of personal interest and do so likewise. The result can be a general loss of morale, bad decisions, and inefficiency.

So far, we have focused on direct personal interest. A direct personal interest exists, for example, when a judge is paid only from fines collected (*Tumey v. Ohio*, 273 U.S. 510 (1927)). However, a less direct relationship to personal interest can produce partiality. A case sometimes cited as involving an indirect conflict of interest is *Ward v. Monroeville* (409 U.S. 57 (1973)). In that case, the Supreme Court held unconstitutional an arrangement in which the mayor heard traffic cases and a substantial part of the village's revenues came from traffic fines. However, *Ward* probably should not be considered a case of personal interest or impartiality; instead, it is one of independence. The mayor's duties in controlling the financial affairs of the village conflicted with his duties in hearing traffic cases.

A clear case of indirect personal interest is *Gibson v. Berryhill* (411 U.S. 564 (1973)). This case involved the Alabama Optometry Board which licensed and regulated optometrists in the state. Only members of the Optometric Association could be members of the Board, and the Association excluded optometrists employed by others—almost half the optometrists in the state. The Board had charged some optometrists with unprofessional conduct for being employed by a corporation. Had the charge been upheld, the corporation would have been forced to cease operations, resulting in significantly more business for independent optometrists.

In this case one could not identify a particular customer who would come to a member of the Board if the corporation closed. Nor could one specify precisely the increase in business a Board member would obtain, because competition among the independent optometrists would significantly affect that. Nonetheless, the Board's composition ensured that its members had a personal interest in decisions contrary to those of employed optometrists. If members of a licensing board are to be chosen only from the members of an association—bar, medical, accounting, barbers, and so forth—then that association should be open to all members of the licensed occupation. Otherwise, a built-in conflict of interest exists between the members of the board and the excluded members of the occupation.

Bias Personal bias does not involve any personal benefit to the decisionmaker other than satisfaction of a pre-existing preference unrelated to the merits of the matter. One can distinguish three possible types of bias as predispositions toward law or policy, the facts in the situation, or a party (Davis 1972, 245; see also Redish and Marshall 1986, 492). A preconceived view toward a law or policy does not constitute procedural injustice. Indeed, one expects, even requires, judges to have views on legal principles. As then Justice Rehnquist put it, "Proof that a Justice's mind at the time he joined the Court was a complete *tabula rasa* in the area of constitutional adjudication would be evidence of lack of qualification, not lack of bias" (*Laird v. Tatum*, 409 U.S. 824, 835 (1972); see also Flick 1984, 164). Similarly, administrators in various agencies are to be committed to previously adopted policies. Even if a policy has not yet been officially adopted, officials are not disqualified because they have expressed preferences for a particular policy. Again, such preferences are often a reason for appointing them.

The law with respect to prejudgment of facts is less clear, because it is often mixed with other considerations such as prejudgment of policy, animosity toward parties, and independence (separation of functions). However, if a decisionmaker has reached conclusions about facts in particular cases prior to hearing or receiving evidence, then the person should be disqualified. Judges and jurors who have personal knowledge of alleged facts in trials are usually disqualified from hearing them (28 U.S.C. § 455(b)(1)); the probability of their having already reached a conclusion regarding them is too great. Sometimes a decisionmaker has already reached a conclusion about the facts in a case. For example, a chairman of the Federal Trade Commission made a speech in which he condemned specific oil and tire companies, including Texaco, for price fixing, price discrimination, and overriding commissions. In a subsequent hearing before the FTC, Texaco was charged with forcing its dealers to purchase tires, batteries, and accessories from Goodrich (another named company). The court held that the chairman should be disqualified from participating in the decision (*Texaco, Inc. v. FTC*, 336 F.2d 754 (D.C. Cir 1964)). Although one might consider this an example of bias against a party, it is more plausibly viewed as one in which the chairman had already decided that Texaco engaged in the offenses charged.

Bias or prejudice against a party affected by a decision is unjust. A classic case involved a judge in a trial of German-Americans for espionage during World War I; he commented that it was hard to be impartial toward German-Americans, whose "very hearts are reeking with disloyalty" (*Berger v. United States*, 255 U.S. 22, 33–34 (1921)). Bias can be shown in the way a hearing is conducted, although it is quite difficult to prove. In one case, a hearing examiner uniformly believed the witnesses for one side and disbelieved those for the other. Nevertheless, the Supreme Court held that this was insufficient to show bias (*NLRB v. Pittsburgh S.S. Co.*, 337 U.S. 656 (1949)). The legal test is whether an examiner's decision can be supported by the evidence. As appellate courts rarely overturn findings of fact, especially those dependent on the credibility of witnesses, a bias operating to discredit witnesses at the hearing stage is difficult to overcome at the appellate level. If no record is kept of testimony, as in informal hearings, and the sole evidence is the report of the presiding officer, bias is nearly impossible to ferret out on review. The evidence in such a situation has already been filtered through the personal bias of the decisionmaker and so will likely support the decision.

The test of whether a decision is supported by evidence is inappropriate. It tests bias only by whether an erroneous decision occurred. It is thus purely instrumental and is too broad even on those grounds. Being supported by evidence does not mean being supported by the preponderance of the evidence; less than that will suffice. In close cases, biases can change the perception of facts sufficiently to yield a different decision. At least if a real likelihood of bias exists and the decision is not supported by a preponderance of the evidence, a decision should not stand. Even with a decisionmaker's probably biased construal of facts, the decision is not supported by the weight of the evidence. Thus, good instrumentalist grounds exist for thinking the decision is wrong and will not further substantive justice. As the procedure appears improper, people also have a reason of avoiding demoralization for rejecting the test.

Bias toward parties or its appearance can also arise from special relationships with parties. Judges are to disqualify themselves if they or a lawyer with whom they were associated previously acted in the matter, they have acted for the government in the matter, or a close relative is a party, official of a party, or is a lawyer for a party (28 U.S.C. § 455(b); see also *SCA Servs. v. Morgan*, 557 F.2d 110 (7th Cir. 1977) (judge's brother member of legal firm representing a party)). These grounds for bias operate like the appearance of personal interest. A judge could have great animosity toward his or her brother and thus be biased against a party the brother represents, but that is not the normal expectation. In all these situations, the appearance and perhaps the likelihood of partiality are great.

Necessity In some situations, it is infeasible to find a qualified decision-maker who does not have a personal interest or possible bias in the matter. The doctrine of necessity is that disqualification for interest or bias is not required if it removes the only tribunal capable of making the decision. In *United States v. Will* (449 U.S. 200 (1980); see also *Evans v. Gore*, 253 U.S. 245 (1920); *Re the Constitutional Questions Act*, [1936] 4 D.L.R. 134 (Sask. C.A.), *aff'd* [1937] 2 D.L.R. 209 (P.C.); Flick 1984, 174), the Supreme Court decided whether Congress could reduce previously authorized cost of living increases for federal judges. It reasoned by the doctrine of necessity that it should do so, claiming that otherwise the case could not be heard. Similarly, in *In re New Mexico Natural Gas Antitrust Litigation* (620 F.2d 794 (10th Cir. 1980)), a district court judge had disqualified himself, because a decision would affect utility rates and his own utility bill. The appellate court held that the judge could hear the case, since all other judges in the district were similarly affected and the likely effect on the judge's bill was small.

The doctrine of necessity cannot simply be applied whenever no tribunal would be capable of deciding an issue. Recall *Gibson v. Berryhill* in which the Optometry Board consisted of only independent optometrists. Disqualification of the Board meant that no tribunal could consider the charge of unprofessional conduct against the employed optometrists. One commentator has suggested that the doctrine of necessity should not be applied when the interest or bias "will infect the tribunal in every case" (Schwartz 1976, 316). However, the interest in *Gibson* would not infect the Board in every case. It would not affect it in a charge of unprofessional conduct against an independent optometrist on grounds unrelated to the economics of the profession.

Nor can one easily constrain the doctrine by analysis of the concept of necessity. In *Gibson*, under state law no other tribunal could hear the case. In *Will*, although the Supreme Court said the case could not be heard if it did not hear it, alternatives did exist. For example, state judges could have heard the issue for federal judges within their state's jurisdiction, but this would not have guaranteed uniform decisions (Redish and Marshall 1986, 492–93). Moreover, in *In re New Mexico*, the case could have been assigned to a judge from another district who would not be affected, but the cost would have been great and the judge's interest was small. Consequently, necessity is not actual necessity; instead, it involves balancing various considerations to determine whether avoiding partiality or the appearance thereof is worthwhile.

Perhaps a sufficient condition for the acceptability of possible partiality is the consent or waiver by possibly adversely affected parties (see Flick 1984, 171; Hewitt 1972, 50). Often the consent is prior to an issue arising, as in joining an association with a decision procedure. But it can be after an issue has arisen. Thus, in *In re New Mexico*, the parties charged with price-fixing might reasonably have consented to the assigned judge despite his potential conflict of interest, especially in view of the additional litigation costs likely in moving the trial to a different forum and assigning a different judge. Nevertheless, parties cannot be expected to consent in all cases in which the doctrine of necessity might operate. Moreover, even if all the parties agree, injustice might be involved even if outweighed by consent. The appearance of injustice could still have demoralizing effects, especially if people were not aware of the parties' consent.

Another important consideration in applying the doctrine of necessity is the consequences of not allowing a tribunal to hear a case (see also Flick 1984, 176). Failure to hear a case usually means that one party wins, for the status quo is continued. This result can involve as much injustice as having a case decided by a potentially biased or interested person. If all judges were in fact disqualified in a case like *In re New Mexico*, then possible price-fixing could not be rectified. In *Gibson*, the result would be the continuation of competition in the optometry business. Consequently, in determining whether to disqualify the only possible tribunal, one needs to balance the likelihood that bias or interest will operate to produce injustice against the possible injustice of not permitting a decision on the merits. Usually, it is possible to obtain an impartial hearing on the merits, but the question is the cost and difficulty of so doing. In *Will*, alternative decisions at the state level were possible, but they might not give a uniform resolution. In *Gibson*, the legislature would have to modify a statute, but that is not too difficult. Moreover, as the injustice was structural, a statutory change would prevent partiality in many cases, not just the one.

Independence

The independence of decisionmakers involves two elements: not being subject to the control of a party or group with an interest at stake and not mixing decision making with incompatible functions. Both elements have been noted in passing above. Placing administrative law judges under the Merit Systems Protection Board rather than the agencies whose policies they apply helps ensure the first element of independence. The separation of functions is achieved by not assigning them tasks incompatible with their judicial duties. The MSA also provides for the separation of functions (MSA § 4-214).

Control Independence from control is not always possible or desirable. Not all burden/benefit decisions in administrative agencies, far less than half, are decided by administrative law judges. Most applications for social security benefits, contracts, and grants are determined, at least in the first instance, by employees subject to an agency. In nongovernmental organizations, decisionmakers are almost always subject to authorities whose policy is being applied. Consider an employee assigning and reassigning offices to other employees. No doubt there are some policies about larger and more desirable offices going to more senior people, efficiency of location, and so on. This person should follow any such policy, and any judgment could be overridden by a superior.

The point of independence from control by interested persons is to avoid influences that prevent impartial application of rules or policies. Not all control of decisionmakers prevents impartial application of rules or policies. Much control by superiors does not involve any adverse interest. The superiors' concern is a predisposition toward rules or policies, and, as we have seen, such a predisposition does not affect impartiality. Similarly, it does not adversely affect a concern for independence, because it does not inhibit but supports the appropriate application of those policies. Loss of independence is objectionable when interests contrary to the person being judged or the policies being applied affect or might affect decisions. Moreover, there are good instrumental reasons for permitting policy control by superiors. Misinterpreted and misapplied policies also create unjust or incorrect decisions. Proper supervision can sometimes reduce such mistakes.

Nevertheless, superiors can be biased or partial and exercise control for purposes other than the appropriate administration of rules and policies. Persons subject to the policies often do not know whether such control is being properly exercised, and if they receive an adverse decision often believe it is due to improper influence. Thus, such control can create at least the appearance of impropriety. As with the appearance of partiality, four possibilities exist: possible influence that is not operative with just or unjust outcomes, and operative influence with correct or incorrect outcomes. If only the first three exist, then a procedure might be the best that procedural justice can achieve.

If control of decisionmakers by policymakers creates only the possibility of injustice and good reasons exist for such control, then the control is acceptable. The principle of independence is outweighed. Good reasons include the probability of eliminating more mistakes than those created and the prohibitive expense in many small organizations of obtaining independent decisionmakers. One can frequently protect against abuse of such control by providing subjects of burden/benefit decisions an independent authority to appeal to if influence is being improperly applied. Thus, employees might be permitted to go over their supervisor's head or to appeal to an ombudsperson. Nonetheless, differences can exist between explicit and implicit policy. The explicit policy might say one thing, but the actual practice, supported and encouraged by the whole administration, might be another. For example, the law might state that welfare payments should be denied if a claimant does not help find a spouse but the practice be to deny payments if the spouse is not found even though the claimant fully cooperates (Davis 1969, 11).

The degree of independence needs to be analyzed for different situations. Above, we noted the steps taken to provide independence for administrative law judges. Yet, they are not completely independent of agencies, and some people think they should have more independence (see Redish and Marshall 1986, 499–500). For example, administrative law judges are removable for cause, and agencies make performance appraisals of their work. A major question recently is whether low productivity (significantly fewer than average cases decided) constitutes cause (see generally Rosenblum 1984). If judges decide only half the average number of cases of other judges per month and no significant explanation (such as more difficult cases) is given, are there grounds for removal? Doing so does not violate independence, because no reason exists to think that a higher decision rate will be more favorable to one type of outcome than another. One might also be concerned about a judge who decides far above the average number of cases. He or she might not be providing adequate attention, and one might expect less thorough reviews to be likely to favor the agency. However, decisions are reviewable by courts, so there is an external control if agency pressure for efficiency results in hasty decisions adverse to individuals.

In contrast, removal for reversing agency decisions significantly above average does threaten independence, for it relates directly to types of outcomes. Even here, however, one must look more closely (see also Rosenblum 1984, 616–17 (distinguishing control of fact-finding from policy determination)). If the charge against the judge is simply the number of reversals, that does threaten independence. It is like objecting that juries find too many criminal defendants innocent. Besides, if the agency does not like the results, it can change the policy. However, the complaint might be that the judge is subtly misinterpreting policy. It is like a jury thinking that mental illness alone is sufficient for an insanity defense. This control is of policy and does not interfere with the independence needed for impartiality.

Commingling functions The primary concern of the second element of independence is that combining the functions of investigating or prosecuting with deciding might result in prejudgment of facts. A prosecutor will usually have had access to information and reached a conclusion from it without having heard or considered all the evidence for the other side. This concern chiefly applies to burden-imposing and benefit-terminating decisions. It is odd to even speak of a prosecutorial function with respect to benefit-conferring decisions, although an analogous function can occur in some situations, for example, a person assigned to develop arguments against conferral of a benefit. Some administrative agencies, such as the Securities and Exchange Commission and the Federal Trade Commission, investigate cases, bring charges against parties, and then try them. Such a commingling of functions, it is claimed, prevents the decisionmakers being impartial.

A secondary concern is respect for the doctrine of separation of powers—legislation, execution or administration, and adjudication—which is probably strongest in the United States. Parliamentary forms of government, as in Canada and England, do not have as complete a separation. The judiciary is practically independent, but the legislative and administrative functions are closely tied because cabinet members are also legislators. Thus, the concept of combining both policy making and administration is not so foreign to parliamentary systems of government as to that of the United States.

In *Withrow v. Larkin* (421 U.S. 35 (1975)), the Supreme Court appeared to hold that mixing investigatory and adjudicatory powers does not violate due process. Larkin was a licensed physician practicing in Wisconsin. The medical examining board held a closed investigatory hearing (with Larkin's attorney present) into aspects of Larkin's practice. Subsequently, the board charged Larkin with practicing under an assumed name and other professional violations, and it set a date for a hearing of the matter. The issue before the Supreme Court was whether the same board could both investigate the sufficiency of evidence for holding a hearing and then sit in judgment at the hearing. The Court did not find actual bias and thought the risk of bias was acceptable. Moreover, it would not be inconsistent for the board to decide that a hearing on suspension of Larkin's license should be held and subsequently decide against suspension.

Both the APA and the MSA have sought to separate investigatory and adjudicatory activities. Among other things, the APA provides that employees involved in investigation or prosecution cannot participate or advise in a decision (5 U.S.C. § 554(d)). A general exception is made for heads of agencies and members of commissions (see also *FTC v. Cement Institute*, 333 U.S. 683 (1948)). If federal statutes governed, this exception would include the members of the medical examining board in *Withrow*. The MSA provides that a person who has served as an investigator, prosecutor, or advocate in a case or is subject to the control of one who has done so cannot preside or assist a presiding officer (MSA §§ 4-214(a) and (b)).

If the primary reason against commingling functions is prejudgment, then the focus should be on whether a function structurally commits a person to a point of view. In *Withrow*, in deciding whether a hearing was required, the medical board was not actually performing an investigatory task. Instead, its task was to determine whether sufficient evidence existed to establish probable cause. This is an adjudicatory function—determining whether a minimum degree of evidence of wrongdoing exists. It is not incompatible with having an open mind as to whether a high degree of evidence will exist when all the facts are developed. Consequently, the MSA distinguishes between determining probable cause and investigating (MSA §§ 4-214(a) and (c)).

The central threat to impartiality is not investigation or prosecution but advocacy which structurally commits a person to a viewpoint. An advocate's function is to muster all possible arguments to support a position. Such a task functionally predisposes a person toward one point of view and makes impartiality unlikely. Much of the concern with combining investigatory and adjudicatory functions stems from the adversary adjudication model. Contesting parties perform their own investigations and present information supporting their position to an impartial judge. Because investigation is oriented toward advocacy, finding evidence for a particular side, it predisposes an investigator toward a particular view of information.

Other conceptions of investigation do not involve the advocacy orientation of the adversary model. In the continental inquisitorial or investigatory model, the judge has the primary responsibility for investigating the facts—calling and questioning witnesses and so forth. The investigatory task is not oriented toward one side of the issue rather than another. In science and ordinary life, one person commonly investigates and decides matters. Persons are not considered partial merely because they have investigated an issue. Indeed, failure to investigate, rather than investigating, would commonly be taken to disqualify one as a decisionmaker. Indeed, even advocacy after investigation does not make impartiality suspect. Only advocacy directing investigation blocks impartiality. Consequently, on these conceptions of investigation, no necessary incompatibility exists between investigatory and adjudicatory functions.

Matters are otherwise when one considers the combination of prosecutory and adjudicatory functions. These two functions should never be combined (Davis 1972, 270; Schwartz 1976, 329–30). Almost by definition, prosecution is advocacy. It is logically possible to combine prosecutory and adjudicatory functions; one might develop all the arguments against someone and yet not be committed. It is perhaps even psychologically possible, but the likelihood of predisposition is too great for a procedurally just system to permit the combination.

Although the APA prohibits the combination of prosecutorial and adjudicatory functions in formal on the record adjudication, the prohibition does not apply to rule making, rate making, or applications for initial licenses (5 U.S.C. § 554(d)). The underlying argument is that rule making is a form of legislation, and that in legislation access to information from various sources is important and particular parties, as opposed to classes of individuals, are not at issue. Rate making is classified as a form of rule making (5 U.S.C. § 551(4)). Although not classified as rule making, perhaps applications for initial licenses were thought to be closer to rule making than adjudication for these purposes, because decisions are prospective rather than retrospective.

Good reasons exist to treat applications for initial licenses, rate making, and even some rule making as more like adjudication than legislation. The American Bar Association and the Administrative Conference have both recommended extending the separation of functions to initial licensing and formal rule making (Pierce, Shapiro, and Verkuil 1985, 502). The underlying principle is to distinguish on the general/particular basis instead of the prospective/retrospective basis (see MSA §§ 1-102(5) and (10); see also Pierce, Shapiro, and Verkuil 1985, 248–52). Applications for initial licenses are benefit-conferring decisions for individuals. Frequently, as before the Federal Communications Commission, these are competitive applications. If commission staff present evidence for or against various applicants, then they should not be involved in the decision making. By supporting or opposing a particular party, they have chosen sides and assumed an adversarial position even if the original orientation was neutral. They have arrived at factual conclusions. Similar considerations apply in noncompetitive cases, such as applicants for the bar or a medical license. If the staff presentation opposes an applicant, say, on the grounds of lack of good character, then a predisposition adverse to the claimant exists. Similarly, in some rate making, staff are often arguing against the position of the company involved. Finally, some formal rule making amounts to an adjudication, for only one or two parties are directly affected by the rule (see Flick 1984, 38–39 (natural justice applies when by-laws deal with one instance)).

The discussion so far, like the APA, primarily applies to formal hearings. More difficult is the extent to which functions should be separated in informal decision making, which is by far more frequent. The reason for separation is the advocacy of one position. In informal procedures, roles are often not clearly defined; indeed, that is one sense in which procedures are informal. The Social Security Administration's informal procedure is largely an inquisitorial one at both the initial and appellate decision stages (Schwartz 1976, 252–54). Usually, even in appeals, the claimant is not represented by counsel, although he or she can be, and the administration does not have counsel to present its side. Instead, an administrative law judge prepares the case for hearing, does most of the questioning trying to bring out points both for and against a claimant, and then decides. In noncompetitive benefit-conferring situations, the notion of advocacy, except by the claimant, is largely out of place. Even in many competitive benefit-conferring situations, such as evaluating grant applications, the concept does not really apply. Moreover, some informal burden-imposing procedures do not so structure the situation, for example, a principal considering punishment of a student usually has no more reason to pursue the case for discipline than that against.

Separation of functions in informal procedures is necessary only if advocacy is an element of certain roles. If that element is absent, then there is no structural predisposition toward facts. Consequently, one should examine the informal procedure to determine whether the decisionmaker is or has been expected to advocate one outcome more than another. If so, there is a built-in advocacy bias that should be corrected. If not, the combination of functions does not provide a reason to object to it.

Ex Parte Communications

The issue of ex parte communications could be considered in the next chapter as well as this one, because objections to ex parte communications rest on the opportunity to be heard as much as impartiality. The problem is clearest in formal hearings. If one party communicates to the decisionmaker without the other party present, then there is an appearance of partiality; the decisionmaker appears to have a special relationship to the communicating party. If the communication involves information relevant to the decision, the opposing party might also lack an opportunity to rebut that evidence. Consequently, there are strong reasons against ex parte communications.

The APA clearly prohibits ex parte communications, provides that if they nonetheless occur their occurrence and substance be made part of the record, and provides some penalties such as denial of claim (5 U.S.C. § 557(d)(1)). The MSA makes the same general provisions and also permits disqualification of the presiding officer and sealing that part of a record if necessary to eliminate its effect (MSA § 4-213, esp. (f)). Moreover, courts have extended such a prohibition to some informal rule making affecting particular parties (*Sangamon Valley Television Corp. v. United States*, 269 F.2d 221 (D.C. Cir. 1959); *Action for Children's Television v. FCC*, 564 F.2d 458 (D.C. Cir. 1977)). Indeed, the prohibition has even been applied to pressure by Congress (*Pillsbury Co. v. FTC*, 354 F.2d 952 (5th Cir. 1966); *D.C. Fed'n of Civic Ass'ns v. Volpe*, 459 F.2d 1231 (D.C. Cir. 1971)). The latter, it is argued, helps insulate administrators from improper congressional pressures to deviate from application of the law as enacted. Contrarily, one might well contend that it decreases supervisory control by Congress to ensure that policies are properly applied.

Protection of an opportunity to be heard in formal or informal processes does not require prohibition of ex parte communications. It only requires making them known to the other party and providing a fair opportunity to reply.

The relationship to impartiality is more complicated and less easily handled. If communications are from nonparties, then the decisionmaker's independence is in question. For example, pressure by members of Congress in particular cases threatens impartial application of policy, because members of Congress have a strong interest in securing benefits for their constituents. The appearance and probability of improper influence is thus great. However, congressional pressure in rule making can be viewed as appropriate control by senior policy makers. Of course, this claim cannot apply to ex parte communications by other nonparties.

Ex parte communications by parties suggests personal bias. One again confronts the distinction between the appearance of influence or partiality and its actual existence. Only the latter directly prevents just outcomes. The same arguments for condemning the appearance of personal interest and bias apply here. However, the grounds for believing that partiality might result are less, because the connection between receiving communications and partiality is weaker than that between personal interest or bias and partiality. Personal interest and bias are reasons for preferring an outcome, having received a communication is not necessarily a reason for so doing. Instead, it is at best evidence of bias. Consequently, the MSA's permitting but not requiring disqualification of a decisionmaker on a case by case basis is appropriate.

The concept of ex parte communications is most at home when the decisionmaking process is structured adversarially. It suggests one of at least two competing parties communicating information. If a procedure is not so structured, then the notion has less hold. Thus, in the Social Security Administration's informal investigatory hearings, one merely has communications in the absence of the claimant. (Claimants are not present at the preliminary stage.) There is no opposed party disposed to communicate or construe information against the claimant. An independent medical examiner is not predisposed for or against a claim, so communication of an exam's results is not likely to bias an examiner. Thus, impartiality does not provide an argument against an examiner or administrative law judge receiving information from other sources. Although the partiality objection to ex parte communications does not apply when the decision-making process is not structured adversarially, the concern for opportunity to explain and rebut any relevant information does. Consequently, the information should still be made known to the person and an opportunity provided to rebut adverse information.

Summary

An impartial decisionmaker is a fundamental principle of procedural justice recognized in human rights codes, constitutions, common law, and legislation; it is one that rational persons would adopt. Partiality is a predisposition to one outcome rather than another. Predisposition on the basis of previous judgments of law or policy does not prevent impartiality toward particular parties. Personal interest in an outcome, preconceived conclusions of fact, and animosity or favoritism toward parties prevent impartiality. Certain standing relationships to parties, such as familial ones, at least create the appearance of partiality because they often predispose decisionmakers to favor them. Even the appearance of partiality should be avoided, because of the difficulty of determining whether it operates and its possible demoralization effects—weakening confidence in impartiality and justice, making compliance appear pointless, and consequent noncompliance. The possibility of partiality should be accepted when the risks of it are small, the costs to parties of an alternative decisionmaker are great, and a failure to decide on the merits might also involve significant injustice.

Independence of decisionmakers is an aspect of impartiality, for decisionmakers lacking independence might decide on grounds irrelevant to the merits of a case. Independence can involve not being subject to the control of a person with an interest in the outcome of a decision as well as not combining functions incompatible with impartial decision making. Independence from control by policymakers is not always desirable. Control appropriately extends to administrative efficiency and prevention or correction of misunderstandings or misinterpretations of policy. It should not extend to determinations of fact.

Although such control might create the appearance of lack of independence, it is justifiable if good reasons exist for such control.

The separation of functions is crucial to prevent an advocacy orientation impairing impartiality. Advocacy involves commitment to a particular outcome. Thus, anyone who at some stage has had a role with an element of advocacy, whether prosecutorial or investigatory, should not be a decisionmaker. An investigatory function is not per se incompatible with impartial decision making, only when it involves investigating for an adversarial party or conclusions have been reached before a hearing. A prosecutorial function is per se incompatible with impartiality.

Ex parte communications are objectionable as indicating possible partiality as well as preventing an opportunity to explain or rebut adverse information. The latter difficulty can be controlled by ensuring that parties are informed of any ex parte communications and provided an opportunity to counter them. Some ex parte communications can threaten decisionmaker independence. Ex parte communications are less likely to produce partiality than personal interest or bias, because they are only evidence of possible bias. In nonadversarial situations, the objection to ex parte communications on the basis of impartiality does not generally apply but the objection on the basis of an opportunity to be heard does.

CHAPTER 3

OPPORTUNITY TO BE HEARD

It is almost universally recognized that persons should have an opportunity to be heard in their own behalf. The process for being heard can vary significantly depending on the type of burden/benefit decision involved. The most stringent requirements arise in the criminal law, because punishment involving incarceration and stigma is normally the most serious type of burden that can be imposed on persons.

Human rights statements and constitutions largely agree on the basic requirements for a just hearing in criminal cases. These requirements include a public hearing within a reasonable time, notice, adequate time to prepare, the assistance of counsel, an opportunity to present witnesses and to examine adverse ones, a presumption of innocence, a privilege against self-incrimination, no double jeopardy, and a right to appeal. Table 3.1 indicates recognition of these elements in the International Covenant on Civil and Political Rights (UN 1966), American Convention on Human Rights (OAS 1969), European Convention for the Protection of Human Rights and Fundamental Freedoms (CE 1950), United States Constitution, and the Canadian Charter of Rights and Freedoms.

The support for several of these rights is even stronger than might appear from the table. Although not specifically mentioned in the U.S. Constitution, the presumption of innocence is constitutionally required (Whitebread 1980, 3; *In re Winship*, 397 U.S. 358 (1970)). Most common-law systems grant criminal defendants an appeal as of right (see Abraham 1975, 247; Jones 1981, 558). Although these rights are for criminal cases, some of them also apply to civil cases. For example, subject to certain limitations, the UN International Covenant and the European Convention also require civil hearings to be public. The due process clauses of the U.S. Constitution impose many of these requirements on civil and administrative procedures (amends. V and XIV(1); see *Goldberg v. Kelly*, 397 U.S. 254 (1970)). The same is true of the Canadian Constitution's requirement of fundamental justice (Cdn. Charter § 7).

Many of these same rights are also found in common law and administrative law. Besides an impartial tribunal, the right to a hearing, with special emphasis on notice and an opportunity to be heard, is the second fundamental common-law requirement of natural justice (Schauer 1976, 56–57; Hewitt 1972, 99). A similar concern can be found in French administrative law (Lefas 1978, 202–14). The common-law principle of an opportunity to be heard has typically been taken to include rights (1) to adequate notice, (2) to pre-hearing discovery, (3) to an adjournment, (4) to present evidence, (5) to rebut evidence and often to cross-examine adverse witnesses, (6) to a copy of the transcript, and (8) to reasons for a decision (Macdonald 1987, 237 n. 36; Flick 1984, 69). As after due reflection many persons have found these rights central to a just hearing, there is a presumption in favor of them even though there may be no articulated general rationale for including these rather than others.

TABLE 3.1
Procedural Rights in Criminal Cases

RIGHT	UN	OAS	CE	US	CDN
Public hearing	14(1)	8(5)	6(1)	6	11(d)
Reasonable time	--	8(1)	5(3-4)	6	11(b)
Notice	14(3)(a)	8(2)(b)	6(3)(a)	6	10(a), 11(a)
Time to prepare	14(3)(b)	8(2)(c)	6(3)(b)	--	--
Counsel	14(3)(d)	8(2)(d-e)	6(3)(c)	6	10(b)
Examine witnesses	14(3)(c)	8(2)(f)	6(3)(d)	6	--
Innocence	14(2)	8(2)	6(2)	--	11(d)
Self-incrimination	14(3)(g)	8(2)(g)	--	5	11(c), 13
Double jeopardy	14(7)	8(4)	--	5	11(h)
Appeal	14(5)	8(2)(h)	--	--	--

Note: the references for UN, OAS, and CE are to articles, for US to amendments, and CDN to sections.

Although the APA does not specify when a formal hearing must occur, that being determined by statutes for different agencies, it does specify that all interested parties have an opportunity for a hearing on notice (5 U.S.C. § 554(c)). It also provides hearing officials a variety of powers usually needed for adjudicatory decisions (5 U.S.C. § 556). The specific procedures are usually determined by agency regulations. Unless otherwise provided, the MSA also requires notice and a hearing with opportunity to present evidence and argument, to cross-examine, and to respond (MSA §§ 4-206 and 4-211(2); see also RSA § 9).

The two central issues in U.S. constitutional law as well as common law have been what procedures should be followed and when the law should require them. As these questions cannot be answered save as part of an adequate theory of procedural justice, we leave them for consideration in chapters 7 and 8. There can be little doubt that rational persons would accept a principle of an opportunity to be heard for trial-type hearings. No one has a good reason to accept a procedure for decisions significantly affecting him or her without an opportunity to be heard in his or her behalf. More debatable is what such an opportunity should include. Our present concern is to delineate the main elements of an opportunity to be heard recognized in the traditional adversary adjudication model. Some suggestions are made concerning revisions that rational persons might accept as better balancing competing considerations. Occasional comments will also be made on informal procedures, which primarily merely omit some elements of a formal hearing (see MSA § 4-402(3)).

Although the adversary adjudication model is of a trial-type hearing, not all elements of the criminal paradigm apply. The requirements of presumption of innocence, privilege against self-incrimination, and no double jeopardy do not apply in most noncriminal burden/benefit decisions. Absent the presumption of innocence, the burden of persuasion often has a different standard—the preponderance of the evidence or balance of probabilities rather than beyond a reasonable doubt. Self-incrimination is restricted to criminal law. Double jeopardy does not apply to benefit decisions, although doctrines such as res judicata can have a similar effect for some benefit decisions.

Two important principles are not explicitly recognized as human or constitutional rights, although they may be assumed or implied by general principles such as due process. One is that the decision be based on the information presented at the hearing (Flick 1984, 105). We already observed one aspect of this principle in the previous chapter—the restriction on ex parte communications. The second principle is a corollary of those of deciding on the hearing information and of appeal, namely, that a record of the hearing be made.

Consequently, we have the following basic requirements of a just adversarial hearing: (1) an open and (2) prompt hearing with (3) adequate notice and (4) time to prepare in which a directly affected individual can (5) with the assistance of counsel (6) present and rebut evidence (7) for a record (8) on which a reasoned decision is based and (9) an opportunity to appeal the decision. The rest of this chapter explores these elements, except for (8), in more detail. The requirement of a reasoned opinion based on the hearing information is considered in the next chapter.

An Open Hearing

Public trials, both civil and criminal, have long been recognized as fundamental to justice. Table 3.1 of human rights and constitutional requirements makes this clear. When the government brings its full power to bear on an individual, public awareness is a useful check on arbitrariness and injustice. Most formal administrative hearings are also open (Davis 1969, 111–12). The APA requires that, with some exceptions, agency meetings be open to the public and that final opinions of adjudication be made public (5 U.S.C. §§ 552(2)(A) and 552b(b)). Moreover, citizens can obtain access to most agency records. Similarly, the MSA requires formal hearings to be open to the public except in accordance with laws expressly providing for closure (MSA § 4-211(6)).

The public nature of rules and principles is sometimes taken to be a criterion of moral rules and principles (Baier 1965, 100–05). Secret laws have been condemned by many writers. However, it is one thing to claim that rules and principles used in burden/benefit decisions must be public, another to claim that proceedings applying them must be open. Public rules and principles allow people to plan their activities to conform to them, and this reason applies whether the rules impose burdens or confer benefits. But this consideration does not pertain to the rule-applying process.

The point of open application of rules is to let people see that justice is done. Like avoidance of the appearance of impropriety, open hearings help prevent demoralization. If people cannot see that justice is done, then they might conclude that it is not. A common (though not always just) charge against secrecy is that people have something to hide. If just rules are unjustly applied, public pressure can often correct the injustice.

Sometimes individuals subject to burden/benefit decisions do not want hearings public, for example, because the publicity might destroy their reputations. Even then, benefits can result from procedures or decisions being public. Consider the case of a housewife convicted of shoplifting close to Christmas (Heine 1981). She received a seven day jail sentence instead of the usual $50 fine, because the judge was cracking down on shoplifters. The woman's husband pleaded with the local newspaper editor not to run the story. Although the trial was open, few people knew about it, and the publicity would be especially severe on the couple's young children. The editor ran the story, and the result was public outrage that prevented any more jail terms for minor shoplifting. Consequently, an affected individual's desire for secrecy is not necessarily sufficient to justify closed hearings.

Of course, legitimate claims of privacy must be considered. Often privacy can be protected by closing portions of a hearing or carefully deleting identifying or private information from a record. Moreover, many formal and informal hearings are likely to concern private matters of little interest to the public. Persons' informal meetings with welfare case workers, discussions with the internal revenue service about disallowed deductions, applications for social security disability, and so forth are not of burning public interest. Furthermore, many of these situations involve information to which there are legitimate privacy claims (see Mashaw 1983, 91–92 (privacy concerns in social security disability claims)). Perhaps such cases should be closed unless the person waives a claim to privacy. This procedure respects privacy, but permits individuals to make glaring cases of injustice public. Still, there is a problem of lack of public interest. To arouse public concern, often many people must complain about improper applications of rules or unjust exercises of discretion. While openness is not a cure-all for substantive injustice, it is a procedural check that can help prevent it. Because the public exposure of unjust procedures and decisions can prevent future injustices, the public concern is great. Rational persons might accept a presumption favoring public access to formal and informal hearings, with provisions to protect central privacy rights, such as to medical information, trade secrets, and so forth. This balance prevents major burdens on individuals, yet should serve the public interest.

Timeliness and Notice

The requirements of a prompt hearing with adequate notice and time to prepare are closely connected. If a hearing is held too quickly, the time to prepare might not be adequate. Contrarily, the more time for preparation, the less prompt the hearing. And one cannot prepare adequately until one has received sufficient notice of the matters at issue.

Timeliness A prompt hearing includes more than the time before a hearing begins; it includes both the length of the hearing (adjournments) and the time for a decision to be rendered. A prompt hearing with a decision delayed a year or so is no better than a hearing in a year with an immediate decision. The APA recognizes this point by stating that an agency shall conclude a matter "within a reasonable time" (5 U.S.C. § 555(b)). The MSA is more explicit. It requires responding to an application within 30 days, beginning a formal hearing within 90 days of receipt of a completed application, and a decision 90 days after a hearing (MSA §§ 4-104(a)(1) and (2), and 4-215(g)). This time-frame still permits seven months plus the length of the hearing for a decision.

An instrumental concern with the accuracy of decisions can favor a hearing and decision sooner or later. An early hearing can facilitate the preservation of evidence; with the passage of time, memories fade and evidence can be lost. Delay in holding a hearing and reaching a decision can also sometimes facilitate correct decisions. Greater time between the notice and hearing can permit a more complete gathering of evidence and preparation of arguments, and more time between a hearing and a decision can permit a decisionmaker better to assess the evidence and reason to a conclusion. Delay has these benefits only if the time is used for these purposes and not other matters.

A more central reason for a prompt hearing is to permit individuals to plan their lives and activities. For example, an applicant for a nursing license might not be able to obtain a nursing job until a decision is made. Even if the state permits applicants to work until the results of nursing board exams are known, many hospitals will not hire and train nurses who might have to be dismissed should they not have passed the exam. Meanwhile, the nurse is either unemployed or working in a lower scale position, such as a nurse's assistant. Many of a nurse's life decisions, such as moving, renting an apartment, and so on might have to be delayed pending the licensing decision because of its effects on employment and income. Similar effects result from almost all burden/benefit decisions. These difficulties are largely independent of the actual decision—whether a benefit is conferred or a burden imposed. They result from uncertainty; a decision either way removes the uncertainty and permits people to make decisions and act. Consequently, the requirement of a prompt hearing and decision does not rest solely, or even primarily, on its contribution to correct decisions.

Promptness of hearings and decisions often competes with adequate time for preparation of evidence and decision making. The underlying considerations are different. While the chief reason for a prompt hearing and decision is to permit individuals to plan and act, the chief reason supporting later hearings and decisions is accuracy. No algorithm resolves the conflict. If rules establish maximum times, as in the MSA, and the full time is used, avoidable delay is often permitted; if the time permitted is quite short, more hasty and incorrect decisions are likely.

Notice Three aspects of notices are important: when they are issued, to whom they are issued, and what they contain. They should issue as soon as it is determined that a hearing should be held on a matter. Of course, one must set a date for a hearing before notice can be given, but a date can usually be set when a decision is made to hold a hearing. Determining the availability of a presiding officer might take a little time, but if it will take significant time, a notice with an approximate date could be sent and persons later informed of a definite date and time. Bureaucrats often provide a specific date and time that will almost certainly have to be changed. Recipients would find it less frustrating were they merely informed of approximate dates instead of spurious specific ones.

Who should receive notice is usually easy but occasionally difficult to determine. The MSA specifies that notice should be sent to all parties and all persons having filed a petition to intervene. The APA states that all interested parties should have an opportunity to be heard and defines as parties persons admitted as such or properly seeking and entitled to be such (5 U.S.C. §§ 554(c) and 551(3)). Consider the situation in *Ashbacker Radio Corp. v. FCC* (326 U.S. 327 (1946); see also Davis 1972, 209–10; Schwartz 1976, 269–71). Two applications had been received for radio station licenses on the same frequency in Michigan. The Commission found that granting both would create interference, so it granted one and set the other for a hearing in accordance with the law's requirement of a hearing before denial of an application. The Court struck down the procedure, for the hearing would have been meaningless; a denial would be necessitated by the prior grant of a license for the same frequency. Instead, comparative hearings must be held.

The *Ashbacker* rule requires a refinement. If all applicants for a mutually exclusive license must be heard in a comparative hearing, then it might never occur. Subsequent applications could be received, and these applicants would also have to be included. Consequently, agencies use cut-off dates so that only applications received by then need be considered.

These types of cases involve a further difficulty. In radio and television station licensing and renewal, listeners also have a significant interest. The courts have held that listeners, or at least selected representatives, can legitimately claim to be parties with a right to participate in hearings (*Office of Communication of United Church of Christ v. FCC*, 359 F.2d 994 (D.C. Cir. 1966)). But if listeners are potential parties, then should they receive notice? Fortunately, in renewals stations can broadcast a notice to listeners. However, that is a fortuitous circumstance of regulation of public communications, and even there it will not work for initial licensing decisions. For other matters, such as setting rates for individual firms, the APA classifies the activity as rule making and requires notice in the Federal Register (5 U.S.C. §§ 551(4) and 553(b)). Licensing is not considered rule making (5 U.S.C. § 551(6)), so the present remedy is for agencies to take it upon themselves to publish notices of hearings. The reasonable solution is to require publication of notices of all hearings in which members of the public are potential parties.

As the point of a notice is to enable parties to appear and present relevant evidence (see de Smith 1980, 196), a notice should provide adequate information to enable parties to prepare all relevant evidence to support their positions (Flick 1984, 51; Hewitt 1972, 120). The fundamentals are captured in the APA requirements of time and place, legal authority and jurisdiction for the hearing, and the matters of fact and law asserted (5 U.S.C. § 554(b); see also MSA § 4-206(c); RSA § 9(b)). The facts given need not be all the evidentiary facts to be developed at the hearing, only the so-called "ultimate" facts on which a decision might be based (Lorch 1980, 129). Moreover, a notice should indicate the consequences of an adverse decision (Flick 1984, 60). The potential consequences can significantly affect the time, effort, and money a person might expend to prepare; indeed, if the consequences were minimal, one might not even bother to attend a hearing.

Discovery is a procedure commonly used in civil cases to help parties prepare for hearings. One party can ask another for information that it has relevant to the case (see Fed. R. Civ. P. 26). Discovery is not widely available in administrative agency hearings (Schwartz 1976, 278–79; Evans 1983; Flick 1984, 78). The arguments for increased discovery are essentially the same as those which led to its recognition in civil law—decreased surprise and increased resolution of issues without formal hearings, although the second reason might not be as strong for administrative matters. Many agencies fear that people might be given license to go through all their files. With the adoption of freedom of information laws permitting access to agency files, this argument cannot primarily rest on privacy. Moreover, if discovery were limited to information to be presented as evidence, a concern for wide ranging searches of agency files would be largely mitigated (Lorch 1980, 139). Agencies can find out almost everything about the subject of a burden/benefit decision, but the individual often cannot find out much about the agency case (Lorch 1980, 138). A greater use of discovery would further the purposes of adequate notice, namely, enabling persons to prepare all appropriate evidence for hearings. The MSA permits discovery orders to the extent permitted in civil procedure (MSA §§ 4-205(b) and 4-210(a)). Unfortunately, civil procedure arguably permits too broad of discovery, which is often used as a delaying tactic. If civil discovery were appropriately constrained (see Bayles 1987, 54–55), this standard would also be appropriate for administrative hearings. People have no reason to accept a rule denying them access to agency information that is directly related to their claims; to do so might deny them favorable decisions or result in their wasting time pressing unmeritorious claims.

Presentation of Evidence

Interested persons should have an opportunity at a hearing to present information and rebut adverse evidence. Three features of this principle are briefly examined: the written or oral nature of the presentation, the opportunity to rebut adverse evidence, and the admissibility of evidence.

Written or oral The APA provides that agencies may receive "[a]ny oral or documentary evidence" (5 U.S.C. § 556(d)). The MSA requires the presiding officer to allow all parties to "respond, present evidence and argument, conduct cross-examination, and submit rebuttal evidence" (MSA § 4-211(2); see also RSA § 9(c)). Little difference exists between these provisions. The federal act does not require, only permits, agencies to receive oral testimony, and the MSA does not specify whether the evidence and argument are to be written or oral. People are rarely denied an opportunity for oral presentations in formal hearings; indeed, an oral presentation is the ordinary meaning of 'a hearing'.

In informal processes, oral presentation is often but not always necessary or desirable. The Supreme Court has held that in welfare termination proceedings mere written evidence is not adequate (*Goldberg v. Kelly*, 397 U.S. 254 (1970)).

The clientele are often incapable of expressing themselves well in writing and might not have access to someone else who can adequately write for them. Moreover, the facts involved often depend on the credibility of persons.

However, in pretermination procedures for social security disability benefits, the Court did not think oral presentations necessary (*Mathews v. Eldridge*, 424 U.S. 319 (1976)). One reason is that the statute places on individuals the burden of showing a continuing disability by "medically acceptable clinical and laboratory diagnostic techniques" (42 U.S.C. § 423(d)(3) (1976)). Because the disability must be medically established, it is more readily ascertainable by written evidence. Furthermore, because of the sensitivity and privacy of some matters that might arise, some claimants might prefer written evidence to the embarrassment of a face-to-face presentation (Mashaw 1983, 91–92). Of course, claimants are entitled to post-termination hearings in which oral testimony and argument can be given. An even stronger case for written evidence alone can be made for revocation of a driver's license for three suspensions within a ten year period (*Dixon v. Love*, 431 U.S. 105 (1977)). It is hard to see how oral testimony could be better than written evidence that suspensions did or did not occur, although an oral presentation might be important for a mercy plea for an exception.

In deciding whether oral or written evidence is preferable, at least two, and sometimes three, factors need to be considered. One is the ability of the individual involved to present evidence orally or in writing. The second is the type of evidence supporting the ultimate fact in question—medical and statistical or credibility of persons. Of course, the ability of administrative law judges and others to determine by observation whether witnesses are telling the truth or lying is probably a myth. If one strongly doubts that they can, then the credibility of persons provides no reason to prefer oral over written testimony. In any case, video tapes would provide an alternative to live witnesses. A third possible factor is the privacy or possible discomfort of the individual.

Although the ability of hearing officials to determine accurately the credibility of witnesses from their behavior in giving evidence is questionable, the opportunity to cross-examine witnesses does provide a reason for oral testimony. By asking appropriate questions, one can often bring out facts that show inconsistencies or support an alternative view of the matter. The opportunity to cross-examine does not require that testimony be given live before a hearing official. It only requires that it be given before the other party or representative who has an opportunity at that time to ask questions. Such questioning occurs in depositions, and again video taped testimony might suffice. Interestingly, natural justice has not included a general right to cross-examine (Hewitt 1972, 129). It does require an opportunity to rebut evidence concerning disputed facts, but cross-examination is only one method and is not necessary if other equally effective means of rebuttal are available (Flick 1984, 84–85).

If oral testimony is to be taken, then each party should be permitted to present witnesses. Permitting one party but not another to present witnesses would deny equal participation. By biasing information, it would also contribute to incorrect outcomes. Even if it did not affect the outcome in a particular case, the appearance of injustice could have demoralizing effects. Thus, rational persons would not accept differential opportunities. The same applies to the power to subpoena witnesses.

Opportunity to rebut adverse evidence This principle is an important one. We have already seen that it provides a reason against ex parte communications and sometimes supports oral testimony, and it has other significant implications. It supports adequate notice and discovery. If people do not know in detail what is alleged against them, a proper defense cannot be prepared. This applies not only to the ultimate factual claims in a notice, but also to specific evidence produced to support those claims. If an unanticipated piece of evidence is introduced during a hearing, one can ask for an adjournment to prepare rebuttal evidence. However, this delays the decision, is inconvenient, and increases costs.

The reasons for the principle are readily apparent. First, if a person does not have an opportunity to rebut adverse evidence, then the evidence on which a decision is based can be significantly incomplete. Without the full evidence, the findings and decision might be incorrect. Second, even if a decision is correct, without having had an opportunity to rebut all adverse evidence, an adversely affected party will not be likely to believe justice was done. The person will have been denied a full opportunity to be heard, a chance to make the case as best as he or she could. Such a denial can also demoralize others.

A final point, unique to administrative law, is an opportunity to respond to a hearing official's report. The adversary adjudication model is drawn from the legal trial. In a trial, the judge or judge and jury are present at the hearing and render a decision. In administrative adjudications, this is often not the case.

The person who hears a case can be an agency head, administrative law judge, senior official, or low level employee such as a social worker, or a panel of such persons. Herein, 'hearing officer'and 'hearing official' are used to refer to any such person, and 'presiding officer' is a hearing official in charge of conducting a hearing. Prior to the APA, hearing officers (predecessors of administrative law judges) rarely made decisions. Now, federal agencies can require that cases heard by administrative law judges be certified to them for decision (5 U.S.C. § 557(b)). Initial decisions by employees are almost always subject to review by superiors. Under the MSA, unless the hearing officer is the agency head, initial decisions are made subject to review by agency heads.

If a hearing official only makes a recommendation to another person, then the hearing report essentially constitutes evidence for the decision. Consequently, in the United States, parties are entitled to "a reasonable opportunity" to respond to the recommendation (5 U.S.C. § 557(c); see also MSA § 4-216(e) (opportunity to present briefs on review)). In England, however, the reports are considered private to the agency (Lorch 1980, 145), although there is some support for the claim that natural justice requires it being made available to parties (Hewitt 1972, 11). The U.S. rule is the better one, for rational persons would want an opportunity to respond to all information given to the decision-maker, even if that information is developed or prepared after the hearing. Nonetheless, as a hearing official's report constitutes preliminary findings by an impartial person, they could accept it having significant weight.

Admissibility of evidence The central issue is whether administrative hearings should conform to the rules of evidence used in courts or to more generous ones. Little agreement exists on this issue. The APA permits the presentation of "[a]ny oral or documentary evidence" but requires the exclusion of "irrelevant, immaterial, or unduly repetitious evidence" (5 U.S.C. § 556(d)). The MSA also includes constitutional, statutory, and evidentiary privilege grounds for exclusion (MSA § 4-212), but the first two are not significant additions since they also apply to hearings under the APA. The MSA explicitly recognizes that findings can be based on evidence inadmissible in civil trials, although it must be evidence reasonable prudent persons would rely on (MSA § 4-215(d); but see RSA § 10(1) (with some exceptions evidence restricted to that admissible in court)). The common law permits evidence not admissible at trial (Flick 1984, 70, 92).

The central question should be: "Why exclude offered evidence?" To the extent judicial rules of admissibility are based on adversary adjudication and the presence of a jury, they are unnecessary or inappropriate for many nonadversarial burden/benefit decisions (Flick 1984, 72). Two reasons for excluding evidence are to save time and to avoid misleading decisionmakers. Irrelevant evidence wastes the time of those involved. If information is unreliable, it too might waste time and be misleading. However, an opposing party should have an opportunity to point out its defects, and a decisionmaker can take them into account. Of course, if there is no opposing party, say, in a social security investigatory hearing, the unreliable and misleading character of evidence will not be pointed out. Nevertheless, a presiding officer would have to recognize evidence's unreliability to exclude it, so usually he or she should be able to evaluate it properly.

Perhaps the evidence most likely to be affected by a choice of rules of evidence is hearsay testimony. The chief difficulty with hearsay evidence is that the person making the claim cannot be cross-examined (Lorch 1980, 134). Yet, technically hearsay evidence need not be unreliable. Consider the issue in *Richardson v. Perales* (402 U.S. 389 (1971)). This case involved a social security disability claim. As noted above, disability must be shown by medical evidence. At the hearing on Perales's disability, the agency submitted reports from several physicians who had examined him, and the hearing officer had another physician explain the medical aspects of the physicians' reports. Without the examining physicians present for cross-examination, the medical reports technically constituted hearsay evidence. Nevertheless, the Court found their admission proper.

Two points about evidence are involved in this case. First, hearsay evidence was permitted. The hearsay evidence involved is more reliable than a report of a conversation with another person; these were reports written by physicians. Although Perales did not have an opportunity to cross-examine, he could have subpoenaed the physicians. Moreover, he had adequate opportunity to present his own medical evidence.

The second point pertains to the so-called residuum rule that there must be some evidence admissible in court, no matter how slight, to support a finding. That was not required in *Perales*. The Court pointed out various reasons for not following the residuum rule, such as the reliability of written medical evidence, the operations of the social security system, and Perales's failure to subpoena the physicians. The crucial point is that some evidence inadmissible in court is quite reliable, and one should look to the reliability of evidence, not technical rules, in determining its admissibility. As one commentator has noted, "There is more danger from the exclusion of competent, relevant, and material evidence than from inclusion of the opposite" (Lorch 1980, 132). The MSA rule that the evidence be the type reasonable prudent persons rely on in important matters is preferable to the residuum rule (MSA § 4-215(d)).

Another point about evidence is official notice—cognizance by decision-makers of facts not presented in evidence. First, one needs to distinguish between legislative and adjudicative facts. The latter pertain to the particular party or parties or events or conditions involved in a decision, while the former pertain to more general matters for developing law or policy (see Davis 1972, 296). Second, in civil cases, judges are permitted to take notice of adjudicative facts only if they are not reasonably disputed because generally known or easily and reliably determined, for example, by looking them up in an almanac (Fed. R. Evid. 201(b)). Third, besides facts of which judicial notice can be taken, the MSA also permits official notice of the record of other proceedings before the agency, technical or scientific facts within its expertise, and codes or standards adopted by governments or national organizations (MSA § 4-212(f); see also RSA § 10(4) (technical or scientific facts); Flick 1984, 97). Natural justice principles also permit tribunals to use their expert knowledge to draw inferences from evidence (Flick 1984, 112–16; Hewitt 1972, 114).

Two reasons for permitting official notice of facts are costs and accuracy (see Davis 1972, 314 (convenience)). It would often be a waste of time and money to produce evidence of generally known or easily ascertainable facts. If agencies cannot bring to bear their technical and scientific expertise, decisions are less likely to be correct. A reason for administrative agencies is to use expertise not readily available to legislatures and courts.

The crucial problem with official notice is that the information noticed might be disputable. As notice is usually taken in an officer's report of a hearing or the actual decision making, parties might not have an opportunity to contest the information. Consequently, parties should have an opportunity to contest or rebut information of which notice is taken (5 U.S.C. § 556(e); MSA § 4-212(f); RSA § 10(4); Fed. R. Evid. 201(e); Davis 1972, 314; Lorch 1980, 141; Flick 1984, 97). The net effect, then, is to shift the burden of proof to parties contesting officially noticed facts (Flick 1984, 105). If parties have an opportunity to rebut the information, then they are not treated unfairly. Again, the opportunity to rebut adverse evidence plays an important role.

Counsel

As noted in discussing *Goldberg v. Kelly* (397 U.S. 254 (1970)) at the beginning of the previous section, some persons are incapable of clearly organizing and presenting written evidence. The *Goldberg* decision thought this especially true of welfare recipients, so it required an oral hearing for termination. Many persons who cannot present evidence well in writing are also incapable of doing so orally. Indeed, some people who can present material well in writing cannot do so orally. Consequently, the Court recognized a right of welfare recipients to be represented by counsel, although few of them can afford counsel.

Besides the inability to express oneself well, two other reasons for counsel exist. Counsel can have a range of experience and knowledge of rules, policies, and procedures that laypersons lack. Counsel also usually have a more objective perspective on the evidence and proceedings than a client. The adage that a lawyer who represents him or herself has a fool for a client reflects clients' lack of objectivity, for the lawyer might have all the knowledge of independent counsel.

The APA recognizes a right to counsel in all cases in which a person is compelled to appear before an agency (5 U.S.C. § 555(b)) and constitutional due process requires it in many other situations such as *Goldberg*. Counsel need not be a lawyer, although agencies can usually restrict the persons who can appear as counsel (5 U.S.C. § 555(b); Lorch 1980, 144). Because the APA right is restricted to cases in which one is compelled to appear, it is largely restricted to regulatory agencies that impose burdens. The *Goldberg* decision and most others acknowledging a right to counsel extend only to benefit-terminating decisions. In important benefit-conferring decisions such as veterans benefits and social security, agencies have effectively limited access to legal counsel by severely restricting the fees that can be paid (Schwartz 1976, 286). The MSA is perhaps more generous, permitting counsel in all formal hearings and incorporating other state law regarding whether counsel must be a lawyer (MSA § 4-203(b)). Some doubt exists whether traditional natural justice entitled one to have counsel (Hewitt 1972, 125).

A drawback of a right to legal counsel is that it pushes procedures toward trial-type hearings. Lawyers are indoctrinated with court procedure, so they often push matters toward the full adversary adjudication model. As one commentator harshly puts it, "Lawyers breed procedure, procedure breeds lawyers, and both breed sluggish and high-priced justice" (Lorch 1980, 144). The presence of legal counsel thus tends to turn informal, inexpensive procedures into formal, expensive ones. The costs are financial and the timeliness of decisions. These considerations are less relevant if people are accompanied or represented by nonprofessional counsel, such as relatives and friends.

A right to have counsel provided is not recognized in administrative procedures. The Supreme Court has required it for all criminal cases involving the possibility of incarceration, and on a case by case basis for some types of civil actions (*Gideon v. Wainwright* (372 U.S. 335 (1963); *Argersinger v. Hamlin*, 407 U.S. 25 (1972); *Lassiter v. Dep't of Social Servs.*, 452 U.S. 18 (1981)).

Whether rights to counsel and to have one appointed are and should be recognized seems to depend on three factors. The chief one is whether a severe burden might be imposed; a second one is the formality of the proceeding; and the third is the expertise provided. These factors go together, for the greater the burden imposed, the greater the need for procedural protection and likelihood the hearing will be formal, and thus the more legal expertise will be useful. Absent these factors, counsel, especially legal counsel, are not necessary and often undesirable for burden/benefit decisions. For example, suppose a faculty member submits a grant application. No burden will be imposed, no hearing is involved, and most lawyers would have less expertise than the applicant. At best, counsel might have a useful role in evaluating and complying with the terms of a grant.

Identifying the chief factors, however, does not settle the rational balance for various types of situation. In general, permitting counsel imposes few costs and can be beneficial to individuals and the administration of justice. Any tendency of lawyers to push informal procedures into more formal ones can be successfully resisted by hearing officers. Agencies need not indirectly bar them by restricting fees that can be paid. However, in some circumstances, such as departmental faculty meetings, even the presence of nonlegal counsel or advisors can be detrimental to informal give and take. The provision of counsel, especially legal counsel, can be very expensive. The importance of the decision to the individual and the benefits of counsel must, therefore, be great enough to outweigh these costs. A theoretical principle for such balancing is given in chapter 6.

The Record

Interest in the record is not an obsession with files. Instead, it relates directly to the opportunity to rebut evidence and for a decision based on the evidence (see chap. 4). If a decision is based on material that is not part of the record, then a party is not likely to be aware of it and have an opportunity to respond to it. If there is a review or appeal to a court to determine whether a decision is arbitrary, the reviewer or court must know the decision's basis. The record constitutes that basis. Of course, all decisions involve matters not part of a record, matters so obvious that no one thinks them worth proving or noticing, such as that it is daylight at noon. Many other considerations that go into a decision, such as policies and attitudes, relate to legislative matters or do not prejudice a person's case.

In formal hearings, what belongs to the record is fairly clear. The MSA prescribes that records in formal adjudications consist of notices; pre-hearing orders; pleadings, motions, briefs, rulings, and so forth; evidence received; matters officially noticed; offers of proof, objections, and so on; proposed findings and objections to them; a record used at the hearing along with any transcript used in making a decision; the order; all staff memoranda submitted to the hearing officer or decisionmaker; and matters from ex parte communications (MSA § 4-221(b); see RSA § 9(e)). We have also seen that if a hearing officer only makes a recommendation, that too should be considered part of the record and parties given an opportunity to respond to it.

The MSA also provides for the contents of a record in informal hearings. Actually, it provides for two types of informal hearings—conference hearings and summary hearings. Although it does not specify what the record is for a conference hearing, as it is only a somewhat reduced version of a formal hearing, presumably it would include anything on the list for a formal hearing. For a summary hearing, the MSA merely specifies the record as the documents considered or prepared by the official and notes that such a record need not be the sole basis for a decision (MSA § 4-506).

Given the purposes of a record to ensure an opportunity to respond to and to evaluate a decision, the criterion should be everything considered in making a decision (except for common-sense matters noted earlier). Individuals and reviewers cannot evaluate decisions if significant relevant grounds for them are unknown. Records of informal hearings, especially summary ones, rarely meet this requirement. For example, an agency employee might meet with a person and simply write a summary of the discussion. Such a summary might not be written for several days, and faulty or selective memory can result in better recall of items supporting a decision than those opposing it. Even worse, the record might include no account of the conversation, only conclusions; perhaps merely a note that a meeting was held; or nothing at all.

Keeping a record or file in informal procedures exhibits a basic tension. Pulling in one direction is the desire for written evidence of the basis of a decision—a record. Pulling in the opposite direction is administrative efficiency. Preparing files takes time and generates much of the condemned bureaucratic paperwork. The flow of paperwork increases as more people are involved in the decision-making process. A person who interviews an applicant might not make the final decision, and several other persons might make recommendations or comments before a decision is made. Much of a record is often not considered by the decisionmaker. Even in informal procedures, files often become large and the volume of decisions can be enormous, so decision-makers rely on summaries and at best a selective look at the file. To do otherwise means bureaucratic delay and less timely decisions.

These considerations have to be balanced. Requiring transcripts or tape recordings of every contact individuals have with persons involved in burden/benefit decisions would be intolerable and pointless, yet, no record at all is also intolerable. Reasonable judgments can be made. Just as the minutes of a board meeting do not include all the discussion, only the relevant actions, so people can determine what is important for the majority of cases. One should not be guided by the exceptional case in which the ordinary information is insufficient and thus require collecting such extra details in all future cases. Much useless bureaucratic paperwork results from that type of policy, and the costs outweigh the benefits. One might object that this is the price of justice in particular cases. But that is to forget that the price includes delayed decisions, which can mean injustice in many cases. However, even in informal interviews, agency personnel can jot down the salient facts either during the meeting (which involves no extra time) or immediately afterward.

Appeals

The right to appeal in criminal cases is widely recognized. It is also generally recognized in administrative law, but appeals in administrative cases are more complex. First, there are administrative appeals. In formal adjudications, either the individual or agency can request agency review of the decision (5 U.S.C. § 557(b); MSA § 4-216). Usually, an agency can exercise the full powers of the hearing officer; that is, all findings of fact, conclusions of law or policy, and applications of law and policy can be considered. A similar review can occur for informal adjudications (see MSA § 4-504). Second, usually after administrative appeals have been exhausted, appeal can be made to the courts (5 U.S.C. § 702; MSA § 5-102; RSA § 15). These appeals are generally restricted to matters of law and their application to facts; findings of fact are overturned only if clearly erroneous or unsupported by evidence (see chap. 4).

These structures of appeals, especially of administrative appeals, raise significant espistemological and normative questions. The primary purpose given for permitting appeals is to ensure accuracy in decision making. The idea is that if a superior or other person reviews a decision, mistakes are likely to be corrected. However, for that to be true, the second decision must be more likely to be correct than the first. Eventually, there must be an unreviewed decision, and accuracy can be no better than that of the last decisionmaker. Reviewers supposedly have greater experience and knowledge of law and policy. Initial decisionmakers, however, hear all the evidence and arguments and observe witnesses, while reviewers look only at records, perhaps selectively.

There might be a loss of impartiality in appeals. In formal adjudications, considerable effort is made to provide impartial and independent persons to conduct hearings. Much of that effort might be wasted if appeal is made to agencies. In informal procedures, a superior might have various reasons independent of the merits of a case to support a subordinate's decisions (see Davis 1969, 144–45).

An appeals system often has high costs and a built-in bias. If an initial decision is that a burden ought not to be imposed or a benefit should be granted, the individual involved is not going to appeal. If the individual loses, then he or she might as well appeal since the whole decision will be made again and the person has nothing to lose but time and effort (see Schwartz 1976, 406–09). If appeals are as of right, agencies will be burdened with appeals from practically all decisions adverse to individuals no matter the appeals' merits. This increases the general costs of the procedure. The only practical solutions to this problem are to make appeals discretionary or to limit the scope of review to specific errors.

In informal procedures in which agency employees make initial decisions, an agency might be unable to appeal a decision. As no one represents the agency against the decisionmaker, no one from that side will appeal (the agency might be forbidden to appeal such cases). Consequently, appeals can only be taken from decisions adverse to individuals, not from those that unjustly favor individuals. One might expect that agency employees would thus be cautious and not inclined to impose burdens or confer benefits, but the opposite might also be true. They might be generous to avoid the difficulties and possible adverse effect on their careers of many appeals being taken from their decisions (see Davis 1969, 143 (systematic effort to discourage appeals common)).

Consequently, the argument from increased accuracy for a right to an administrative appeal is weak due to lack of assurance of increased accuracy, loss of impartiality, higher costs, and a possible biasing of issues appealed. Nonetheless, an individual adversely affected by a decision would not be pleased to have no chance for appeal. Mistakes can be made, and an adversely affected person is likely to think one has been. A reversal constitutes a correction in this person's eyes. Even if no reversal occurs, the assurance that two people concur might increase confidence that a correct decision has been made, or at least weaken the confidence that a mistake has been made. The appeal might thus help prevent demoralization. Sometimes even asking a decisionmaker to review a decision helps. Thus, students are often more satisfied with a grade lower than they thought appropriate if a teacher rereads a paper or exam. Nonetheless, these considerations do not support a right to have the full case rather than specific alleged errors reviewed.

Finally, a few comments about double jeopardy are appropriate. The criminal law prohibition of double jeopardy applies only to acquittals from burden-imposing decisions on a final determination of facts in a particular allegation. Thus, it requires (1) a final decision (2) favorable to the defendant (3) on a particular charge or alleged fact situation. Double jeopardy is irrelevant to many burden/benefit decisions, because one or more of these elements is missing. First, denials of benefits and of burden relief as well as termination of benefits are adverse to a person, so the concept underlying double jeopardy does not apply. No reasonable person would object to having an adverse decision rejected and a new one made, especially when the new one could not be worse. Decisions to confer or not terminate benefits and to relieve burdens are favorable to a person, so something analogous to double jeopardy can apply. That is, a person might claim that once such determinations are made, it is unfair to reconsider them.

Second, however, the underlying fact situations must be the same, and they frequently change for benefit conferral or termination and burden relief. The basis for granting welfare benefits or parole can change, for example, if one obtains a job or violates a condition of parole. Whenever it is alleged that facts have changed, reconsideration is appropriate. The particular facts for many burden-imposing decisions also change. Even if one successfully argues that certain income or property should not be taxed this year, next year is another matter. Whether an agency or decisionmaker should be required to come to the same conclusion absent a change in law or regulations is a matter of consistency and adherence to precedent (see chap. 5).

Summary

The fundamental principle of an opportunity to be heard is that an individual "who has a sufficient interest or right at stake in a determination of governmental action should be entitled to an opportunity to know and to meet, with the weapons of rebuttal evidence, cross-examination, and argument, unfavorable evidence . . ." (Davis 1972, 160). The principle requires an open and prompt hearing with notice providing sufficient information and time to prepare. Open hearings provide an important safeguard against improper decisions, for others can observe whether justice is done. Determining how promptly a hearing and decision should occur involves balancing possibly increased accuracy from time for preparation against the possibly decreased accuracy and extended uncertainty of delayed decisions. Notice should be given as soon as possible and sufficiently inform a person of the issues and possible consequences to enable him or her to determine what evidence is relevant and the significance of the decision to be made.

At a hearing, persons should usually be able to present both written and oral evidence if reasonably relevant to the issues. Oral presentation of evidence and argument is not always necessary. A person should not only be permitted to present evidence and witnesses, but to rebut all adverse evidence. The opportunity to rebut evidence has important implications for ex parte communications, cross-examination of witnesses, hearing officers' reports or decisions, official notice, and hearsay evidence. The main reasons for excluding evidence are that it wastes time or is misleading. Irrelevant and repetitious evidence wastes time, and unreliable evidence can but need not waste time and be misleading.

Finally, counsel should usually be permitted, an adequate record made, and appeals allowed. Counsel can help people present their cases coherently and objectively. Legal counsel are not always desirable, for they can make processes more formal and longer. An adequate record in informal processes will contain the salient evidence on which a decision is made, but the compiling of files and records can delay decisions and promote inefficiency. Appeals can contribute to accuracy of decisions, although perhaps not as much as one might at first expect. Perhaps as importantly, they can help assure persons of the correctness of adverse decisions.

CHAPTER 4

GROUNDS FOR DECISIONS

Unlike the principles of an impartial decisionmaker and an opportunity to be heard, human rights codes and constitutions do not generally recognize a principle requiring provision of the grounds for decisions. It is widely recognized that for criminal conviction, conduct must violate a previously established law and a person must be informed of the charges against him or her (UN 1966, art. 15; CE 1950, art. 7; OAS 1969, art. 9; Cdn. Charter § 11(g); LRCC 1982, 12). The general requirement of notice also includes informing persons of the basis on which action will be taken. Thus, a person must be informed of the substantive standards on which a burden/benefit decision is to be made. Presumably, one is then found to meet or not meet these grounds. But these principles do not require that persons be informed of the findings and reasoning involved in the decisions in their cases. It is one thing to be told, say, that one is charged with assault and the tribunal has decided that you did assault someone on April 23rd; it is another to be told why the tribunal has so decided.

The common-law principles of natural justice have never clearly required that standards or reasons be disclosed (Galligan 1986, 270; Flick 1984, 117, 127). Some support exists for a third natural law principle requiring the giving of reasons (Hewitt 1972, 10; Verkuil 1986, 702). So far, any such right seems to be limited to a few contexts and usually to require that one request that reasons be given (see also Macdonald 1987, 237 n. 36). However, administrative agencies might have difficulty justifying their decisions to reviewing courts if no reasons were given (see Wade 1982, 373–74).

Thus, for a general requirement that one be given reasons for decisions, one must look to statutory law. For all formal hearings, the APA requires a statement of "findings and conclusions, and the reasons or basis therefor, on all the material issues of fact, law, or discretion presented on the record" (5 U.S.C. § 557(c)(3)(A)). Similarly, in formal adjudications involving agency discretion, the MSA requires "separately stated, findings of fact, conclusions of law, and policy reasons" for all aspects of an order including remedies (MSA § 4-215(c); see RSA § 12). For the denial of written applications and other requests in connection with agency proceedings, the APA requires that a notice of denial "be accompanied by a brief statement of the grounds for denial" (5 U.S.C. §

555(e)). It is unclear whether this applies to all written applications or primarily to those in connection with other proceedings. The MSA requires a notice of a summary proceeding to provide a statement of findings of fact, conclusions of law, and policy reasons (MSA § 4-503(b)(2)).

Central problems surrounding the reasons requirement stem from the significant discretion legislatures usually give administrative agencies to deal with matters delegated to them. Kenneth Culp Davis has commented on the scope of such discretion (Davis 1969, 48). He notes that often the legislature has in effect told an agency, "Here is the problem. Deal with it." Sometimes the practical content of the legislative direction is even less clear, merely telling the agency to find the problems and deal with them. If an agency has such wide discretion, then even if in formal hearings it is confined to the evidence in the record, can it not decide any way it wants? If so, what good are reasons and is there any way to criticize them?

Discretion is a central issue of procedural justice. There are various concerns with the discretion of persons making burden/benefit decisions (see Goodin 1988, 193–204). To the extent they have discretion, their decisions may seem arbitrary. Moreover, they can often use their discretion to manipulate and exploit those subject to them by giving or withholding favorable decisions. Furthermore, as decisions might go either way, uncertainty and unpredictability result. Finally, in a search for full information, decisionmakers might intrude on the privacy of persons who might not object for fear of an unfavorable decision.

Many of the issues in the rest of this book relate one way or another to such discretion. This chapter and the next focus on traditional legal methods of controlling or limiting discretion. This chapter focuses on requirements of grounds for decisions—standards, giving findings and reasons based on such standards, the burden of proof, and judicial review of administrative decisions. The next chapter considers various "formal" requirements that presumably limit discretion.

Discretion

First, however, the concept of discretion requires analysis. It is most at home in contexts in which people are criticized or held accountable for decisions on the basis of some standards or norms (see Dworkin 1977, 31; Christie 1986,

752; Galligan 1986, 21). As we shall see (chap. 8), the types of standards involved affect the type of discretion and people's accountability. Various authors have distinguished several senses of 'discretion'. In one sense, someone has discretion if that person must exercise judgment in making a decision (Dworkin 1977, 31–32; Galligan 1986, 8). Thus, if a person is told to pick the three ripest apples from a tree, judgment will be required in deciding which are the ripest. Let discretion$_1$ be the sense in which judgment is required. This sense is not the central one for analyzing burden/benefit decisions, because decisionmakers almost always have discretion$_1$ (see Goodin 1988, 191–92 (ineliminable)). One can conceive of some decisions that do not require judgment. If the decision is merely the amount of a burden or benefit as based on a mathematical formula, for example, the amount of tax owed on a given amount, then judgment is not required. A decision whether or not a person owes tax and on what amount, however, usually requires judgment.

Let discretion$_2$ stand for the sense of a person's decision being final or ultimate, of no one being able to review and overturn it (see Dworkin 1977, 32; Goodin 1988, 189). Actually, this sense has two subsenses. (a) Normatively, no one is authorized to review and overturn the decision. For example, in professional football, instant replay officials can overrule some decisions of officials on the field, but they cannot overrule all of them. So officials on the field have final normative authority to make certain types of calls. Often the normative basis for review is a matter of degree depending on the scope and stringency of review. Even in the football case, replay officials are to overturn decisions only on the basis of incontrovertible evidence. (b) Practically, no one has the power to overturn the decision (see Davis 1972, 91; Davis 1969, 4; Fletcher 1984, 273–74, 276). Although theoretically Supreme Court decisions interpreting the Constitution can be overturned by constitutional amendments, in practice this is nearly impossible. For the most part, for our purposes the difference between normatively and practically final decisions is not important.

Discretion$_2$ has a role in analyzing burden/benefit decisions, but it is often dependent on another sense. For example, a judge can have discretion$_2$ to impose a prison sentence of four years. Provided the sentence is within statutory limits for the offense, appellate courts do not overturn such decisions. They grant trial judges discretion$_2$, because the judges' have discretion in some other sense.

It is this other sense that is crucial for administrative law and burden/benefit decisions. Let discretion$_3$ stand for the sense of having a choice between permissible alternatives (Davis 1972, 91; Davis 1969, 4; see Goodin 1988, 187 (weak discretion)). Consider the following statement about the receipt of evidence in a formal adjudicative hearing: "Any part of the evidence may be received in written form if doing so will expedite the hearing without substantial prejudice to the interests of any party" (MSA § 4-212(d)). This subsection confers discretion on a presiding officer to accept or not accept written evidence. It is part of the presiding officer's authority to manage the hearing, and it leaves the officer a choice among possible courses of action.

Other senses of discretion do not adequately account for this type of case. The MSA statement does not indicate whether the presiding officer's decision can be reviewed, so it does not provide discretion$_2$. Obviously, the presiding officer will have to exercise judgment as to whether written evidence will expedite the hearing or cause substantial prejudice to a party, so discretion$_1$ will be required, but it is not the heart of the matter. Nor does the presiding officer straightforwardly have discretion$_4$—the 'strong discretion' of not being bound by standards (Dworkin 1977, 32; Goodin 1988, 187). If written evidence will cause substantial prejudice to a party, the presiding officer is not permitted to admit it. Standards do apply to the decision, but they do not completely control it. Even if written evidence would expedite the hearing and not cause substantial prejudice, the presiding officer does not have to admit it. The presiding officer has a choice between two permissible alternatives. (Dworkin (1977, 32 n. 1) suggests that this might be considered either limited discretion to admit written evidence or full discretion to decide whether to admit written evidence that expedites a hearing and is not substantially prejudicial.)

We can think of standards as limiting permissible choices to various degrees. Consider two circles with the same center, one larger than the other one. Let a point represent a decision or judgment. The area of the larger circle represents all the logically possible judgments that can be made about a matter; it represents the constraint of the subject or jurisdiction. The smaller, inner circle represents the choices that are left after a standard applies—the possible judgments meeting the standard. The more stringent the standards or the more there are, the smaller the circle and area for discretion. The most stringent standards provide for one and only one correct or permissible decision—a particular point, say, the center. The degree or scope of discretion corresponds to the size of the inner circle in proportion to the larger one. When there is no inner circle or it is the same size as the outer one, a decisionmaker has discretion$_4$. The decisionmaker has discretion$_3$ until the inner circle collapses to a point. In practice, a person would rarely be said to have discretion$_3$ if the inner circle were quite small even though not a point.

D. J. Galligan has suggested that even within the area of discretion, decisions can only be made for good reasons (Galligan 1986, 7). However, that is too stringent a requirement or at best misleading. It suggests that sufficient reasons exist to determine a decision and that decisionmakers are merely exercising personal judgment in determining what they require. But as the analogy with circles indicates, sometimes existing standards provide no reason for choosing one rather than another alternative that meets them. However, some reasons for choosing amongst permissible alternatives might be excluded as bad, for example, imposing a greater burden because a person is black. In short, there might not be good reasons for choosing within the area of discretion but there can be bad or unacceptable ones.

Indeed, Galligan also suggests that decisionmakers can be viewed as creating, giving more specific meaning to, or ranking standards by importance (Galligan 1986, 11). But if decisionmakers create standards, it is misleading to say that they must decide for good reasons. With perhaps a few exceptions, if they create the standards, then so long as they follow them their reasons are good or permissible. The same applies in a muted way to giving meaning to and ranking standards. It is their creating, giving meaning to, or ranking that makes the reasons good, so the requirement is no constraint on them.

These ideas about discretion can be illustrated by rules incorporating different standards. Suppose everyday my daughter is to bring me an orange for a snack. If the rule is for her to bring the biggest orange in the refrigerator, then only one correct choice exists, although she will have to exercise discretion$_1$ in making it. If it is to bring a big orange, then she often has alternative choices and both discretion$_1$ and discretion$_3$. Finally, if the rule is merely to bring me an orange, then there is essentially no standard and she has discretion$_4$. Of course, even here, there is a subject matter jurisdictional standard—peaches are out!

This example also makes clear the sense in which discretion$_2$ often rests on discretion$_3$. If the order is to bring a big orange, then so long as my daughter brings a reasonably large orange, there are no grounds for claiming she made a mistake. She need not have good reasons for picking this orange over other large ones, although a thoroughly rotten though large orange would be excluded (a bad reason). If, however, she brought one the size of a walnut, then her decision would be incorrect and might be overridden, unless that was all that was left in the refrigerator. In short, so long as her decision reasonably falls within the scope of permissible choices, it should stand. She abuses her discretion if she does not use any evidence, for example, arbitrarily reaches in and gets an orange without looking. But a good faith effort with some evidence to back it up should suffice for compliance with the rule. We thus see how $discretion_2$ fits with $discretion_3$ (see Galligan 1986, 13)

The common legal technique of factorial analysis often provides $discretion_3$ (see Christie 1986, 766–70). Factors often pick out a subclass but do not identify a particular choice. Suppose my daughter were told to bring a big, ripe, juicy orange. This specifies three factors—big, ripe, and juicy. Each factor picks out a subclass of oranges—big oranges, ripe oranges, juicy oranges. The more factors there are, the narrower the range of permissible choices, for each factor needs to be satisfied. Nevertheless, several different choices might satisfy all factors; there might be several big, ripe, and juicy oranges. Moreover, often the factors will need to be balanced against one another; that is, the factors operate as principles (see Galligan 1986, 11 (ranking standards)). One might take a somewhat smaller orange that is juicier than a larger one, or at least the two oranges might tie for satisfying all three criteria. Because burden/benefit decisions often involve application of such a set of factors or criteria, they often involve $discretion_3$.

The Requirement of Standards

If $discretion_4$ results from the absence of any standards and has undesirable aspects, then one would expect significant legal doctrines requiring standards for decisions. In two major areas the U.S. Supreme Court has not very successfully required standards. One is requiring Congress to prescribe standards for administrative agencies. The other area concerns standards for imposing the death penalty. A brief consideration of these two areas sheds light on problems of discretion.

Nondelegation According to the constitutional nondelegation doctrine, Congress cannot delegate legislative power because the Constitution assigns it to the Congress alone (art. 1, § 1). Legislative power is unconstitutionally delegated when no standards or intelligible principles are given defining the area in which, and basis on which, administrative decisions are to be made (*Butterfield v. Stranahan*, 192 U.S. 470 (1904); *J. W. Hampton, Jr. & Co. v. United States*, 276 U.S. 394 (1928)). In effect, the nondelegation doctrine requires that administrative agencies always be bound by legislatively imposed standards and thus not have $discretion_4$.

The nondelegation doctrine has largely become a dead letter, except for some deprivations of individual rights and some state agencies. The Supreme Court primarily relied on it to overturn congressional delegations of power in only two cases (*Panama Refining Co. v. Ryan*, 293 U.S. 388 (1935); *Schechter Poultry Corp. v. United States*, 295 U.S. 495 (1935); see also *Carter v. Carter Coal Co.*, 298 U.S. 238 (1936) (primarily based on the commerce clause but also using nondelegation)). The cases involved New Deal legislation and provided part of the motivation for President Roosevelt's court-packing plan. Before and since then, extremely vague standards such as regulating in the public interest have satisfied the requirements (see Schwartz 1976, 42–45). In recent years, some scholarly and judicial support has developed for reinvigorating the nondelegation doctrine (see Symposium 1987, Part I; *Industrial Union Dep't, AFL-CIO v. American Petroleum Inst.*, 448 U.S. 607, 671 (1980) (J. Rehnquist concurring); *American Textile Mfrs. Inst. v. Donovan*, 452 U.S. 490, 543 (1981) (J. Rehnquist dissenting)).

One might contend that even a vague and imprecise standard such as the public interest still prevents agencies having $discretion_4$. In particular contexts within regulatory areas, the public interest standard can yield a clear decision, for example, not licensing two radio stations on the same frequency in the same area, because it would be impossible for anyone to receive either station clearly. Nevertheless, for many important decisions, such as whether competition should be fostered or prevented, it provides no useful guidance. A public interest standard permits so many alternative choices and is so close to no standard as to be better described as providing $discretion_4$ than $discretion_3$. In other countries such as Great Britain, Parliament is not constrained from delegating authority without any standards (Schwartz 1976, 44). Consequently, administrative agencies and many other burden/benefit decisionmakers often practically have $discretion_4$.

Much of the concern about legislatures' failure to prescribe standards focuses on their failure to prescribe rules (clear-cut criteria) for making choices within jurisdictional limits (see Davis 1972, 23; Davis 1969, 38–39). There are various reasons why rules cannot be formulated for problems. (1) The matter might not admit of any precise answer. How many clients should a lawyer accept at one time? (2) One has not had experience with the problem and does not know what rule will work. When should physicians be permitted to use artificial hearts? (3) There might be many unforeseeable fact situations for which a rule would be inappropriate. (4) People cannot agree on a rule.

Except for the last, these are not necessarily good reasons for failing to prescribe more general standards presenting factors to be taken into consideration. Even though one cannot give precise answers or anticipate fact situations, one can usually indicate what sorts of factors should be considered; that is, one can prescribe some principles. Even without experience in an area, one can usually formulate some criteria for what a good outcome would be. As factorial analysis narrows permissible alternative choices, it converts discretion$_4$ to discretion$_3$.

Nonetheless, legislatures have much on their agenda, and the standards that can be formulated are sometimes too general and vague—perhaps no more than public interest and fairness. What more would one prescribe for regulating a new industry such as airlines or radio stations? But standards such as these hardly need to be prescribed, because one can ordinarily assume that administrative authorities will have them in mind.

The death penalty The Supreme Court's most interesting and perhaps tortuous confrontation with discretion has concerned the imposition of the death penalty. As the death penalty is the greatest burden anyone can impose on an individual, the Court's struggle with discretion in imposing it magnifies difficulties in all areas. We can only look at the highlights as illustrating both the importance of standards and, surprisingly, of discretion$_3$. The series of decisions almost resembles a ping-pong game bouncing from the too much to too little discretion sides of the net.

The first two cases (for our purposes) appeared to bounce from one extreme to the other. In *McGautha v. California* (402 U.S. 183 (1971)), the Court held that due process does not require juries to be given instructions as to when the death penalty should be imposed. The next year produced a slam shot in the opposite direction. The major theme of the several opinions in *Furman v.*

Georgia (408 U.S. 238 (1972)) was that the Georgia statute resulted in arbitrary imposition of the death penalty with no rational or meaningful basis for distinguishing who did and did not receive it. However, Chief Justice Burger's dissent forewarned further bounces of the ball, for he thought the movement away from mandatory sentences an enlightened development and indicated that he could more easily be persuaded that mandatory sentences were arbitrary (408 U.S. 238, 402).

Three issues central to present concerns arose in subsequent cases. The major one is the requirement of standards to control discretion$_4$. A second issue pertains to the finding and balancing of factors for and against the death penalty. The third issue is the requisite specificity of the standards—whether they are vague like the public interest or more precise.

The requirement of standards was the focus of a set of cases decided in 1976. In *Gregg v. Georgia* (428 U.S. 153) and *Proffitt v. Florida* (428 U.S. 242) the Court upheld two similar statutes. Both provided a set of legislatively identified aggravating circumstances at least one of which had to be found for a death sentence, entitled decisionmakers to consider any mitigating factors, and required the state supreme court to review all cases. Juries could consider additional nonstatutory aggravating factors. In a companion case, the Court emphasized that the jury must be permitted to consider all relevant evidence in mitigation (*Jurek v. Texas*, 428 U.S. 262 (1976); see also *Lockett v. Ohio*, 438 U.S. 586 (1978)).

If control of discretion is crucial, one might expect that mandatory sentences would be best. They would essentially eliminate discretion$_3$ in sentencing. However, the Court has consistently held that mandatory sentences are unconstitutional. Indeed, the Court has claimed that mandatory sentences provide no guidance or control of jury discretion$_4$! When the death penalty is mandatory on conviction, a jury has discretion$_2$ not to convict. Consequently, a "mandatory death penalty statute provides no standards to guide the jury in its inevitable exercise of the power to determine which first-degree murderers shall live and which shall die" (*Woodson v. North Carolina*, 428 U.S. 280, 302 (1976)). Even a statute that includes an aggravating factor in the definition of a crime but imposes a mandatory death penalty fails, because it does not permit consideration of mitigating factors (*Roberts v. Louisiana*, 431 U.S. 633 (1977)).

Two conflicting considerations are at work in these cases on requiring standards. First, there is a desire to eliminate discretion$_4$ by requiring standards to guide judgment and narrow the scope of discretion. Mandatory death penalty statutes fail in this respect, because the jury always has discretion$_2$ not to convict. Second, a conflicting consideration is for "an *individualized* determination on the basis of the character of the individual and the circumstances of the crime" (*Zant v. Stephens*, 462 U.S. 862, 878–79 (1983)). Because no list of mitigating factors can cover all possible grounds, the defendant cannot be foreclosed from raising any factor he or she thinks relevant. The tension is between limiting discretion and providing for individualized determinations based on all relevant information. Now one could permit an open-ended list of mitigating factors but a closed set of aggravating ones. However, the Court has permitted decisionmakers to consider aggravating factors not on a legislative list provided one on the list is also found (*Gregg v. Georgia*, 428 U.S. 153, 197 (1976)). Thus, the requirement of standards or factors only amounts to directing the decisionmaker's attention to certain common factors without preventing consideration of others.

The second issue concerns how one finds and balances aggravating and mitigating factors. Juries seem to have discretion$_2$ to determine whether or not a factor is present. Moreover, even if one has closed lists of factors, if decisionmakers can balance them as they desire, then discretion$_4$ seems to result. The balancing issue was raised in *Proffitt*. The Court responded that such balancing is no more difficult or arbitrary than the validity of traditional criminal defenses, such as insanity (428 U.S. 242, 257–58 (1976)).

Finding an aggravating factor is another matter. First, juries might determine them after conviction. Although a decisionmaker might find an aggravating circumstance in the face of evidence, review by courts should overturn such a decision; thus initial decisionmakers do not have discretion$_2$. Second, legislatures can make the finding of an aggravating factor part of the conviction judgment. The purpose of aggravating factors is to narrow the class of persons for whom the death penalty is a possibility. Thus, a legislature can define a crime as involving risk of death to more than one person and then have a parallel provision for the jury to find as an aggravating circumstance (*Lowenfield v. Phelps*, 108 S. Ct. 546, 555 (1988); see *Jurek v. Texas*, 428 U.S. 262 (1976)). However, although conviction indicates the presence of an aggravating factor, it does not mandate the death penalty because the jury is still free to consider mitigating factors that would outweigh it. What a legislature cannot do is prevent consideration of such mitigating factors, because that would prevent the individualized determination necessary to do justice in individual cases.

Finally, the legislatively identified aggravating factors "must channel the sentencer's discretion by 'clear and objective standards' that provide 'specific and detailed guidance,' and that 'make rationally reviewable the process for imposing a sentence of death'" (*Godfrey v. Georgia*, 446 U.S. 420, 428 (1980) (notes omitted)). The issue of vague standards has concerned two particular aggravating factors, both of which were initially approved. The first was a Georgia factor that the murder was "outrageously or wantonly vile, horrible or inhuman in that it involved torture, depravity of mind, or an aggravated battery to the victim." In *Gregg*, the defendant contended that this was so broad that it could apply to any murder case. However, the Court upheld it on the assumption that the Georgia Supreme Court would not give it such a broad construction (428 U.S. 153, 201 (1976)). A similar conclusion pertained to the Florida factor that the murder was "especially heinous, atrocious, or cruel" (*Proffitt v. Florida*, 428 U.S. 242, 255–56 (1976)).

Subsequently, the Court's expectations of the Georgia Supreme Court were not fulfilled. The Georgia court failed to construe narrowly the phrase outrageously or wantonly vile, horrible and inhuman. Consequently, the Supreme Court found that it implied no "inherent restraint on the arbitrary and capricious infliction of the death sentence" (*Godfrey v. Georgia*, 446 U.S. 420, 428 (1980)). A similar fate befell 'especially heinous, atrocious, or cruel' as construed by the Louisiana courts (*Lowenfield v. Phelps*, 108 S. Ct. 546 (1988)). In both cases, the phrases were construed so broadly that they could apply to any murder. To return to our analogy of circles, the standards did not serve to make the inner circle smaller than the outer one. Thus, they did not reduce discretion$_4$.

This review of the nondelegation doctrine and the death penalty establishes several important points. First, standards are necessary to limit discretion$_4$ and prevent arbitrary and capricious decisions. Second, the complete elimination of discretion$_3$ is often not possible or desirable. Not all relevant considerations can be foreseen. Consequently, to have individualized decisions it is important to allow some scope for alternative judgments—discretion$_3$. Third, to narrow discretion$_4$ to discretion$_3$, standards must significantly operate to narrow the subject class. Standards such as the public interest and outrageously or wantonly vile, horrible and inhuman do not do so. Finally, when several factors arguing both for and against a determination are involved, as they often are, both discretion$_3$ and, within limits, discretion$_2$ will be involved.

Findings and Reasons

In the death penalty cases, the decisionmakers are required to state the aggravating factors found to support its imposition. In Florida, where the sentencing is by a judge with the recommendation of a jury, written findings supporting the sentence of death are required (*Proffitt v. Florida*, 428 U.S. 242, 250 (1976)). The existence of discretion$_3$ does not prevent giving reasons. One can at least cite the factors that were found. Indeed, even discretion$_4$ does not preclude having and giving reasons for decisions. No standards are set for decisions about what to eat for dinner, but a reason can be given for one's choice, even if it is the minimal reason that one wanted it tonight. Usually, more reasons than that can be given, for example, not to have stew because one had it last night, and so on. In burden/benefit decisions, more complex reasons can be given. Usually the decisions are instrumental to achieving some purpose or purposes, so they can be evaluated by their effectiveness, as well as rationality and fairness (see Dworkin 1977, 33; see also Galligan 1986, 266). Thus, not only can reasons be given, but the reasons and decision can be rationally criticized, even if the decisionmakers have discretion$_2$ and discretion$_4$. However, unless the decisionmaker relied on a bad or excluded reason, within the area of discretion decisions are not wrong or incorrect—only better or worse.

Although closely connected, the requirements of stating findings, conclusions, and reasons are distinct. The law and commentators often fail to distinguish them adequately. Findings concern the fact situation as viewed by the decisionmaker. They operate as premises in an argument. One needs to distinguish between evidence, findings of basic fact, and findings of ultimate fact. The evidence consists of the material presented at a hearing or included by official notice. Evidence is often conflicting, and inferences must be made as to whether, say, a given rate increase would produce ten or thirteen million dollars in additional profits. This sort of finding is one of basic fact. One has a further question of whether such an increase in profits would be in the public interest. Findings stated in the terms of statutes or rules or standards, such as the conduct being price fixing, are ultimate findings of fact. Even ultimate facts do not always automatically settle the matter. For example, a proposed rate decrease in long distance phone charges by AT&T might be an appropriate reduction in profit margins but also be unfair to competitors.

The term conclusion is not used in its full logical sense; only some logical conclusions are intended. As just noted, the logical conclusions from evidence are findings of basic fact. Conclusions in the special sense are normative. Conclusions of law are general normative statements of the relevant law. A normative statement that a burden (benefit) should or should not be imposed (conferred) on an individual can be called the particular conclusion or judgment.

Reasons are statements or beliefs that support other statements or beliefs or decisions. Usually, when a person is asked to give reasons for a decision, various premises and logical rules of inference are not given, but they are also involved in the reasoning from the reasons given to the conclusion. A requirement of reasons is thus ambiguous between giving (a) supporting statements or beliefs and (b) explaining how these statements or beliefs lead to a statement or decision (reasoning). Thus, when reasons are asked for findings of basic fact, what is called for is both evidence and how that evidence supports the findings, at least if there is any complexity in the latter. Diagram 4.1 illustrates the structure of a decision.

Elements of a Decision

evidence
↓
(reasoning)
↓
findings of basic fact
↓
(reasoning)
↓
findings of ultimate fact
+
conclusions of law
↓
(reasoning)
↓
particular conclusion or judgment

Diagram 4.1

The requirement of a statement of findings usually applies to basic facts. Were it to include only ultimate facts, it would not be significant. Boilerplate language could be developed stating that it is found that such and such would be unfair and contrary to the public interest. Some agencies do strongly tend to couch their findings in this language. Were a statement of findings to include evidence, it would practically amount to the record. However, a statement of the reasons for findings of basic facts will refer to some of the evidence as well as how it supports the findings.

The most common reason given for requiring statements of findings and reasons is to facilitate judicial review (Schwartz 1976, 421; Davis 1972, 320; Friendly 1975, 1292). Although judicial review is discussed in the last section, we shall not emphasize it as a basis for giving findings and reasons. It does not apply to unappealable or unreviewable decisions. We are looking for reasons that might apply to all burden/benefit decisions.

Although there are similarities and overlaps, there are differences in the reasons for requiring statements of findings, conclusions, and reasons. Two central reasons for requiring a statement of findings are (1) to encourage careful consideration and (2) to enable parties to plan better (see Davis 1972, 320; Flick 1984, 121). The first reason needs little explanation. If one has to state explicitly one's findings, then one has to formulate explicitly what one believes to be the case rather than operate from general impressions. Getting the facts correct improves the accuracy of decisions. Even if no basis exists for evaluating the decisions as correct or incorrect, perhaps because they are a matter of discretion_4, different fact situations can prompt different decisions. Consequently, a more careful and accurate assessment of basic facts can lead to different decisions.

By knowing the findings, parties can better plan for a rehearing, appeal, or future conduct. Suppose one's grant application is turned down. If one is told that the methodology involves insufficient statistical analysis and that the cost estimate for principal investigator time is excessive, one can better plan and prepare future applications. If no such findings are given and one is merely told that the grant is not awarded, one has no idea how to improve future applications. In this example the decisionmaker has discretion_3, but an indication of factors judged weak can guide applicants.

As we saw in the previous chapter, records of formal hearings must include all evidence on which a decision is made. Thus, the evidence for findings of basic fact must come exclusively from the record and parties thus have had an opportunity to rebut it. If decisionmakers were able to use other evidence, then the whole point of a hearing in which one could present evidence would be blunted. Thus, a third purpose of requiring a statement of findings, and of reasons for them, is (3) to help ensure that decisions are indeed based on the evidence in the record and not extraneous material. To ensure this, more than a bare statement of findings of basic fact is needed; one also needs an indication of what evidence in the record supports the findings and how it does so.

The requirement of statements of conclusions of law is supported by several reasons. (1) Their statement is likely to increase accuracy. (2) They are crucial premises in the argument, and without them the individual subject to a decision cannot understand the normative grounds of a decision. (3) Doing so can lead to revision of principles. Expressly formulating the particular rule or principle used can lead one to recognize the need for qualifications and exceptions. (4) As we shall see in the last section, review of legal conclusions is much stricter than for factual findings; that is, no $discretion_3$ exists for conclusions of law. Hence, for effective judicial review, the precise legal conclusions used must be known.

A requirement of a statement of conclusions is easily supported. Stating particular conclusions is hard to avoid. The requirement basically amounts to informing a person of a burden/benefit decision. Not to state the particular judgment would be like awarding a grant but never telling the recipient. A more important concern is that once made, the decision be promptly conveyed to the subject. Conclusions of law are important premises connecting findings of fact with particular conclusions. Without them, one would not know what standards were used. Thus, the reasons for requiring them are closely tied to those for requiring reasons.

A statement of reasons, including conclusions of law, is perhaps the most important aspect of the principle of reasons and findings. Although the APA requires the reasons for findings and conclusions on all material issues of fact or discretion (5 U.S.C. § 557(c); see also MSA § 4-215(c)), courts have been fairly lax in enforcing it (Schwartz 1976, 421; Gellhorn, Byse, and Strauss 1979, 359–60). The requirement amounts to one of providing a reasoned opinion. If only findings and particular conclusions need be stated, a party can still be left in the dark as to how the decisionmaker got from the findings to the particular judgment. Sometimes the connection is obvious and does not require stating

(*State ex rel. St. Louis Public Serv. Co. v. Public Serv. Comm'n*, 365 Mo. 1032, 291 S.W.2d 95 (1956)), but usually inferences need explanation.

Several reasons exist for having a decisionmaker state the reasons (supporting claims and reasoning) for findings and conclusions. (1) It can prevent arbitrariness (Davis 1972, 318, 332; see also LRCC 1985, 63; Lorch 1980, 146). To state reasons, there must be reasons, and if there are, the decision cannot be arbitrary. A reason must provide some support for one decision rather than another. "I just felt like it" or "it was a whim" does not provide a reason based on any feature of the persons or their situations for one outcome rather than another and so cannot be a reason. Thus, decisions on such a basis are arbitrary and capricious.

(2) A statement of reasons can prevent wrong or incorrect judgments (Friendly 1975, 1292; Flick 1984, 118). Of course, this requires that the notions of correct and incorrect apply. In stating (usually writing) reasons, one is more apt to discover lapses in logic and correct them, perhaps leading to different (and correct) decisions. This increased accuracy is much less likely to occur in agencies in which the people who write the statement are not those who make the decisions (see Schwartz 1976, 424–25).

(3) If reasons are stated, decisions might be more uniform (Friendly 1975, 1292; LRCC 1985, 63). The same decisionmaker will be apt to follow the same line of reasoning in other cases. It can also lead to more uniform decisions by several decisionmakers in an agency if they are aware of each other's reasoning and accept it (see chap. 5).

(4) A person can know why a decision was given and whether an appeal is reasonable (Davis 1972, 322; Flick 1984, 118). Most people want to know why a decision affecting them was made. Granted, their curiosity is greater when burdens are imposed and benefits denied than when the opposite occurs; still, even when benefits are conferred, for example, a grant, one often wants to know why. One reason is that one might be better able to make an acceptable application for another grant. The reasoning involved is often complex, and the various steps need to be indicated.

(5) When a decision is adverse to a person, a statement of reasons might make the decision more acceptable (Friendly 1975, 1292; Lorch 1980, 146). One is more apt to accept a decision when reasons are given, even if one disagrees with them. One at least thinks that one's concern was not arbitrarily dismissed and that one received consideration. Even if the person affected does

not accept the decision, reasons might increase the others confidence in the process and prevent demoralization (see Flick 1984, 119)

Providing a statement of findings and reasons is in tension with administrative efficiency (LRCC 1985, 63; see also Flick 1984, 119). Preparing statements of findings and reasons involves administrative time and expense. A one hundred page statement of findings and reasons is not needed for every case (see Gellhorn, Byse, and Strauss 1979, 359). Indeed, extremely long statements can be more than parties desire or need. They can be too complex and detailed for ordinary citizens to understand. Their intelligibility is also often decreased by cumbersome bureaucratese and legalese. Consequently, the requirement of a statement of findings and reasons should allow for differences in how elaborate they are. For some cases, merely checking a box indicating which of the common reasons applies is sufficient, but still a major improvement over providing no reason at all (see Davis 1969, 104–05).

Another method to decrease the burden of providing findings and reasons, common in Canada and England, is to provide them only on request. This approach has at least two difficulties (LRCC 1985, 64). First, if reasons need be given only on request, then often they will not be formulated until well after a decision has been rendered. Why draft a statement of findings and reasons if one does not need to do so? Such a practice severely weakens the benefits of requiring findings and reasons. It does not encourage decisionmakers to be more careful or reason more accurately. Moreover, after a decision has been reached, a plausible rationale can usually be developed for almost any decision. Consequently, decisions that were in fact arbitrary can be given a plausible basis. Second, sometimes reasons are not given until after the time for appeal has passed. Although this can be corrected by running the time to appeal from the date of the presentation of reasons, this will not remedy the first defect.

The Law Reform Commission of Canada has proposed that reasons be required only for decisions that in whole or part deny a request or otherwise adversely affect a party (LRCC 1985, 63). This proposal has much to recommend it. If a decision is favorable, few people are likely to protest or be concerned about its basis. Still, people do sometimes want to know why they received a favorable decision. If reasons are provided only for adverse decisions, many of the benefits of providing reasons will not be attained. Uniformity of favorable decisions will not be enhanced, and that can lead to incorrect and arbitrary favorable decisions. Thus, it will not increase fairness between parties. It is unfair if both X and Y have similar fact situations, but a benefit is correctly denied X and incorrectly granted Y (see chap. 5).

Therefore, providing findings and reasons for all decisions encourages decisionmakers to be more careful, resulting in more accurate findings, better reasoning, more correct judgments, less arbitrariness, and uniformity of decisions. It also helps parties and others to know why a decision was made, to plan future conduct better, and to accept adverse decisions. The elaborateness of the findings and reasons can reasonably vary with the complexity and importance of the decision. Perhaps as Kenneth Davis forecasts, in the long run findings and reasons will be required for all informal governmental administrative decisions except where the inconvenience outweighs the probable benefits (Davis 1972, 342).

Burden of Proof

An important feature in providing reasons for decisions is the burden of proof. There are two distinct burdens of proof—the burden of production and the burden of persuasion. The burden of production requires that one raise an issue and present some evidence supporting one's side. The burden of persuasion requires one to meet some standard of support for one's position. These burdens usually go together, that is, if one has the burden of production one also has the burden of persuasion, but they need not and do not always coincide.

The burden of persuasion is the more crucial one. Suppose people had the burden of production for social security retirement benefits, but the Social Security Administration had the burden of persuasion beyond a reasonable doubt that people were not at least sixty-two years of age. People could easily meet the burden of production by applying and providing some evidence, but the government would face a monumental task in proving improper claimants were too young. Errors would likely be much more numerous than when people have the burden of persuasion as to their age.

In formal adjudications, the APA imposes the burden of proof on the proponent of an order unless otherwise provided by statute (5 U.S.C. § 556(d)). Presumably, this means the burdens of both production and persuasion. Thus, if an agency claims that an individual has violated a regulation, then the agency has the burdens. Contrarily, if an individual claims an exception to a regulation, the individual carries the burdens. Similarly, an individual claiming benefits carries the burdens, while an agency seeking to terminate benefits carries the burdens of showing ineligibility. Exceptions to this general policy exist. For example, a person claiming social security disability has the burden of production, but the administration has the burden of persuasion that the person is not entitled to the benefits (Schwartz 1976, 351; see also Mashaw 1983, 188–89).

The standard of proof to be met is normally the civil procedure standard of preponderance of the evidence. In some cases it is increased to clear and convincing proof, primarily when the government seeks to impose a severe burden on an individual such as deportation, termination of parental rights, or revocation of a broker-dealer license (*Woodby v. Immigration and Naturalization Serv.*, 385 U.S. 276 (1966); *Santosky v. Kramer*, 455 U.S. 745 (1982); *Collins Sec. Corp. v. SEC*, 562 F.2d 820 (D.C. Cir. 1977)). In license revocation and similar matters, the criminal law principle of innocent until proven guilty is also carried over (Lorch 1980, 131).

It has been suggested (Schwartz 1976, 351) that a similar standard should apply to termination of benefits, such as welfare benefits in *Goldberg v. Kelly* (397 U.S. 254 (1970)). An incongruity would then exist in different standards for benefit conferral and benefit termination. To secure welfare benefits, individuals need only prove by a preponderance of the evidence that they qualify. Why should a stronger burden be required to terminate the benefits? A preponderance of evidence that a person is not qualified would defeat an original application for the benefit. In areas such as welfare where people's eligibility varies frequently, different standards of proof for conferral and termination can lead to many incorrect outcomes. If the standard of persuasion for conferral is 51% of the weight of the evidence and for termination it is 75%, then incorrect outcomes will result in all those cases in which circumstances have changed so that recipients have 26–50% of the weight of the evidence for receipt of benefits.

A justification for differential treatment is not obvious. The impact on individuals does not obviously justify a difference. If persons truly need welfare, then failure originally to receive it seems as bad as its termination. Yet, persons having only 45% of the weight of the evidence would not qualify for initial granting of benefits, but they would qualify for their retention if the state had to prove ineligibility by the perhaps 75% needed for clear and convincing proof. One might contend that in benefit-terminating decisions, due to reliance there are often consequential losses not present in original refusals. Welfare recipients make various plans in reliance on benefits. However, the reliance must be reasonable. The reasonableness of reliance partly depends on the standard of proof required for termination, so it is circular reasoning to use the reliance to support a higher standard. We return to this issue in chapters 6 and 7.

Another issue arises when criminal conduct is transferred from courts to administrative agencies, for example, traffic offenses might be transferred from criminal court to an administrative tribunal. One might claim that in such situations a higher standard of persuasion should be required, perhaps the criminal law standard of beyond a reasonable doubt. The courts have rejected this claim (Schwartz 1976, 352). After the transfer, the issue is no longer a criminal law one, so the criminal law standard of persuasion need not apply. A deeper reason is that such matters need not, and probably should not, have ever been committed to the criminal law (see LRCC 1979). Two common reason for transferring such matters are efficiency and that they seem improperly placed in the criminal law. Even if one accepts the severity of the sanction as a basis for requiring a higher standard of proof, the sanction in traffic court and many other matters so transferred is not severe. Furthermore, severe sanctions, such as deportation, do not call for the criminal standard but only clear and convincing proof.

Judicial Review

This section merely outlines the range of review as a check on administrative discretion. As one commentator puts it, "[D]iscretion is at the heart of agency power. Indeed, what is administrative law about if not the control of discretion?" (Schwartz 1976, 606). The central issues are whether review is available and the stringency of the review. By 'the stringency of the review' is meant the standards by which administrative action is evaluated. Some legal scholars use 'area of review' to mean what can be reviewed, and the 'scope of review' to mean generally what is here meant by 'stringency' (Davis 1972, 470).

The availability of judicial review of administrative action is a complex topic involving issues of standing, ripeness, and so forth. We shall only consider whether legislatures should be permitted to delegate power to make burden/benefit decisions that are not subject to judicial control. To so delegate is to grant administrative agencies discretion$_2$. Legislatures do often try or seem to try to make such grants, albeit with varying success. In the United States, the presumption is that courts can review administrative actions. Indeed, the Supreme Court has permitted it in the face of strong statutory language barring it (*Shaughnessy v. Pedreiro*, 349 U.S. 48 (1955); *Ortwein v. Schwab*, 410 U.S. 656 (1973)). However, occasional cases hold that judicial review is not available (*Switchmen's Union v. National Mediation Bd.*, 320 U.S. 297 (1943)). In Canada, Parliament and provincial legislatures have sometimes used "privative clauses" to bar judicial review. However, courts have often found ways to recognize Parliamentary sovereignty and yet provide review (see Macdonald 1987, 231–34).

The central objection to assigning administrative agencies discretion$_2$ is the lack of assurance of the justice of their exercise of authority. Administration within executive departments or ministries is subject to control by the cabinet officer, minister, or president. However, executive control does not protect against administrative injustice carrying out executive policy. Illegal administrative conduct (contrary to statutory authority) is neither unknown nor rare (see Davis 1969, 12–15). Consequently, the Law Reform Commission of Canada has recommended that privative clauses be abolished (LRCC 1985, 42).

A central reason legislatures try to bar judicial review is to prevent courts substituting their judgments for those of administrators. This concern goes to the stringency of the review or how much discretion$_3$, if any, administrators should have. Presumably, matters are delegated to administrative agencies because they are better able to handle the problems than legislatures or courts. They can be more flexible and bring expertise to bear. If judges can simply substitute their own judgments for those of administrative agencies, then these advantages are lost.

American administrative law distinguishes the stringency of review for questions of law and questions of fact. Although many questions are mixed ones of law and fact, such as whether conduct is negligent or reasonable, the American principles for judicial review hinge on this distinction. Questions of law fall within the expertise of judges; questions of fact fall within the expertise of administrators. Consequently, on legal questions judges will substitute their judgments for those of administrators. In short, administrators must get their answers to legal questions correct; they have no discretion$_3$. Common-law natural justice also largely follows this practice (Flick 1984, 122–23). In Canada, administrators are accorded significant discretion$_3$ concerning the interpretation of statutes they administer, and the Law Reform Commission of Canada partly predicates its rejection of privative clauses on this deference. The Commission believes courts should accept administrative interpretations of law unless they are "patently unreasonable" (LRCC 1985, 42). The difference between the United States and Canada on this point is probably not as large as appears. U.S. courts do in fact accord weight to administrative interpretations of statutes they administer; the extent of such deference has been the subject of debate under deregulation (see Hirshman 1988).

The APA specifies that courts can declare administrative actions unlawful and set them aside if they are (1) "arbitrary, capricious, an abuse of discretion, or otherwise not in accordance with law;" (2) contrary to constitutional provisions, (3) "in excess of statutory jurisdiction"; (4) do not conform to legally required procedures; (5) "unsupported by substantial evidence" in formal cases on the record; or (6) "unwarranted by the facts" if the court is authorized to hear evidence anew (5 U.S.C. §§ 706(2)(A)–(F)). The MSA essentially includes (1) through (5), although (1) is optional. It also adds the following grounds: (7) not all issues were decided, (8) the law was erroneously interpreted or applied, (9) the persons taking action were improperly constituted or motivated or subject to disqualification, (10) the action is outside the agency's discretion, (11) the action is inconsistent with an agency rule or prior practice (MSA §§ 5-116(c)(3), (4), (6), and (8)(i)–(iii)).

Our concern here is with administrative discretion$_3$ in fact finding, which primarily involves grounds (1), (5) and (10). The basic standard for review is the reasonableness of the administrative finding of fact (Schwartz 1976, 596, 606). At one time, a weaker interpretation was given to the arbitrary and capricious test, but now it is usually given the stronger reasonableness interpretation (Pierce, Shapiro, and Verkuil 1985, 361–62). An essentially similar standard applies in England (Flick 1984, 133–34). The reasonableness standard leaves administrators discretion$_3$. In our analogy of circles, judgments can fall anywhere within the inner one. Where the decision falls is a matter of administrative discretion$_1$. In short, administrative decisions or findings of fact are final (discretion$_2$) if they are the result of judgment (discretion$_1$) within a reasonable range (discretion$_3$).

Perhaps the clearest example is the APA criterion that administrative decisions and findings can be overturned if they are not supported by substantial evidence (5 U.S.C. § 706(2)(E); see MSA § 5-116(c)(7); see also RSA §

15(g)(5)). The evidence must be that contained in the whole record, not just that for one side. However, substantial evidence for the agency's position can exist, even though the court would have decided the issue the other way. If a reasonable person could have concluded from the evidence as the agency did, then courts should allow the finding or decision to stand (Pierce, Shapiro, and Verkuil 1985, 357). This point can be stated in terms of the strength of evidence supporting an administrative agency's position. Obviously, any position which is more than 50% probably correct is established by the preponderance of the evidence. However, the substantial evidence requirement means that some findings or decisions less than 50% probably correct will also be permitted. A position that to the judge seems to be only 45% probable will be upheld. A reasonable person might interpret the evidence so that such a claim appears more than 50% probable.

The reasonableness standard is the fundamental one that rational persons could accept. Without good evidence, actions are not rational or reasonable (Galligan 1986, 314). People have no good reasons to accept unreasonable administrative findings. Yet, they recognize that reasonable people can interpret evidence differently and thus reach different conclusions about the probable truth of factual claims. Moreover, a more stringent standard would greatly handicap the functioning of administrators and thus significantly thwart the benefits of assigning decisions to them.

Finally, for an agency's decision to be upheld, the reasons it gives must be reasonable (*SEC v. Chenery Corp.*, 318 U.S. 80, 87 (1943); see Flick 1984, 136–37 (inadequate explanation)). If an administrator's reasons are not reasonable, then a court must strike down the judgment and remand the case to the agency. A court cannot provide its own reasoning to the same conclusion. This rule upholds administrative discretion$_1$. The agency might not accept the court's rationale, and on reconsideration it might still reach the opposite conclusion. The decision is one for the agency to make; if its decision (findings, conclusions, and reasoning) are not reasonable, then it must reconsider. It is not the court's job to make the decision; only to ensure that it is a reasonable one based on a correct interpretation of the law.

Summary

An impartial decisionmaker and an opportunity to present evidence will be of little value if decisionmakers do not have to have grounds, or those grounds need not be given, or they do not have to be reasonable. The question is often put as whether or how much discretion decisionmakers have. Decisionmakers can be said to have discretion in at least four different senses: (1) exercising judgment, (2) having final authority, (3) having permissible choices among alternatives, and (4) not being limited by any standards. These various senses are closely related and often confused with one another. (4) is a limiting case of (3). If a decisionmaker has a choice among permissible alternatives, then judgment will need to be exercised in choosing. Even when standards are given, they need not remove all alternatives and a decisionmaker may have to interpret or rank standards. If a decisionmaker can exercise judgment among permissible alternatives, then often others will not be entitled or able to overturn decisions and the decisionmaker's judgment is final.

Standardless governmental burden/benefit decisions can result in arbitrariness, exploitation, uncertainty, and intrusions on privacy. Consequently, standards are important for such decisions, and the Supreme Court has required legislatively determined standards for administrative agencies and persons deciding on the imposition of the death penalty. Standards are required for governmental burden/benefit decisions. However, often clear-cut criteria are impossible and consideration of the unforeseeable and varied factors in individual cases make them undesirable. Consequently, often standards merely provide some limits on choices, changing discretion$_4$ to discretion$_3$. Moreover, contrary standards can permit discretion$_3$ in weighing and balancing them. Some standards are so vague or general as to provide no effective limit on alternative choices.

An important principle of procedural justice is that a decisionmaker's findings, conclusions, and reasons be stated or made known at the time of decision. This principle helps ensure that decisions are based on evidence presented, carefully considered, uniform, and not arbitrary or incorrect. It also helps people to know why decisions importantly affecting them are made, to plan better, and perhaps to accept adverse decisions. The provision of findings, conclusions, and reasons requires time and effort and can reduce administrative efficiency; a balance must be struck between the benefits of providing findings, conclusions, and reasons and the costs of doing so.

The acceptability or adequacy of reasons for decisions often depends on the burden of proof. The burdens of production and persuasion should normally fall on the party originally proposing an order or decision. The burden of persuasion should ordinarily be the preponderance of the evidence. For some burden-imposing or benefit-terminating decisions, a higher standard should be required. For example, if the burden is imprisonment, the case for a more stringent standard of persuasion is credible. A special difficulty is justifying a stronger burden of persuasion for terminating benefits than for refusal to confer them when the eligibility conditions of many persons change frequently.

Finally, judicial review should usually be available, although various procedural conditions and standards for review might often make it impractical. The standard for review of law should be more stringent than for facts. Agencies should be required to be correct about the law, although in determining what the law is courts should and often do give significant weight to administrative interpretations. In short, the legal standards, principles, or rules applied in burden/benefit decisions should be the correct ones. More leeway should be permitted decisionmakers in determining facts, including findings of mixed law and fact. Such findings should be upheld provided a reasonable person could so conclude.

CHAPTER 5

FORMAL JUSTICE

Standards narrow the scope of discretion$_3$ but often do not eliminate it. Decisions with discretion$_3$ and even discretion$_4$ can be criticized. One form of criticism is based on the consistency of decisions. Moreover, even if decisions are originally discretionary, once a decision is made, future discretion$_3$ can be limited by treating previous decisions as precedents to be followed in future cases. Furthermore, rules can restrict discretion$_3$ and often even eliminate it by indicating that only one decision is correct.

This chapter explores the requirements of consistency, adherence to precedents, and conformity to rules as elements of procedural justice and thus limits to the scope of discretion. Each of these requirements effects an equality of treatment among individuals and thus promotes justice, even though the reasons for them include considerations not usually considered those of justice, for example, efficiency. Because straightforward requirements to be consistent and to follow precedents and rules say nothing about the subject matter of decisions, they are often called elements of formal justice (see also Lyons 1984, 582). However, one must distinguish principles not specifying subject matter from their being justified for all substantive contexts. As we shall see, adherence to precedents and conformity to rules are not appropriate for all substantive contexts. Whether these three principles are a matter of procedure or substance is perhaps moot. Nonetheless, because use of precedents and rules are often used to distinguish different procedural methods, they are appropriately considered here.

Distinctions Consistent decisions, use of precedents, and rule following are closely related but distinct concepts. Prominent legal scholars have confused them, especially consistency with the other two (see Lyons 1973, Lyons 1985, and Winston 1974, for especially good analyses of these confusions). Consistency is often rendered as treating like cases alike and different cases differently. This formulation contributes to confusion with using precedents and following rules which are also sometimes similarly described (see Coons 1987, 59–60 (calls treating like cases alike 'consistency' and applies to cases under a rule)). Thus it is better to start with the root notion of logical consistency. Two propositions are inconsistent if they cannot both be true. Assertions of both of two inconsistent propositions are incoherent, for example, the spot is brown and red.

We can preliminarily characterize use of precedents as taking previous decisions to prescribe decisions in present similar cases. The use of precedents thus provides consistency, but it is not necessary for consistency. One can have a perfectly consistent system considering each case on its individual merits without regard to previous decisions. Many teachers do precisely this in grading papers. They do not look to see what grade they gave to previous similar papers; they independently evaluate each by a set of standards. The resulting grades can be quite consistent. Adherence to precedent provides consistency over time, whereas logical consistency concerns only simultaneous or atemporal judgments.

Following rules means deciding cases as a given rule or set of rules prescribes. The rules in question pertain to a person's conduct in making a decision. Decision rules constraining discretion have the form "If F, then D" where 'F' stands for the factual features made relevant by the norm and 'D' for the decision or judgment. (Power-conferring rules do not have this form, but they do not constrain discretion although they can delimit the subject for decision.) Although rules provide clear-cut criteria, they need not eliminate discretion$_3$. If F or D is a standard permitting discretion$_3$, then the rule will not eliminate discretion$_3$. For example, a rule requiring a sentence of life imprisonment or the death penalty for persons convicted of murder is clear-cut, but it permits discretion$_3$. However, it clearly limits discretion$_3$ by excluding lesser sentences. Decision rules without such standards can be called nondiscretionary.

Strictly following nondiscretionary rules provides consistency. This claim requires a narrow interpretation of 'following rules'. If whenever the antecedent condition F is fulfilled one decides D, then there is consistency. Discretionary decision rules, for example, about sentencing convicted murderers, permit inconsistency (see Coons 1987, 63–64, 89). One might object that following even nondiscretionary rules does not necessarily provide consistency, because in applying a rule the first time there is no similar case with which to be consistent (Lyons 1973, 852). However, it would also be wrong to claim one was inconsistent. Whenever the concept of consistency applies, accurate application of a nondiscretionary decision rule will provide it. By a broader interpretation of 'following rules', consistency does not necessarily result. In this broader sense, one can follow rules with unspecified exceptions or choose between applying two or more rules whose antecedent conditions are both met (see Winston 1974, 36). On this interpretation, one can follow rules but not be consistent, for example, sometimes apply one rule and sometimes another.

One can also be consistent and not follow rules (see Lyons 1973, 851; but see Winston 1974, 38); there is no logical difficulty in consistently not following a rule. For example, although a university rule might prohibit giving an examination during the last week of classes before the final exam period, a teacher can quite consistently always give an examination that week. One might object that consistency always entails conformity to a nondiscretionary rule, for it requires conformity to the normative grounds for a decision. Whatever reason the teacher has for giving exams during the last week, this constitutes a rule which is consistently followed. However, this sense of conformity to rules does not involve following announced rules. Moreover, the teacher might not be consciously applying any reason or rule. If so, the teacher is conforming to a rule only in that there is a regular pattern of behavior; as a rule, the teacher gives an exam the week before finals. Our concern is with following rules in the sense of being consciously guided by them.

One can follow rules without looking to previous decisions applying them for guidance, without adhering to precedents. Contrarily, one might follow a precedent which is an incorrect application of a rule. Thus, in one ordinary sense, in following the precedent one is not following the rule; one is following a mistaken interpretation of the rule. And one can follow precedents without following announced rules.

Legal requirements Administrative law has somewhat different requirements for consistency, adherence to precedent, and conformity to rules. In apparently similar cases treated differently, agencies must either treat them the same or explain the difference (*Contractors Transp. Corp. v. United States*, 537 F.2d 1160 (4th Cir. 1976)). If an agency gives inconsistent decisions, such as granting a stay of deportation for the spouse of one person but not another similarly situated person, sometimes one decision will be overturned as an abuse of discretion (*Del Mundo v. Rosenberg*, 341 F. Supp. 345 (C.D. Cal. 1972)).

Following precedent is closely related to consistency, because it involves consistency over time—between one case and a previous one. The MSA provides for judicial relief if action is inconsistent with "prior practice" unless "facts and reasons" are given to show that the inconsistency is "fair and rational" (MSA § 5-116(c)(8)(iii)). If an agency does not follow its previous decisions, for example, by permitting a regulated company extra charges for a service which was previously included in a basic charge, then an agency must clearly explain why it is not following its precedent (see *Secretary of Agriculture v. United States*, 347 U.S. 645 (1954); *Atchison, Topeka & Santa Fe Ry. Co. v. Wichita Bd. of Trade*, 412 U.S. 800 (1973); see also Galligan 1986, 282). Thus, administrative law does not require that precedents be adhered to, only that failure to do so be explained.

Finally, administrative agencies and executive departments are required to follow their own rules (MSA § 5-116(c)(8)(ii); *Nader v. Bork*, 366 F. Supp 104 (D.C.D.C. 1973); *United States v. Nixon* (418 U.S. 683 (1974)). If a rule has been appropriately adopted and not rescinded or altered, the agency must comply with it. Unlike inconsistency and failure to adhere to precedent, the executive and agencies are not permitted merely to explain why they do not follow their own rules. One reason for the greater stringency of the requirement to follow their own rules than to adhere to precedents is that agencies can always change their rules; explaining why precedent is not followed is similar to changing a rule.

In one area, agencies, like courts, need not follow their own rules precisely. Some discretion[3] is permitted in complying with procedural rules, provided there is sufficient compliance to secure the ends of justice (*American Farm Lines v. Black Ball Freight Serv.*, 397 U.S. 532 (1970)). A narrow interpretation is that one need not conform to procedural rules only if doing so would cause unnecessary delay or other procedural disadvantage and no party is prejudiced. In short, no party is harmed and gains are achieved by noncompliance with procedural rules.

To many persons, especially those trained in law, the justification for the requirements of consistency, adherence to precedent, and rule following will appear obvious. Nonetheless, the justifications are more complex than at first appears and imply significant limits to them. A more detailed analysis is necessary to determine precisely what they require and when the requirements are appropriate.

Consistency

The main difficulty in applying the requirement of consistency is determining when two cases are similar enough so that different decisions would involve inconsistency. Decisions rest on both factual and normative grounds. For an inconsistency to arise, both the factual and normative grounds for decision must be the same in two cases but the judgments differ. It is sometimes said that no two cases are alike, there is always some factual difference, so no inconsistency can arise. However, not all factual differences are relevant. Language and perhaps the structure of reality place some limits on determining similarities (see Schauer 1987, 582–88). The primary determinants of the relevance of factual features are the normative grounds and purposes. For example, the color of hair or eyes of the parties is rarely relevant, because few decision criteria depend on that. Hair color could be relevant if one were seeking to hire a natural redhead to test a hair color.

Logical basis The problem of consistency and incoherence is as follows. Suppose two situations both have features $F_1, F_2, \ldots F_n$. If the decision in one is D but in the other not-D, one of three explanations is possible. First, an invalid inference has been made in one situation, but an invalid inference is a logical inconsistency (the premises and conclusion cannot both be true). Second, two different decision norms have been applied. Use of any standard yields decision norms; if the standard is met, decide one way; if it is not, decide another way. Decision norms often correspond to norms for the conduct of persons subject to the decision. For example, a norm requiring people in situation S to pay a tax will have a corresponding decision norm requiring a decisionmaker to impose the tax on persons in situation S. On the supposition, one will have used the norms "If F, then D" and "If F, then not-D." But these two norms are logically inconsistent. Third, the relevant factual features are not the same, but this is inconsistent with the hypothesis. In short, if the same relevant features are present in two cases and the same norm is to be applied, different decisions are inconsistent.

Consistency does not require any specific content. Given discretion_4 and only a requirement of consistency, a decisionmaker can choose to use any norm and thus pick out any set of features as relevant. Moreover, as different cases always do have some features that differ, a decisionmaker can always avoid inconsistency by specifying a norm that makes different features relevant. In doing so, however, a decisionmaker is apt to violate other requirements of procedural justice, such as impartiality. For example, this would occur in a norm making being a close relative of the decisionmaker a relevant feature.

Moral basis Besides being incoherent, inconsistent decisions result in unequal and unfair treatment of persons (see also Pierce, Shapiro, and Verkuil 1985, 127). This point is most clear when the appropriate norm imposes a burden or terminates a benefit. (For the present, we assume the norm is given, although the same results follow if the decisionmaker can choose a norm.) Suppose the norm imposes a tax, and the cases of X and Y have relevantly similar features. Further suppose the correct application of the norm requires payment of the tax. (1) If X is made to pay, but Y is not, then the burden is unequally imposed. X is treated unfairly in comparison to Y (see Davis 1969, 167–68). (2) Inequality or unfairness also results if X is made to pay the tax but Y is made to pay more than X. In this case, Y is treated unfairly with respect to X. This result occurs whether or not the tax itself is a fair one, for the injustice or unfairness is comparative between X and Y.

It is often claimed that no injustice results in cases of type (1). If the tax is fair and X is correctly liable to it, then X deserves the burden and is not done an injustice. If this is so, then consistency is not always a requirement of justice and thus is not intrinsically valuable but only instrumentally valuable. Because this claim is quite important, it must be examined in detail.

The claim that no injustice is done to X is based on noncomparative justice. For present purposes, noncomparative justice concerns persons receiving what they deserve; comparative justice, equal or fair treatment, concerns similar treatment of relevantly similar persons. In cases of type (1), if the tax is fair or just, X cannot complain of noncomparative injustice, but the situation is comparatively unjust (see Davis 1969, 169).

One might contend that X cannot suffer even comparative injustice if he or she is not harmed and that X is not harmed by Y not having to pay the tax. One reply to this contention is to hold that X is harmed. If the government must raise a certain amount of revenue, then X's taxes will have to be proportionately higher the fewer payers. Granted, X is not adversely affected any more than any other taxpayer, but that does not mean X is not adversely affected. Second, it is unclear why X must suffer harmful consequences to be treated unjustly. Equality, which is the basis for comparative justice, is not a consequentialist concern.

A possible counterexample to the injustice or unfairness of all cases of type (1) is as follows (see Lyons 1973, 846–47; see also Galligan 1986, 158). Suppose the decisionmaker is certifying persons to be sent to an extermination camp. The norm is that all Jews are to be sent. If both X and Y are Jewish, it is surely not unjust, indeed, it is commendable, for the decisionmaker not to certify Y. Thus, although inconsistent decisions are rendered, no injustice is done. Again, X is not adversely affected by the decision; it does not make X's situation any worse.

Several points should be noted about this objection. First, it might be confusing the conceptions of justice everything considered and just in a particular respect. In many complex situations, different just-making features point to opposite conclusions. The inconsistency can point to the injustice of the decisions in one respect, while the gross immorality of the norm point to their being just in another. The latter may be so much more important, that the decisions are just everything considered.

Second, one could also confuse noncomparative and comparative justice. Noncomparatively, Y is treated justly, and that does not by itself give X a complaint of injustice. X of course has a noncomparative justice complaint, but X might also have a comparative one. The comparative complaint is that since the decisionmaker did not certify Y, X should not have been certified either. No basis existed for certifying X but not Y. Now one can concoct various stories as to why, independent of the features specified by the norm, the decisionmaker could not refuse to certify both. Perhaps a superior was present when the decision about X was made. Nonetheless, it makes perfectly good sense for X to want such an explanation and to complain of unfair treatment if none can be given.

Third, the objection assumes that X is not treated unjustly if not harmed. As noted above, comparative injustice does not seem to require consequential harm. If one believes it does, the claim advanced here can be modified. One can hold that inconsistency often (sometimes) results in unequal or unfair treatment, not that it always do so.

Similar results can occur if benefits are conferred. Suppose a norm confers a benefit, such as disability payments, and X and Y are relevantly similar and deserve the benefit. (1) X receives the benefit but Y does not. Then Y is unfairly treated, both noncomparatively and comparatively. Y does not receive a deserved benefit and is treated unfairly compared to X. (2) X receives the benefit, but Y receives a greater one. One might contend that X was not treated unfairly, because X received the benefit he or she deserved (see Lyons 1973, 857). Again, this contention rests on noncomparative justice. X might object that he or she was treated comparatively unjustly because he or she received less than Y. Moreover, those who have to provide the benefit (taxpayers) are harmed or wronged. Again, even if no one is harmed, that does not necessarily imply no comparative injustice occurred.

Consequently, inconsistency often results in adverse effects on persons. Even if it does not in some cases, one might well object that comparative unequal treatment is unjust. However, one might finally object that consistency is not morally desirable. Perhaps it encourages greed and envy (Coons 1987, 105–06). People only object to inconsistency when they think it will benefit them, and the comparative aspect encourages envy of persons who fare better. However, the greed objection could be made to almost any moral principle. People rarely raise them to their detriment. Envy is not intrinsic to comparative considerations; 'envy' is appropriate only when people are unhappy about others' deserved greater advantages. Consequently, we can conclude that inconsistent decisions are morally objectionable.

This point is widely recognized in some contexts, and, inconsistently, not in others. Few people would deny the unfairness if a teacher raised one student's grade to one higher than deserved, from a C to a B, but did not do so for other similar students. Although no student could complain of receiving a lower grade than deserved, the action would be condemned as unfair. However, it is often thought unobjectionable to fail to prosecute some criminal suspects whose cases are relevantly similar to those of others who are prosecuted. Assuming that the prosecutor had a reasonable case, no prosecuted suspect can complain that prosecution was not deserved. Logically, however, the situation is no different from the situation of students who did not receive a higher grade.

One might contend that comparative justice is appropriate for the student grading context but not the prosecutorial context. Part of the purpose of grades is to compare students. Criminal prosecution, however, is not a competitive and thus comparative situation. Two replies are possible. First, criminal prosecution does have a comparative function. Prosecution stigmatizes in a way having charges dropped does not. It thus distinguishes those persons who are reasonably believed to have committed crimes from others. Second, and more importantly, whenever people are judged by standards, consistency and thus comparative justice is involved. Logical consistency requires that if the same standard is applied to two relevantly similar cases, the judgments be the same. This is true even of cases not involving justice, for example, measuring two lengths of rope. When the standards and judgments concern the distribution of burdens and benefits to people, then justice is involved.

Thus, the Supreme Court in the death penalty cases was too hasty to reject defendants claims of injustice due to prosecutorial discretion. The Court claimed such discretion merely involved showing mercy (*Gregg v. Georgia*, 428 U.S. 153, 199 (1976); *Proffitt v. Florida*, 428 U.S. 242, 254 (1976)). Implicit in the Court's judgment is that defendant X has no complaint if mercy is shown to defendant Y. However, elsewhere the Court was sensitive to differences in mercy shown by different juries, emphasizing that state supreme courts would review the cases for consistency. Thus, the Court should have at least permitted defendants to show that prosecutorial discretion is exercised inconsistently.

Limitations The Court's reference to mercy relates to a final objection which indicates a limit to consistency. Suppose Z is gratuitously bestowing a benefit on two people X and Y, say, giving candy to two unknown twin children on the street. If Z gives more to X than to Y because Z just felt like it, a charge of inconsistency cannot get a foothold. In effect, the only feature indicating D is Z's feeling like choosing it, but this is not a reason! Without a reason, the question of inconsistency is out of place; it does not make sense because there is no decision norm to generate an inconsistency. Any such decision is thus arbitrary and capricious. It violates the requirement of standards.

Actually, few burden/benefit decisions are like this. People give gifts, say, wedding gifts to nieces and nephews, for reasons, not mere whim or feeling like it. These reasons constitute a decision norm. Without a relevant difference, it would be comparatively unjust to give a wedding gift to one niece and not another. Moreover, people usually use various standards in deciding to whom to give. Prosecutors, in particular, have various reasons of efficiency and so on for charging and plea bargaining. The requirement of consistency does not limit their choice of those purposes (although moral considerations do), only their inconsistent application. Consequently, although comparative justice applies, it is easily met because the decisionmaker's purpose or standard can produce almost any result. For example, one can give wedding gifts only to nieces one frequently sees. The constraint is sincerity or good faith—the standard must be one a person actually accepts. Of course, these reasons might be silly and irrational and in that sense arbitrary and capricious. Courts often use 'arbitrary and capricious' in that sense, requiring decision norms to be reasonable. However, decisions can be arbitrary in that sense but logically consistent.

Another limitation or difficulty arises in requiring consistency in burden/benefit decisions by organizations. Inconsistency arises when a person makes different decisions in relevantly similar cases. However, if two people make different judgments about relevantly similar cases, neither one need be involved in an inconsistency (see Lyons 1985, 509). Consequently, if different employees of an organization make different decisions about relevantly similar cases, no logical inconsistency exists.

The solution is to treat an organization as one individual; its decisions should then be consistent. Good reasons exist to treat organizations—governments, businesses, universities—as individuals (see also Dworkin 1986, chap. 6, esp. 219–24 (distinguishing integrity from consistency); but see Coons 1987, 96 (mistake to personify legal system in one mind)). First, in many administrative agencies, employees exercise delegated authority in the name of the agency head. Thus, in effect, all decisions are those by the agency head, so consistency applies. Second, if one does not require consistency across persons, then the outcome of cases depends on which individual happens to make a decision. This will create inefficiency as people shop for favorable decisionmakers. Third, the substantive benefits expected from the adoption of standards and norms will be significantly decreased if they are applied in inconsistent ways.

Although the requirement of consistency is strongly justifiable as both rational and fair, within the scope of discretion$_3$ it has little effect and sometimes is undesirable. It applies only when the factual and normative grounds are the same in two cases. A difference in facts or norms can justify different results. If a person has discretion$_3$, that person can determine the norms or standards to be used within the scope of discretion$_3$. Suppose two cases have all features $F_1, F_2, \ldots F_m$ in common, but one has an extra feature F_n. This will justify a different decision if the person's norm specifies F_n as relevant. If a norm specifies that features $F_1, F_2, \ldots F_m$ are sufficient for decision D, then the extra feature F_n does not justify a different decision. To treat the cases differently, the norm must specify that features $F_1, F_2, \ldots F_m$ and only those features are sufficient, or more plausibly, that if those features are present and F_n is not, then decision D. If one has been using the first norm and wants to treat the second case differently due to feature F_n, then one must change the norm one is applying. The situation is often more subtle than this. Often one is not completely clear about the normative grounds one is using. Confronted with the first case, one might think that the appropriate norm does not make feature F_n relevant, and it is only when one confronts a case with feature F_n that one realizes more precisely what the appropriate normative grounds are.

Consistency does not prohibit people with $discretion_3$ changing their minds about the normative grounds for decisions within the scope of their $discretion_3$. If they have reasons for so doing, then they are not arbitrary. They are inconsistent over time, but logical inconsistency does not apply over time. Sometimes they will simply decide that the standards or norms being used are not good and thus change them. For many burden/benefit decisions, norms and standards are adopted against a set of background factual assumptions. Rarely do the norms specify these background assumptions, so they are not features picked out as factual grounds for decisions. In particular, they are not features of the individuals about whom burden/benefit decisions are being made. For example, consider an airline company that has been hiring pilots with ten years experience at $95,000 a year. A new job applicant with ten years' experience is offered a job at only $75,000. The company might reasonably claim that changing economic circumstances—less competition, excess supply of pilots in the labor market, and so on—justify a different offer. What the airline cannot consistently do is at the same time offer one pilot $75,000 and another similar pilot $95,000 for similar jobs.

Because decisionmakers can reasonably become more aware of precisely what standards or norms they are using, change them on reconsideration of their merits, or change them because of background factual changes, different decisions in apparently similar cases are not a strong indication of inconsistency. Consequently, one must first ask for an explanation of the apparent inconsistency. Only if one is not forthcoming can a charge of inconsistency stick. Requiring decisionmakers to provide the findings and reasons for their decisions helps indicate whether or not they are inconsistent.

Adherence to Precedents

The use of precedents was preliminarily described as taking decisions in similar previous cases to prescribe decisions in present cases. As noted, adherence to precedents will provide consistency, not only at a given time, but over time. Many difficulties arise in explaining the logic of precedents, but fortunately most details are not relevant here. Two general interpretations are worth noting—the factual and the normative reasons models (see Lyons 1985, 500–02). A third model interprets precedents as rules set by previous courts and thus does not differ significantly from our discussion of following rules in the next section. According to the historical or factual model, if the same or similar factual features are found in the present case as in a previous one, then one should decide as before. In this model, the factual features control the present decision. According to the normative reasons model, it is not the factual features themselves but acceptable norms justifying the previous decision that control the present case. The application of those norms in the present apparently similar case might justify a different decision. The best norms justifying the previous decision might pick out as indicating a different decision a factual element in the present case that did not exist in the previous one.

The differences between the two approaches are not as stark as here indicated. As both factual and normative grounds are required for decisions, both models must accommodate both grounds. On the factual model one can distinguish a present case from a previous one on the basis of an extra feature not mentioned in the previous decision, if one can present good reasons why it is relevant. And the best normative reasons for a previous decision would prescribe the same decision for similar cases unless there was some factual difference. The models differ most clearly when one must choose between competing precedents. On the factual model, the appropriate precedent is the one most factually similar. On the normative reasons model, one develops a set of reasons justifying both precedents and then applies them to the case.

As we have seen, administrative law requires agencies to follow precedent or explain why they have not (see MSA § 5-116(c)(8)(iii)). This principle might seem to be undermined by David Lyons's argument against the claim that there is always a sound reason for following precedent, so that any failure to do so must be justified (Lyons 1984, 581). Fortunately, Lyons' argument need not undercut the principle. The view Lyons attacks contends that there is always a good reason to follow precedent. The legal principle need not assume that there is always a good reason, only that there usually is. A sufficient explanation for not following precedent might be that the usual reasons for doing so do not apply. Lyons would not necessarily object to the principle thus interpreted.

Our question is the extent to which precedents should be used in burden/benefit decisions. The use of precedents depends on two dimensions (cf. Davis 1969, 105). At a general level, adherence to precedent may or may not be accepted as a principle for a context or subject matter. The strength of this principle can vary, depending on considerations discussed below, and it can be balanced against other principles.

At a particular level, a given precedent can be more or less compelling depending on the degree of similarity between it and the present case. At this level, precedents operate like nondiscretionary decision rules; they are either followed or not (Schauer 1987, 594). Any reason that might be given for outweighing or overriding a precedent can be converted into a dissimilarity between the present and past case and so a reason for it not applying. The same applies to choice of precedents. Suppose two precedents, P_1 and P_2, are both similar to the present case but give different results. A decisionmaker must choose which to follow, and in so choosing the person has $discretion_3$, because the standard is a multifactor one (importance of factual similarities or best reasons justifying both). Once one of them is chosen, it applies and decides the case. The other one does not apply. However, unless the principle of precedent is taken as absolute, the decisionmaker could reject following precedent at all and simply decide on the merits of the case.

Moral basis It is useful to begin by considering the reasons often given for the principle of following precedents in law. It is frequently said to be important for treating like cases alike (e.g., Golding 1984, 98). To the extent that this is a requirement of consistency, we have already seen that although adherence to precedent provides consistency, it is not necessary for consistency. Adherence to precedent does more than add consistency over time; it also makes it more difficult to change one's mind about the normative grounds. On the normative reasons model, one should follow the norms justifying previous decisions. On the factual model, one must use norms that give the results in the previous case, so changes of norms make no practical difference for cases deemed similar.

Any significant adherence to precedent must sometimes commit one to suboptimal decisions, even bad ones (see Schauer 1987, 589). To be useful, precedents must generalize, that is, not take all features of a case as relevant; otherwise, they will apply only to exactly similar cases and thus provide little guidance, for there are few if any such cases. Even the best precedent, however, will then include situations in which an alternative decision might have had better results. The more general the description of the precedent, the more suboptimal cases that will fall under it.

One might think that this commitment does not ensue on the reasons model of precedents, because one uses the most acceptable norms that will justify previous results. Nevertheless, the norms must justify most previous decisions. If a number of those decisions are bad, there might not be an otherwise acceptable norm that will justify them. For example, if precedents hold that discrimination against blacks is permissible in various situations, even the most acceptable norm justifying those decisions will not be one that would be accepted were one not trying to adhere to precedent.

At least four reasons can be offered for following suboptimal and even some bad precedents. Several of the reasons do not appeal to considerations that might in some narrow sense be considerations of justice. But as we have noted, our concern is with the morality of procedure whether or not it depends on some narrow conception of justice. The first reason is to provide predictability (Golding 1984, 99; Schauer 1987, 597–98). People reasonably want to be able to predict decisions affecting them. If they can predict what decisions will be given, then they can often plan to conduct their lives to avoid the imposition of burdens and to receive benefits. If decisionmakers follow precedents, such prediction is easier. However, predictability does not require that decisionmakers always follow precedents. Friends and relatives can often predict what I will have to eat, even though I do not decide on the basis of precedent. Similarly, if decisionmakers consistently apply standards or norms, one can often predict their decision.

A second reason is that people might have relied on previous decisions. Although closely related to predictability, reliance is not the same. Predictability pertains to an interest in planning, while reliance pertains to an interest in not having expectations upset. Not all reliance provides a reason for adherence to precedent; it must be justifiable reliance. Reliance on an unreasonable interpretation of a precedent is not justifiable. More importantly, reliance itself would not be appropriate were there not some understanding that decisionmakers would not easily change their minds. Thus, were it not for a principle of adherence to precedent, reliance might be unreasonable and unjustifiable (Lyons 1985, 496). Thus, reliance cannot be a justification for the principle of precedent.

Reliance can, however, affect the strength of the principle vis-à-vis other principles in particular cases. Two factors are involved—the extent and importance of the reliance. The extent of reliance pertains to how many people relied how often. Some precedents might not be relied on at all. The importance of the reliance depends on the amount of the burden or benefit involved. Reliance on a precedent that would relieve one of a \$5.00 tax is not as important as reliance on a precedent that would relieve one of a \$500 tax.

A third reason is efficiency (see also Posner 1977, 426; Schauer 1987, 599). If a decisionmaker or others have carefully addressed a problem on several previous occasions, little gain can be expected from going through the elaborate process of applying standards or norms anew to similar factual situations. Without adherence to precedents, many more losing parties would appeal. Except for the costs of appeal, they have little to lose. But if an appellate decisionmaker will follow a clear precedent, appeal is pointless. Even if a decisionmaker in each case were to consider whether a precedent is good or bad, as much time might be spent as in considering the case afresh (see Lyons 1985, 512).

A fourth consideration closely connected to efficiency is coherence. Whereas efficiency pertains to hearing the same issue debated over and over, coherence pertains to the systematic fit of decisions on different but related issues. For example, suppose a regulatory agency has normally included the cost of a service in the basic charge it allows. If it ceases to follow precedent and permits an extra charge for that service, then it might also want to lower the permissible basic rate. Decisions are often part of a system to achieve some purpose. Following precedent holds one aspect constant so that other decisions can be made on that basis.

Limitations These reasons for the principle of precedent do not support applying it in all contexts. Each of them might not apply to some decisions (see Lyons 1984, 585). Some decisions are largely independent of decisions about other issues. For example, a decision not to award disability benefits for one type of injury has little to do with awarding it for others. There is, of course, some relationship for overall degree of disability. Few people rely on certain types of decisions; they do not even know of them. For example, students do not rely on a teacher's decisions about particular papers submitted a previous semester, although they do rely on general policies of severity of grading. For some decisions, it is more efficient simply to apply standards rather than to consider a surfeit of precedents not precisely on point; moreover, reasons can frequently be given in clearer and more coherent fashion. Finally, although the possibility of planning is often present, it is certainly possible that no one is interested in planning to avoid a burden or obtain a benefit. The chances of the situation arising might be too small to be significant for planning, or other more important reasons might exist to guide one's conduct. For example, most pedestrians avoid walking into the street from behind parked cars to avoid injury, not to avoid contributory or comparative negligence denying or decreasing an award for damages if they are hit by an automobile. (Insurance companies do use decisions about contributory and comparative negligence in planning and setting rates.)

Besides the failure of the reasons for the principle of precedent, other reasons exist for not using it in many burden/benefit decision contexts. First, in some contexts it might simply be inappropriate. If an agency is authorized to award grants to encourage innovative research, that an award was made for a proposal to test the same hypothesis with the same research design the year before is a reason against, not for, awarding this proposal a grant. One might claim that precedent does apply but a crucial similarity is a proposal's innovative character. This year's proposal is relevantly different, because it is not innovative—someone else is already doing that research. This claim is most plausible on the normative reasons model of precedent, because the reason justifying last year's award does not apply to this year's proposal. On the factual model, the claim is at best misleading. Innovation or uniqueness reverses the usual grounds for the operation of the factual model. It operates on the detailed factual similarity of cases, but a standard of innovation or uniqueness operates with dissimilarity. In short, an innovativeness or uniqueness criterion implies that factual similarity is a reason for treating proposals differently and thus undercuts or at least reverses the usual operative basis for factual precedent.

Moreover, even on the reasons model, one often cannot object to the rejection of one's proposal by arguing that it is as innovative as others funded in the past. If agencies have more worthy proposals than they can fund, the issue is not whether a proposal is as innovative as past ones but whether it is more innovative than those funded this year. In short, comparisons with past competitors are not relevant, unless all worthy proposals can be funded. The principle of precedent is thus not appropriate for competitive benefit-conferring decisions. If all worthy proposals can be funded, it is no longer a competitive situation but one of meeting a minimum standard below which no award will be given.

Second, sometimes, although the reasons for following precedent may apply, they are outweighed by other considerations making it undesirable to adopt the principle of precedent for them. Many administrative agencies and other positions of authority are created precisely to provide flexibility in decision making. Following precedents decreases flexibility and increases rigidity (Lorch 1980, 147). By following precedent, one becomes committed to the normative or factual grounds of previous decisions. If one wants decision-makers to be able easily to reconsider and change their minds either on the normative grounds alone or because the background factual situation is frequently changing, adherence to precedent is inimical to that purpose. The faster social and economic background conditions are changing, the less valuable the principle of precedent (Posner 1977, 427). Moreover, sometimes one wants different decisionmakers for different cases to reflect contemporary community values or to support democratic processes. A prime example is the institution of the jury (see also Coons 1987, 79–83, 108). Although juries are given standards, within their discretion3 they are not bound by precedent.

In England, the no-fettering doctrine helps ensure administrative flexibility although it also makes the use of precedents and rules more difficult (see Flick 1984, 142). Basically, the no-fettering doctrine is that agencies may, but need not, adopt standards and norms for decisions (including precedents) provided they are not mechanically applied (Galligan 1986, 270, 281–82; Flick 1984, 142, 144). Each case must be must be considered on its own merits and standards or norms modified if appropriate. This doctrine differs from the American requirement that agencies follow their own rules. It provides individualized justice for each case at the cost of some predictability and efficiency. However, those subject to decisions are not likely to be prejudiced by the doctrine, as agencies are unlikely to deviate from precedent or rules unless the person argues for such deviation.

Adherence to precedent is a weak principle for evaluating burden/benefit decisions. In many contexts it is simply not appropriate because the reasons of predictability, efficiency, and coherence do not apply. In others, it can be more or less appropriate depending on the strength of other considerations such as the rate of change in background circumstances. In particular cases, its weight depends on the above reasons as well as justifiable reliance. These interests need not pertain, and their absence explains or justifies failure to follow precedent in particular cases.

Conformity to Rules

Conformity to rules is deciding cases as a given rule or set of rules prescribes. More precisely, we are primarily concerned with rules announced in advance. Most of the points apply whether a rule is nondiscretionary or has scope for discretion3. Many laws and regulations are obvious examples of such rules. Rules are common in other burden/benefit decision contexts. A teacher can announce rules at the beginning of a course concerning due dates for papers and penalties for late papers. Many businesses have announced rules regarding employment and other matters, for example, a 5% pay raise after one year.

That rules are announced in advance helps clearly to distinguish conformity to rules from adherence to precedent. One can plausibly argue that adherence to precedent involves conformity to rules. Lawyers speak of the rule of a case or its ratio decidendi. On the factual model of adherence to precedents, the factual grounds and decision amount to a rule that on similar facts the same decision should follow. On the normative reasons model, rules are often the basis of the best justification of the decision. Some people who write of the importance of following rules may include the rules in precedents, but here they are excluded. There are two important differences between rules and precedents. First, the rule of a precedent is not "announced" before the first decision, but a rule is. Second, a rule has a canonical formulation, but a precedent does not. Even if the judge in a precedential decision states a holding, subsequent judges following that precedent can still give it a different formulation. This second point does not apply to some versions of the rule model of precedent, for they take the statement of a holding as canonical. On such views, after the first case is decided, one proceeds the same as an agency following its own rules and the discussion in this section applies mutatis mutandis.

As we noted at the beginning, U.S. law requires administrative agencies to comply with their announced rules, except for some procedural rules. Similarly, courts must conform to statutes (unless they declare them unconstitutional, which involves conformity to a superior rule or principle). Administrative agencies have an advantage over courts in conformity to rules, namely, they have the power to change most of the rules they apply. Administratively adopted regulations constitute the bulk of the rules they apply, so agencies can revoke or revise them. Nonetheless, most burden/benefit decisionmakers cannot change the rules they apply. Indeed, most decisions applying administrative regulations are made by civil servants who are not empowered to change them—"I don't make the rules."

Moral basis The same reasons for adhering to precedent support conforming to rules. Conformity to announced rules provides predictability enabling people to plan, and it protects their interests when they have relied on the rules (Barry 1965, 101). Efficiency and coherence are also benefits. Rules are better in these respects than precedents. Because of their authoritative wording, it is usually easier to determine the implications of a rule than a precedent. Rules are often adopted as a group with an eye to their consistency and coherence. Being determined on a case by case basis, precedents frequently lack the systematic coherence of many sets of rules. Indeed, rules are often adopted precisely when it is thought to be important to provide a systematic framework to achieve some purposes rather than rely on case by case determinations.

A further reason for conformity to rules does not apply to adherence to precedents. In formulating and announcing a rule, a person or organization makes a commitment to decide or act, impose burdens or confer benefits, as the rule specifies. The announcement of a rule would not serve any purpose if those people announcing it did not usually intend to conform to it and those people who might be affected by it did not expect them to do so. People can announce rules they do not intend to follow, but doing so is deceptive and would be pointless were there not the usual practice and expectation that announced rules will be followed.

This type of commitment is either completely lacking or at least weaker in precedential decisions. Deciding a particular case need not involve any commitment to decide future cases the same (see also Eisenberg 1979, 123). If the decisionmakers have indicated that they will follow precedent, then there is a commitment to follow a particular decision; but the commitment stems from the prior adoption of the principle of precedent and so cannot be a reason for adopting it. One does not need an additional or prior commitment to follow rules to be committed to following a particular rule; its announcement alone provides the commitment. Thus, the commitment to follow a rule is intrinsic to its announcement, but the commitment to treat a prior decision as precedential is extrinsic to the decision.

The commitment to follow rules also makes the reliance ground for following them stronger than for following precedent. Recall that reliance on decisions as precedents has to be justifiable, but it is not unless the principle of precedent is adopted. With rules, announcing them provides the commitment to follow them. Thus, reliance is justifiable. One might object that reliance is not justifiable if a decisionmaker habitually fails to follow announced rules. In reply, one might distinguish between reasonable and justifiable reliance, it being justifiable but not reasonable to rely in such cases. Anyway, the point does not affect the standard situation.

The intrinsic commitment to follow announced rules faces a difficulty analogous to one about consistency. As no personal inconsistency arises if two different people decide similar cases differently, the commitment to follow a rule pertains only to those who formulate and adopt it. Other people called on to apply the rule have no personal commitment. For example, a new faculty member might confront a departmental rule prohibiting incompletes in graduate courses unless students have a medical excuse. The faculty member might not agree with the rule, thinking that other legitimate grounds exist for giving incompletes. The answer to the problem, as with consistency, is to treat the department as a unit. To uphold the departmental commitment to the rule, each member must follow the rule.

Consistency, adherence to precedent, and conformity to rules often constrain decisionmakers as members of a larger organization. They can apply at the personal level, but usually they apply as consistency of judgment between various persons, adhering to precedents decided by others, and applying rules formulated and adopted by others. The moral force of their application to individuals depends on the individuals' obligations to the organization. One basis of this obligation stems from commitments undertaken in accepting a position in an organization. Sometimes this commitment is explicit, as when judges and other officials take an oath of office to uphold the constitution and laws. More frequently it is implicit; in accepting a position, one implicitly agrees to uphold its commitments and fulfill the tasks associated with it. One can accept a position with no intention of supporting an organization but instead subverting it. As with false commitment to announced rules, doing so rests on the contrary practice. Such deception can be justifiable, for example, a spy or anti-Nazi accepting a position in the Third Reich to help undermine it, but that cannot be the usual or normal case.

Conformity to rules, like adherence to precedent, can involve suboptimal and even bad decisions. Even good rules encompass cases in which the best decision is contrary to the rule, and rules are not always good or morally indifferent. Many rules prescribe silly, inefficient, or iniquitous decisions or conduct. Consequently, even though the justification for conformity to rules is stronger than for the principle of precedent, it is implausible to claim that one must always conform to announced rules.

It is tempting to claim that one should consider whether the factors of predictability, reliance, efficiency, coherence, and perhaps commitment are affected enough to make conformity to a rule better than violating it. Such a practice resembles an act utilitarian approach to rules as rules of thumb (see Smart 1968). Such an approach would undermine the benefits of rules. The benefits of predictability, reliance, efficiency, and coherence depend on rules being followed in most cases, but usually not a particular one. Any one failure to follow rules will not undermine the general predictability of results or the reasonableness of reliance. Consequently, in no particular case do these concerns have great weight. But if they are outweighed in many cases, then predictability and reasonableness of reliance are lost. Moreover, evaluating each case on its merits independent of the rule and then calculating the various effects on rule following is the least efficient method of decision making. Furthermore, many people applying rules in organizations lack the ability or information to determine the benefits of following a rule. It is one thing to develop a rule for one's private concerns and then disregard it when doing so appears best. It is another to allow others to disregard a rule when they think it best. In the latter situation, one is subject to various particular risks one has not knowingly and voluntarily accepted.

Exceptions and limitations Still, allowances must be made for the suboptimality of conformity to rules. Two methods of doing so are exceptions and simple rejection of the rule. Exceptions reduce the number of suboptimal decisions required by a rule. Rejection is appropriate when a rule generally has bad results.

Recall the faculty member confronted with a rule permitting incompletes for graduate students only for medical illness. Suppose the professor has a student whose spouse and young child were killed in an automobile accident the next to last week of the term. One might, as courts sometimes do, try to construe the rule to cover the situation. One might argue that the student is emotionally distraught and so mentally ill. The argument is spurious and probably unsound; granted, the student is emotionally distraught with grief, but in the circumstances grief is completely normal and not a sign of mental illness. However, the faculty who made the rule might not have foreseen this circumstance. One cannot predict all the possible exceptions to rules that might arise. Consequently, this situation might be an unforeseen exception.

More plausibly, the faculty might have foreseen claims for incompletes due to a death in the family but not included it as an exception for fear of misuse. (In one of my classes, one sixth of the students claimed a death in the family the week papers were due.) Rules do or should have purposes. The supposed purpose for no death in the family exception to the no incomplete rule was to prevent fraudulent claims. If the accident and death of the student's family is widely known, for example, appeared in the local newspaper, then this purpose is not defeated by an exception in the case.

The legal permission for administrative agencies not conforming to procedural rules basically appeals to not defeating the purposes of the rules. If exceptions further procedural concerns for efficiency, timeliness of decisions, and so forth without prejudice to parties, then the permission is justifiable. However, one must be careful about what constitutes prejudice to a party. Some recent court decisions have suggested that a party is not prejudiced if the outcome is not wrong (see Smolla 1984, 482–86). And if the judgment is within the decisionmaker's discretion3, a party cannot have been prejudiced. This interpretation makes two mistakes. First, it assumes that if a judgment is within a decisionmaker's scope of discretion3, a difference in procedure would not have resulted in a different judgment. Second, it ignores the possibility of injury due to a failure to follow just procedures independent of the outcome (Smolla 1984, 500–02). That is, it takes a purely instrumental view of the value of procedure. The next chapter rejects that view. In short, failure to follow announced procedural rules is justifiable only if no party is procedurally or substantively prejudiced.

Their purposes can also justify exceptions to substantive rules. Sometimes enforcement of a rule can defeat its purpose. For example, suppose rules require that faculty at the rank of instructor not be retained more than three years and that the highest degree in the field be attained before one can be promoted to assistant professor. Further suppose that a department has an outstanding instructor who has been on the faculty three years, published a dozen major articles, but never completed the Ph.D. Application of the rules in this case would result in the loss of an excellent department member. Conformity to both rules would defeat their purpose. Technically, one could argue that the rules' purpose is to prevent the retention of poor faculty, not to retain good ones, so the purpose is not defeated. That analysis ignores the broader purpose of securing a good faculty, with the rules addressing part of the goal by preventing the retention of poor faculty.

Sometimes rules should be rejected or ignored. Grossly bad rules fall in this category. How bad a rule must be before it is rejected or ignored is a difficult problem not pursued here. Instead, we consider when rules are bad because rules are inappropriate for the problem. In the previous chapter we identified four reasons for not adopting rules—no precise answers, lack of experience, many unforeseeable exceptions, and lack of agreement.

Two related reasons for the inappropriateness of rules are worth emphasizing. First, rules presuppose relatively stable background conditions that are not mentioned in the rules. Precedents also presuppose such background conditions, but as the authoritative language of rules locks one into a normative position more than precedents, they require more stable background conditions. For example, a rule to set utility rates to achieve a net return of 10% on investment is not appropriate in a period of highly volatile inflation as in the late 1970s and early 1980s. Yet, assumptions about inflation rates are not normally part of a rate-setting rule about return on investment.

Second, the clear-cut feature of rules makes them appropriate only when a set of empirical conditions correlates with appropriate outcomes (see also Galligan 1986, 173). This is especially true of nondiscretionary rules. The factual features F are chosen because when they and D are present, a purpose will be realized. If no set of features $F_1, F_2, \ldots F_n$ and D usually advance that purpose, then a rule is inappropriate. For example, reportedly at one time some colleges followed the rule of always hiring Harvard graduates over other candidates for faculty positions. The correlation between being a Harvard graduate and being the best person for a position is too weak to support such a rule.

Many burden/benefit decisions occur in contexts that do not permit the formulation of rules, for example, awarding academic grants. Instead, one should use standards and principles indicating factors that must be weighed and balanced, thus leaving considerable discretion3 (see Mashaw 1983, 114–23 (use of standards in social security disability decisions)). Indeed, this is one reason legislatures often provide only a few general standards for administrative agencies. Nevertheless, on the whole, persons making burden/benefit decisions probably fail to provide rules when they can more than they provide rules when they should not (Davis 1969, 103; but see Rosenblum 1974, 51, 60).

Summary

Three closely related but distinct requirements—consistency, adherence to precedent, and conformity to rules—can limit the scope of discretion. They are considered requirements of justice because they promote equality of treatment of those subject to decisions. Because they do not specify the content of decisions, they are sometimes called requirements of formal justice.

Consistency requires that if one is applying the same normative grounds to similar relevant facts, one must reach the same decision. Personal consistency is a requirement of rationality. Inconsistent decisions create comparative injustice (inequality) between those subject to the decisions, even if the unjustly treated individual is not adversely affected. Consistency of decisions by different persons in an organization goes beyond the requirement of rationality and requires treating the organization as a unit, as though it were one person. Good normative and practical reasons exist to do so. A requirement of consistency is not a strong restriction on decision making, because it applies only to simultaneous decisions and if one has discretion3 to adopt standards or norms, one can always change one's mind about what norm is appropriate either in itself or due to changing background circumstances.

Adherence to precedent goes beyond the requirement of consistency, requiring consistency over time and placing limits on the grounds for decisions. On either the factual or normative reasons model of precedent, grounds are constrained either to previous factual conditions or to the best norms that account for previous decisions. Consequently, less scope for discretion3 exists. Adherence to precedent can thus involve suboptimal decisions and even implementing norms that cannot be justified on their merits. The advantages of the principle of precedent include predictability of decisions enabling better planning, efficiency of decision making, coherence of decisions and purposes, and in particular cases protection of interests in justifiable reliance. None of these reasons can support the principle of precedent in all circumstances, and sometimes the reasons are outweighed by others making adherence to precedent undesirable.

Conformity to rules involves deciding in accordance with previously announced rules. The rule model of precedent basically collapses to following rules. If the rules are nondiscretionary and following rules is narrowly construed, it implies consistency but is not required by consistency. Predictability, reliance, efficiency, and coherence also support conformity to rules; efficiency and coherence are often more likely from conformity to rules than adherence to precedent. An additional reason supports conformity to rules that does not support adherence to precedent, namely, the commitment involved in announcing a rule. This commitment applies directly only to those who adopt a rule. For the commitment to constrain others, it must be indirectly through their commitments or obligations to an organization.

Conformity to rules can also result in suboptimal and even bad decisions. The benefits of conformity to rules will be lost or decreased if one tries to analyze in each particular case whether conformity is the better decision. Exceptions can reduce the number of suboptimal decisions by better achieving a rule's purposes. Exceptions to procedural rules can be justified to further procedural purposes without detriment to those purposes, but one should consider noninstrumental as well as instrumental procedural purposes. Rules can also sometimes be justifiably rejected or ignored. Sometimes the rules are simply bad ones. Sometimes rules are inappropriate for the context, for example, those in which the substantively appropriate outcome is not highly correlated to empirical features. In the absence of such correlation, broader criteria must be weighed and balanced thus allowing discretion3.

Following precedents and rules are central to the traditional adversary adjudication model of decision making and its principles of procedural justice. Because the use of precedents and rules is not always appropriate for burden/benefit decisions, the plausibility of the adversary adjudication model for all burden/benefit decisions is called into question. In Part II we shall develop a more general theory of procedural justice using different models for disparate contexts.

PART II

THEORY

CHAPTER 6

A THEORETICAL JUSTIFICATION

Part I examined traditional principles for administrative procedures in making burden/benefit decisions. There are four general principles—impartiality, opportunity to be heard, grounds for decisions, and formal justice. Each subsumes less general principles such as separation of functions, opportunity to rebut information, adherence to precedent, and so on. While some reasons were given for the principles, no systematic theoretical justification was provided. The principles are for the traditional adversary adjudication model, and there were suggestions that the model might not be appropriate for all contexts. In particular, adherence to precedent and use of rules were not found appropriate for all burden/benefit decisions.

This Part provides a theoretical framework to evaluate procedures. This chapter formulates a fundamental norm for evaluating procedures for burden/benefit decisions and indicates how it supports the general principles considered in Part I. The literature on theoretical justifications of procedure is sparse and primarily pertains to conflict resolution, in particular, legal adjudication. Still, much of that literature can, with some modifications, be applied to the burden/benefit context. The following chapter considers a variant of the constitutional question of when due process is required. But our question is broader—when should law (rather than merely ethics) require procedural justice? The last chapter in this Part then directly considers the limits of the traditional adversary adjudication model. Our question is a variant of the constitutional question of what process is due. Alternative decision-making models are elucidated, the appropriate procedural principles for each indicated, and criteria given to help determine when each is appropriate. The net result is to so limit the use of adversary adjudication that it becomes only one, and perhaps not the most important, of several models for making burden/benefit decisions.

Two purposes are inherent in the concept of burden/benefit decision making—resolving issues and finding the "truth." That a decision is to be made implies a choice or issue, to allocate a burden (benefit) or not. If decisions were not intended to resolve issues, but, say, only to express support for doing or not doing something, they would not be so important. One must be clear about the sense in which an issue is resolved. Even after final judgment, parties and others can still think decisions were wrong and feel aggrieved. Decisions do not necessarily resolve issues at the psychological level, only at the practical level, and even there they are not always successful. As I have learned, being hired by a dean or awarded a salary increase by a university vice-president does not always mean that paychecks reflecting the decision will be issued.

An important subsidiary aim of issue resolution is dispute avoidance or minimization. Dispute resolution is an aim of the legal system, but for many burden/benefit decisions no dispute exists. Criminal law with two disputing parties is not always an appropriate model. Burden/benefit decisions do not necessarily involve two or more parties with conflicting positions. Sometimes only one party is involved, for example, a claimant for social security benefits. It would distort the situation to view the Social Security Administration as opposed to giving benefits. Its concern is to pay valid claims, so its interest does not necessarily conflict with the claimant's (see Mashaw 1983, 81). If the claimant is dissatisfied with the administration's decision, then there is a dispute (see Mashaw 1983, 94). A purpose of burden/benefit decision procedures is to enable those receiving burdens or denied benefits to accept the results, that is, to avoid disputes and appeals from initial decisions.

The purpose of ascertaining truth is also inherent in the concept of burden/benefit decision making. Decisionmakers are to decide issues by the application of standards or norms (in this chapter, 'norm' will usually include standards). Even assuming that the norms are correct, a case will not be properly decided in accordance with them unless the "truth" or correct facts are determined. The truth needs to be found not for its own sake but to apply the norms to the case correctly. The aims of the norms—justice, economic efficiency, public policy—make no difference. If the situation is not accurately understood and described, then the aims cannot be rationally served by the decision either in the particular case or as a precedent for others (see Summers 1978, 123).

Of course, decision making is not a simple application of norms to facts. First, finding facts is not a straightforward descriptive process. Facts must be classified for the application of norms and do not come neatly labeled (Hart 1983, 63). Second, many so-called factual questions are matters of evaluation (Atiyah 1983, 34–36). Determining whether someone is disabled or deserves promotion requires judgment and evaluation—discretion$_2$. Third, even when the facts are clear, it is not always clear what the norms imply. Is a faculty member on leave for a year with no place of residence in the city of his or her permanent job on a temporary job "away from home" for less than a year? Nonetheless, one needs to get core factual matters correct—that the person has a contract for the following year, that the leave is for a year or less, and so on.

The purposes of issue resolution and ascertainment of the truth do not provide sufficient criteria for evaluating procedures; they are too general and omit considerations. Issue resolution is a purpose of all decision making, and of substantive as well as procedural norms. Unlike pure science, burden/benefit decision making does not aim at the truth, the whole truth, and nothing but the truth. That would be too expensive and often irrelevant to the purpose of issue resolution. Yet, matters could be resolved without any concern for the truth. Arbitrary fiats or flips of a coin could be used practically to resolve many issues. Consequently, more specific criteria are needed to evaluate procedures.

In considering more specific criteria, we progress from more simple to more complex ones. The first section considers a criterion evaluating procedures by their instrumental promotion of a single value—minimizing economic costs. The next section considers an instrumental evaluation by two values—minimizing economic and moral costs. The third section then adds consideration of a plurality of values that might be inherent in processes. The final section applies the norm developed to support the principles articulated in chapters 2–5.

Economic Costs

Although this section focuses on economic analysis of procedure, it is merely a specific instance of 'single value instrumentalism'. That is, the underlying concept is to design procedures as a means to maximize a single value (or minimize a disvalue). The economic approach seeks to maximize economic efficiency (or wealth) by minimizing costs. The substantive aims of the decision making can be many valued, but the procedures are evaluated by the single value of efficiency. For example, a farm subsidy program might have several aims—to support farmer's incomes, assure an adequate supply of food, and so on, yet the procedures for allocating the subsidies to individuals be chosen solely for their efficiency in achieving these aims. Like any other instrument, procedure is viewed as an expense incurred in achieving an end, so the aim is to minimize the expense. The costs of incorrect decisions are called error costs, and those of making decisions direct costs. The short statement of the aim is to minimize the sum of error and direct costs (Posner 1973, 399–400; Posner 1977, 429; Tullock 1980, 5–6; see also Mashaw 1981b, 185; Mashaw 1985, 117). If we let 'EC' stand for error costs and 'DC' for direct costs, it can be written as follows:

Minimize Sum (EC + DC)

One does not aim to minimize either cost alone but the sum of the two. If one tried to minimize only direct costs, error costs might become exorbitant. Similarly, at some point the increase in direct costs to achieve accuracy is greater than the savings in reduced error costs.

An analogy might help one understand the view. In purchasing from suppliers, purchasing managers aim to achieve the most value for the least expense. An error cost occurs if they purchase an item from one supplier, when it could have been purchased for less from another. The direct costs are those of obtaining bids from various suppliers and evaluating them. Purchasing managers for private firms often have a limited list of qualified suppliers. That is, they have evaluated most potential suppliers and selected a few to be the best in terms of quality, reliability, and so forth. When an item is needed, they request bids from the short list of qualified suppliers and take the lowest bid. Sometimes they might have obtained a significantly lower bid for an item of comparable quality from a supplier not on the short list. However, the time and effort of securing bids from all potential suppliers and evaluating them on each occasion is not worth the savings in error costs. The purchasing managers are minimizing the sum of error and direct costs.

Error costs arise when an incorrect decision is made. A person deserves a burden or benefit or not. There are thus four possible decision outcomes. A decisionmaker can allocate a burden or benefit to a deserving person (AD), allocate it to an undeserving person (AU), not allocate it to a deserving person (~AD), or not allocate it to an undeserving person (~AU). (In this chapter, the expressions 'the deserving' and 'the undeserving' refer to persons who should or should not receive a burden or benefit; with burdens, 'deserving' is thus used in the sense that 'someone deserves punishment'.) Two of these decisions—AU and ~AD—are incorrect, and two—AD and ~AU—are correct. Each incorrect decision results in an inefficient use of resources and an inappropriate expense, because it is not furthering the substantive purposes. For example, if a violator of a safety regulation is mistakenly found not liable, then the violator will not be deterred; insufficient resources will be spent on safety and the number and cost of accidents will increase. Because decisionmakers might make such incorrect decisions, some others in the industry will fail to invest adequately in safety equipment (Tullock 1980, 6–7).

Direct costs are those of running the decision-making system. In administrative agencies, these include the public costs for officials' salaries, hearings, and so on, and the private costs of parties in hiring lawyers, obtaining expert testimony, and so forth. Although many factors influence decisions to apply for government benefits, such as their size and the estimated chances of obtaining them, as private costs increase fewer applications tend to be made and public costs decrease. A similar sort of analysis applies within a private system. For example, if a faculty member at a private university requests to be considered for promotion, the university incurs costs in considering the request. The faculty member also incurs the costs of time and effort to supply materials to support the request. Faculty do not usually request consideration for promotion unless they think they have a reasonable chance of success.

The U.S. Supreme Court appears to have adopted a variation of the economic cost approach to determine due process requirements for administrative decisions. Although the Court is concerned to minimize costs, it has not restricted them to the single value of economic costs. The Court has specified that in evaluating procedures one should balance the private interest, the chances of error, and the government's interest (*Mathews v. Eldridge*, 424 U.S. 319, 335 (1976)). The government's interest includes most of the direct costs. The private interest includes the cost of errors against the individual. Procedures are thus required if and only if DC < ECp, where 'ECp' is the expectable reduction in error costs to the individual from an additional procedure (see also Pierce, Shapiro, and Verkuil 1985, 264). Presumably, if errors were against the government, it would itself increase accuracy so long as the direct costs of doing so were off-set by its gain from reduced errors. Even if the government does not do this, as it historically has not in checking income tax returns, that is its prerogative. So balancing essentially amounts to cost minimizing.

Three objections are commonly made against the economic approach. First, often the data are not available to make the necessary calculations. In particular, courts are not likely to have access to such information. However, our concern is broader than judicial requirement of procedure, including agencies and other organizations that might make such calculations themselves. Moreover, various methods might be employed to reduce these information demands (see Mashaw 1985, 127–40).

Second, many people claim that one cannot place a dollar value on the concerns involved. A prisoner's application for parole or a parent's interest in continued custody of a child, for example, cannot be evaluated in monetary terms. Nonetheless, an economic analyst can reply that people indicate how much freedom or continued custody are worth to them by how much they are willing to spend to obtain them. Of course, a pure willingness to pay analysis here is unpersuasive, since the amount people are willing to pay is largely controlled by how much they have (see also Mashaw 1983, 81). However, other methods exist for placing an economic value on such goals.

The third and closely related objection is that the economic approach or any other single value analysis omits important values. One can reasonably be concerned about the fairness as well as total cost of procedures. A process might be as accurate as, and less expensive than, another but unacceptable because distinctly less fair. Other suggested values that might be omitted from an economic analysis are privacy and participation. An economic analyst can reply that, as in the other cases, one need only place a dollar value on those concerns and the theory can accommodate them.

These objections can be seen as the basis for two other approaches to evaluating procedures that are discussed in the next two sections. Before turning to them, it is worth noting that even if the economic approach is inadequate as a complete theory, it does at least indicate one important factor to be taken into account in evaluating procedures. All else being equal, anyone concerned with wealth has a good reason to prefer lower to higher economic costs, whether they be direct or error costs.

Moral Costs

Another approach to procedure emphasizes that values other than economic costs are involved in evaluating outcomes. The moral cost approach of Ronald Dworkin (1985, chap. 3) is an instance of 'multi-value instrumentalism', that is, evaluates procedures by seeking to maximize several values of outcomes.

Dworkin contends that utilitarian (including economic) approaches to procedure ignore rights. He focuses on criminal cases in which he claims there is a right not to be convicted if innocent (a right not to have a burden—conviction—imposed if undeserving of it). A utilitarian single value instrumentalism looks at what Dworkin calls the "bare harm" inflicted by mistaken decisions; it considers how much suffering actually results from them. Dworkin contends that the bare harm suffered by convicted innocent persons might not be any greater than that resulting from failures to convict guilty persons. Consequently, there need be no greater reason to avoid convicting the innocent than not convicting the guilty. Utilitarianism or efficiency analysis gives inadequate weight to a right not to be convicted if innocent.

Economic analysts do argue that convicting innocent persons involves greater costs than failing to convict guilty ones (Posner 1973, 410–15; Posner 1977, 433–34). This difference then supports the higher burden of proof required for criminal than civil liability. One reason for lower error costs for failing to convict the guilty than for convicting the innocent is that failure to convict one guilty person will probably not have much effect on deterrence, and an increased violation rate is the chief error cost of failing to convict those deserving it. Nonetheless, the fewer guilty persons convicted, the greater the punishment has to be to maintain an effective deterrent. Thus, as the burden of proof requirement is raised, the amount of punishment also needs to be raised to maintain an equal deterrence. It is not clear that innocent persons benefit from a lesser chance of a greater punishment (Tullock 1980, 82). This same method of reasoning should generally apply to any imposition of burdens for deterrent purposes, such as penalizing workers for mistakes. Of course, not all burdens, taxes, for example, are imposed for deterrent purposes.

The moral cost approach implies that there are at least two types of error costs. Consider the two possible mistaken decisions, allocating burdens to the undeserving (AU) and not allocating them to the deserving (~AD). The first is often worse than the second, regardless of the bare or economic harm involved in the two, because it infringes a right not to have a burden imposed if undeserving of it. Such violations of rights are moral harms or costs. Moral harm is not restricted to criminal conviction. If parents have a right to the custody of their children that might be infringed by an incorrect termination decision, then procedures should be biased against infringing that right and causing moral harm.

The moral cost approach adds moral harm to the economic or bare harm of the economic approach's analysis of error costs. Thus, the aim of procedure can be stated as minimizing the sum of the economic and moral error costs and the direct costs. If we here let 'EC' stand for the economic or bare harm error costs and 'MC' for the moral error costs, then the moral cost view merely adds another term to the economic approach's formula:

Minimize Sum (EC + MC + DC)

Moreover, Dworkin claims that moral cost is an objective and constant factor across cases of the same type (Dworkin 1985, 81, 87). That is, moral harm is the same whenever the same right is infringed, so moral costs are a constant factor for each type of substantive decision.

Moral costs can make a significant difference in the procedures that are justified, because they attach to some errors but not to others. Consider diagram 6.1 of possible decision outcomes for the allocation of burdens. Because there are greater costs in AU than in ~AD, one should bias the procedural system to avoid AU errors. That is, ~AD errors are preferable to AU errors; a false positive is worse than a false negative. This effect can be obtained by shifting the burden of proof to make decisions to impose burdens more difficult.

Possible Error Costs in Allocating Burdens

decision

Outcomes	AD	AU	~AD	~AU
Costs		EC + MC	EC	

Diagram 6.1

For benefit-conferring decisions, consideration of moral harm might give a weighting of error costs the opposite from that for burden-imposing decisions. Diagram 6.2 illustrates the effect on benefit-conferring decisions. If the person has a right to a benefit, then failure to award it violates that right and both economic and moral error costs are involved. However, awarding a benefit to someone who has no right to the benefit does not violate any right of that person. Presumably it does not violate any right of others, because they have no personal grievance or that has already been taken into account in determining the net moral cost. One could, of course, include rights of others, say, of comparative injustice, with a factor of weight attached to each moral cost. In any case, presumably a false negative is worse than a false positive. Consequently, if an applicant has the burden of persuasion, it should be lower than even a preponderance of the evidence!

Possible Error Costs in Allocating Benefits

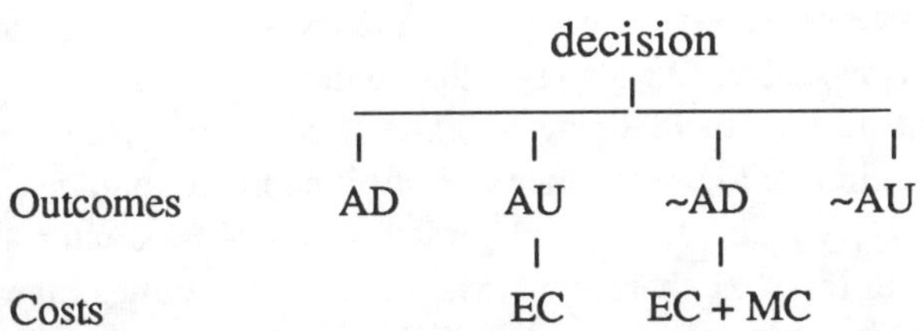

Diagram 6.2

The effects on burden-relieving and benefit-terminating decisions are more complex than for burden-imposing and benefit-conferring decisions. Two factors are involved—who has the burden of proof (persuasion) and which types of errors are preferable. Normally, who has the burden of persuasion shifts from burden-imposing to burden-relieving decisions and from benefit-conferring to benefit-terminating decisions. For example, the state has the burden of persuasion in criminal convictions, but convicted persons have the burden of persuasion for pardons and paroles. For pardons, the issue often remains whether the person should be punished, so presumably ~AD errors are preferable to AU errors. Logically, then, an applicant for a pardon should not have to prove innocence by the preponderance of the evidence, only raise enough evidence to create a reasonable doubt. The matter is complicated by epistemological considerations; for example, a person granting a pardon would be overriding the judgment of a judge or jury. In parole decisions, the issue has plausibly changed. It is no longer whether the person was guilty of a past crime, but whether the person has reformed sufficiently to merit parole. (This can be true of some pardons also.) Here there might not be a reason to prefer one outcome over another, or if there is, it is likely to be to prefer retention over release and risk of further crime. Thus, a parole applicant should have a burden of the preponderance of the evidence or even higher.

In benefit-terminating decisions, there is often no preferred error. To impose a higher standard of proof for terminating benefits, one must contend that continuing benefits to the undeserving (AU) is preferable to discontinuing benefits to the deserving (~AD). This claim must be reconciled with the standard for original conferral. In chapter 4 we considered the claim that a higher burden of persuasion be required for termination of welfare benefits than for granting them. We pointed out the anomaly that would result, namely, that a percentage of persons who were originally granted benefits but were no longer deserving would continue to receive them, but similarly situated original applicants would not receive them. We also saw that to the extent reliance on receipt of benefits depends on there being a higher burden of proof for termination, it would be circular to use reliance to justify the higher burden.

There are two ways to reconcile differential burdens of proof for conferral and termination. First, in the next chapter we will see that sometimes other arguments exist for thinking that terminating benefits is worse than originally failing to confer them. If so, the situation changes so that AU errors are preferable to ~AD errors in benefit-terminating decisions but not in benefit-conferring ones. Second, the same preference might exist for both types of decisions. However, good reasons might exist not to set the burden of persuasion for an original applicant at less than the preponderance of the evidence. It might be difficult for decisionmakers to handle—how much evidence is necessary? Moreover, it could cause demoralization. People might have difficulty accepting X receiving a benefit on the grounds that there was only some chance that X deserved it.

Although Dworkin bases his argument for moral costs on the notion of moral rights being involved, one need not do so (see Galligan 1986, 332). Some rights of various sorts might be assigned because of economic considerations—such as transaction costs (see Calabresi and Melamed 1972). However, even economic analyses of rights admit considerations other than efficiency, for example, distribution. Furthermore, there are other good reasons for admitting various rights (Radin 1987; Rose-Ackerman 1985). However, one need not base moral costs on rights at all. All one needs is a substantive reason to avoid one type of error more than another. Thus, moral costs can be taken to include the costs of failure to achieve substantive aims making one type of error preferable to another. One has good reason to add moral costs to economic costs if one has a good reasons to prefer one type of error over another. Consequently, one should also consider minimizing the moral costs of procedures.

The moral cost approach does not differ from the economic approach as significantly as might appear. First, some economic analysts have recognized that substantive rules might have aims other than economic efficiency (Posner 1973, 401). If the failure to achieve a substantive aim can be evaluated in monetary terms, the same cost minimizing approach can be used. Second, it is difficult to maintain that no monetary value can be placed on moral costs, because the moral cost approach requires balancing monetary error and direct costs with moral costs. One must then have some common factor or method by which to compare moral and economic costs, and monetary value is a plausible candidate. Even if a price cannot be placed directly on moral costs, an indirect pricing occurs. One need only consider how much one is willing to pay in economic costs to avoid moral costs. That amount is the price of the moral costs. For example, the cost of increased crime and greater punishment (when imposed) resulting from placing a high burden of persuasion on the prosecution is the price of the moral harm in punishing the innocent. Third, the moral cost approach is still an instrumentalist one. Procedures for making burden/benefit decisions are simply means to achieving correct outcomes.

The instrumentalism of the economic and moral cost approaches has significant implications for decision-making procedure. Substance and procedure are closely related. The more significant the substantive issues, whether economically or morally, the greater the error costs. A mistaken judgment in a case involving $500 does not impose the error costs a similar mistake in a case involving $500,000 does. Similarly, moral costs vary with the substantive principle involved or the amount of moral harm (different amounts of punishment). Contrary to Dworkin, the moral harm of imposing a burden on a person who does not deserve it increases with the size of the burden. Dworkin is misled by focusing on a right not to be convicted if innocent rather than a right not to be punished. Whereas conviction does not admit of degrees, punishment does. Consequently, fewer direct costs are justified in cases involving less significant substantive matters. This reasoning supports less expensive and less elaborate procedures for smaller matters such as minor discipline of students (*Goss v.*

Lopez, 419 U.S. 565 (1975); Galligan 1986, 332 (principle of proportion)). It also supports the claim that substantive norms and procedures for their application should be evaluated together.

Instrumentalism also implies that one has no reason to prefer one procedure to another unless outcomes are either correct or incorrect and one can determine which is which. The economic approach is assured of outcomes being correct or incorrect, if the aim of substantive principles is economic efficiency. An outcome either is or is not economically efficient. Similarly, one of Dworkin's major theses is that legal cases always have a right answer (Dworkin 1985, chap. 5). But if these claims are incorrect, there are no correct answers and consequently no error costs. If there are no error costs, both the economic and moral cost approaches prescribe minimizing direct costs, that is, deciding in the cheapest way possible.

One must distinguish some or a few cases not having a correct answer from there never being correct answers for certain types of cases. The dire implications above result only if cases of a certain type never, or almost never, have correct answers. If only a few cases of some type fail to have correct answers, then one might design procedures on instrumental grounds for the usual cases with correct answers. Nonetheless, fewer direct costs are justified than if all cases had correct outcomes.

To evaluate a decision-making procedure instrumentally, not only must there be correct answers, but one must be able to determine which are which. If one cannot make this determination, then one does not know whether many or a few errors are being made. Thus, one does not know whether one is spending too much or too little on direct costs to reduce errors. Hence, Dworkin's acceptance, even insistence, that correct decisions are controversial undercuts much of the utility of his procedural analysis though not the theoretical possibility of there being a correct decision (see Dworkin 1985, 137–45; Dworkin 1986, chap. 1). Moreover, if the underlying basis for decision presents a continuum, for example, disability, but decisions are bipolar—disabled or not disabled, then errors near the borderline are plausibly relatively less costly than those at the ends of the continuum (see Mashaw 1983, 81–85). Practically, inability to distinguish correct and incorrect decisions has consequences similar to there not being correct and incorrect decisions.

Inability to determine correct outcomes also supports decisionmakers having discretion$_2$. Given that most decisions are theoretically correct or incorrect, one should use procedures properly designed to avoid error costs. If decisionmakers follow the procedures, they should have discretion$_2$ for the borderline or marginal cases. In particular, as there is little or no reason to believe that others with differing views are more likely to be correct, there is no reason to overrule the initial decision. Consequently, appeals from the original decision should be sparely allowed and decisions overturned only when the original decision is clearly erroneous. Otherwise, one would merely increase direct costs without any assurance of reducing error costs.

If decisionmakers have discretion$_3$, then fewer direct costs are justified to reduce errors. Compare two decisions, one with and one without discretion$_3$. Suppose the issue in both is awarding a salary merit increase. In one case, the criterion gives a determinate decision, $600 being the correct choice. In the discretionary case, the criteria only indicate that an increase of $500 to $750 is appropriate. In the discretionary situation, fewer errors are possible; only decisions outside the limits of discretion$_3$ are mistaken; $585 is not an error. Consequently, fewer error costs are likely and therefore justify fewer direct costs of procedures.

Because they are instrumentalist approaches concerned with the costs of avoiding errors, the economic and moral cost approaches focus on truth finding. If no truth is to be found, no reason exists for any procedure. The instrumentalist approaches are concerned with issue resolution only in that decisions give correct answers to disputes. One can view the next approach as in part and indirectly adding a concern with satisfactorily resolving issues at the psychological as well as practical level and thus avoiding disputes. However, its primary addition is a concern for the realization of inherent values.

Process Benefits

Another approach to procedure considers values or benefits of procedures independent of their effect on the accuracy of outcomes (see Summers 1974; Mashaw 1981a; Mashaw 1983, 88–97; Mashaw 1985, chaps. 4–5; Saphire 1978). Concerns for fairness and participation are not necessarily aspects of correct or incorrect outcomes (error costs) or costs of the procedure (direct costs). Fairness is not necessarily the same as the minimization of error (Tullock 1980, 124). These values might be served by procedures that do not increase the accuracy of decisions. Although most of these values can contribute to accurate outcomes, that is not their sole basis and often not their primary basis. One can describe this approach as an 'inherent process value' approach. The concept of inherent value does not mean that the values are independent of the effects or consequences of a process. Whereas moral and economic error costs result from incorrect decisions, the inherent values served are independent of particular outcomes (see Saphire 1978, 121, 159). Put another way, the causal chain from procedure to economic and moral error costs goes through the specific outcome, while the causal chain from procedure to process values or benefits does not go through the specific outcome. They can, however, depend on there being a decision one way or another. They are satisfactions derived from the process itself (see Frankel 1980, 6).

The process values served by procedure are benefits corresponding to direct costs. Process values are logically in the position of direct costs, which are also independent of the particular outcomes. The economic and moral cost approaches view decision procedures as expenses to be borne only if they contribute to reducing error costs. However, one might prefer one procedure to another even if both have the same direct costs and are equally effective in producing a desired outcome, have the same error costs. An analogy illustrates the point. Suppose one wants to lose ten pounds. Further suppose one can do so equally well by an exercise program of either calisthenics or tennis. One might prefer tennis to calisthenics, even if tennis costs more. One might consider tennis to have other benefits than mere weight loss. Similarly, one might prefer one type of decision procedure to another, even though they are equally accurate. The assumption of equal effectiveness is merely to make the point more clear. One might prefer tennis to golf, for example, both because it is more effective in reducing weight and because one enjoys it more.

An instrumentalist might contend that these alleged benefits can be included in direct costs. For example, if calisthenics are less desirable than tennis, one can consider how much more one would be willing to pay for tennis than calisthenics. To obtain the full costs of a procedure, one compares it with a perfect procedure. For an instrumentalist, a perfect procedure is one that has no costs and is completely accurate. Ignoring errors by assuming equal effectiveness, the question then is how much would one be willing to pay for a costless procedure. Alternatively, one can ask how much one would have to be paid to use a decision procedure instead of a perfect one. (How much would one have to be paid to do calisthenics?) These will give the full direct costs of a procedure.

In one sense, this reply works. One can, at least theoretically, calculate direct costs in this manner. However, the instrumentalist has no reason for a procedure if there are no outcome benefits—correct decisions. One might not have to receive any outcome benefits to play a sport. Golf, for instance, has little value for weight loss or health promotion, and one might not care about either. Some people find it worthwhile in itself. The costs—time, equipment, and so on—are outweighed by the benefits or satisfactions in the playing. Instrumentalists can account for such cases by claiming that golf then has negative costs, but this is to give the game away. Negative costs are benefits! Like golf, decision procedures can have both benefits and costs. Instrumentalists might be correct to claim that in burden/benefit decision procedures, unlike golf, costs are always greater than benefits, but that can only be a conclusion of weighing or balancing the costs and benefits. It is more perspicuous to consider costs and benefits as separate items than to use a conclusory sum. Simply speaking of direct costs can lead one to overlook the offsetting benefits and thus exaggerate total net costs.

The argument so far shows that one might perceive benefits or values in burden/benefit decision procedures independent of their contribution to accurate outcomes and that these benefits should be kept distinct from direct costs. Consequently, the formula for evaluating procedures needs to have another term added to indicate process benefits. If we let 'PB' stand for process benefits, the formula can be represented as follows:

$$\text{Minimize Sum } (EC + MC + DC - PB)$$

Process benefits are subtracted rather than added, because the other terms are costs and the goal is to minimize the total.

This approach avoids one possible problem of instrumentalism, namely, the implication that if there is no correct outcome or one cannot determine which outcome is correct, then the least expensive procedure should be used. Process benefits might offset significant direct costs, so a fairly complex and expensive procedure might still be justified (see also Saphire 1978, 176). Of course, if 'least expensive' is confusingly taken to mean 'the net of direct costs and process benefits', then one should use the least expensive procedure. The process benefits approach retains the instrumentalist implication that substance can affect procedure, because error costs are still relevant whenever they exist and can be determined either individually or statistically.

We have not yet established that there are any process values or the basis on which they can be determined, only that if there are such values, evaluation of burden/benefit decision procedures should explicitly take them into account. Various grounds have been given for process values—autonomy (Saphire 1978), human dignity (Mashaw 1981a), and natural rights (Mashaw 1985; Mashaw 1987). These are ultimate ethical grounds resting on traditional ethical theories. Our ultimate approach rests on the values a fully rational person would accept. Consequently, assuming one is rational, one must ask whether one would accept or hold a particular value. Some arguments are offered to indicate why one would. All these approaches, however, are very general and vague. It would help if a more concrete basis could be indicated.

Some basis for process values exists in the inherent purpose of issue resolution. As we have seen, instrumentalist approaches focus on truth finding, ignoring issue resolution except as it results from correct decisions. Process benefits contribute to both psychological and practical issue resolution. Features of procedure can contribute to issue resolution without contributing to accuracy. Moreover, decision procedures might have benefits that do not even contribute to issue resolution. Without claiming completeness, a number of process benefits and principles can be identified on these grounds (see generally Summers 1974, 20–27; Mashaw 1983, 88–97; Mashaw 1985, 173–82).

People should be able to participate meaningfully in burden/benefit decisions affecting them. One reasonably desires to at least be heard, to have one's say, before decisions affecting one are made. Being permitted to participate also evidences others' respect, that one is to be considered seriously (see Galligan 1986, 333). Participation contributes to issue resolution, because people who have been able to participate are more likely to accept a decision; although they might not agree with the decision, they are more likely to comply with it. Trials in absentia and ex parte hearings violate this principle and are used sparely.

One must not overvalue participation (Bayles 1977; Simon 1978, 94–98). Participation in decision-making procedures can be a very frustrating, incomprehensible, and discouraging task. Many people seek participation merely as a means to a desired outcome. Indeed, it has been claimed that participation "only makes sense" if one hopes to affect the outcome in the current or future cases (Redish and Marshall 1986, 487). This claim overstates the extent to which the value of participation depends on affecting outcomes. If the effect is only on future cases, then it is independent of the correct outcome in the individual case. The decision in a particular case might have nothing to do with future outcomes; it might not be considered a precedent. Moreover, one's concern might not have anything to do with future cases. A woman once told me that she wanted to appear in the divorce action her husband had filed, not because she was going to contest the divorce, but because she wanted someone to know how she felt about it. This is more than mere "steamletting"; it is an opportunity to place one's view on record. Although some scholars doubt that this function has a role in procedure (e.g. Redish and Marshall 1986, 488), it can contribute to practical and psychological issue resolution. If people have not had an opportunity to have their say, they might appeal or fail to cooperate in implementing the decision, producing increased direct costs or decreased effectiveness.

Procedures should be fair—treat persons equally (see also Dworkin 1985, 84–85, 88; Tullock 1980, 124). Fairness here essentially means equality of treatment in the procedures. This consideration is one of comparative justice, comparing the procedures used for one decision with those used for a similar decision about another person. Some students persistently submit late papers and seem to be unaware of the unfairness of their having more time to write their papers than other students. If papers are graded on a noncomparative basis, such extra time does not lower the grade of the other students, yet like inconsistency, comparative injustice can be involved. If grades are on a comparative basis, a benefit for one student can well be to the detriment of another. People are less likely to accept decisions, either psychologically or practically, if they think the procedures used to arrive at them were unfair. The principle of fairness only specifies that people have an equal opportunity to participate; the principle of participation provides a reason for significant participation.

Equality or fairness is also supported by a concern for accurate outcomes. A person with more opportunity to participate is perhaps more likely to obtain a favorable decision, but it does not follow, as some people have claimed (e.g. Redish and Marshall 1986, 484), that fairness is valued only as a means to correct outcomes. In conflict resolution contexts with two parties, inequality might generally be expected to produce errors. That does not apply when one is considering different noncompetitive burden/benefit decisions, for example, making social security disability determinations. Moreover, equality can be achieved by reducing the opportunities of the party in one case as well as by increasing the opportunities of the party in the other. The former would achieve equality, but it might decrease accuracy. Thus, equality is a distinct concern from correct outcome. A counterclaim is that concern for equality pertains to all governance by rules and so applies beyond our context (Redish and Marshall 1986, 484–85). But this is irrelevant. That a value applies to more than a given subject does not imply that it is irrelevant or should not be taken into account for that subject.

One should note the restricted comparative meaning given here to 'fairness'. The term is sometimes used in a broader sense. Thus, persons might object to a procedure not permitting them to participate as being unfair. In this broader sense, procedures with less accuracy than could be justified on instrumental grounds might also be said to be unfair. In short, sometimes 'fair' is used to characterize any morally appropriate procedure or aspect of it. As we do not use it in this broad sense, it plays a smaller role in the theory than one might have expected.

Procedures should be intelligible, especially to the persons affected. Generally, rationality increases intelligibility (Summers 1974, 26). Consequently, the more rational the procedures for ascertaining the truth and arriving at decisions, the more rational persons will assent to the outcomes. That is, if people can understand the process and the reasons for a decision, they are more likely to accept it and disputes will be minimized. Moreover, many people simply want to know why they receive benefits and burdens. It can affect one's self-respect to know that one deserved an arbitrarily denied benefit, even though that does not remove the injustice of the denial (but see Redish and Marshall 1986, 490 (claiming no increased dignity)). It follows that decisions should be articulated by rational rules and principles and information developed in the process.

Again, it has been objected that this concern is really instrumental for accurate outcomes (Redish and Marshall 1986, 485–86). The argument hinges on rationality as the best method for achieving correct outcomes. However, intelligibility extends beyond accuracy. A process can be intelligible even though it results in a mistaken decision. Granted, identifying the mistake increases the chances of convincing decisionmakers to reconsider or render a different and correct decision in that or future cases. It also, however, provides for the ability to plan. If one knows that a decisionmaker holds a particular mistaken interpretation of a rule, one can better plan to avoid burdens or obtain benefits in the future than if one has no understanding of why a decision was reached. For example, one university does not interpret textbooks, even long single-author texts, as research for merit pay increases. Consequently, a faculty member might plan to have a book capable of being used as a text published by a nontextbook publisher. And there is still the concern to know why something happens to one. Thus, although the benefit of intelligibility partly rests on its instrumental value in arranging one's life, this benefit is independent of the correctness of the outcome.

Procedures should provide timely decisions. Timeliness is a mean between the extremes of haste and dilatoriness. Persons do not rationally want decisions made without adequate time to gather information and reflect on its significance. In part, this concern pertains to accurate outcomes; hasty decisions are more likely to be incorrect. However, the concern the other way, to avoid dilatoriness, is not. People do not want to wait longer than necessary for decisions significantly affecting them. The saying that "Justice delayed is justice denied" is not correct substantively, for a delayed decision can be substantively correct. Nonetheless, delay prevents people planning and living their lives, and as we just discussed, this can be independent of the correctness of the outcome. An instrumentalist approach to delay is likely to ignore this aspect, concentrating only on its economic costs (e.g. Posner 1973, 420–21). The principle of timeliness includes the traditional legal concern with repose. If a decision is not final but might be reversed, then people still lack the opportunity to make definite plans.

Finally, we might add the value of confidence or the appearance of justice in the decision-making process. We have already partly considered this concern in discussing the appearance of partiality in chapter 2. If people lack confidence in the justice of a procedure, then demoralization (including noncompliance) can result. This confidence is a second order concern; that is, it is confidence that other values and principles are realized and adhered to in the process. Consequently, to a significant extent it depends on the process producing correct decisions. However, we also saw that it can be reduced even when features, such as partiality, are not in fact present or influential but appear to be. Because appearance and reality are not the same, a concern with confidence and the appearance of justice is not identical with a strict concern for accurate outcomes.

One might object that the theory is unworkable or collapses into a sophisticated single value approach. Process benefits include a multiplicity of values. If these values are incommensurable, one cannot apply the theory because one cannot balance them with one another as well as with economic and moral error costs. If they are commensurable, then they must be reducible to one value, say, wealth or utility.

The objection rests on a literal interpretation of the formula of minimizing the sum of costs plus benefits. However, there are two ways of using this general conception that do not require such a mathematical calculating approach. First, often one can find various values supporting a principle of procedure and only direct costs against. Thus, one might cite intelligibility and reduction of error costs as reasons for a requirement of findings and reasons. This method is primarily used in the next section to support the traditional principles.

Second, the fundamental method of appeal to what norms rational persons would accept for a society in which they expected to live provides another method. Suppose the choice is between two procedures—P_1 and P_2. One can describe each in terms of the factors identified by the formula—error costs, direct costs, and various process benefits. The question then is which procedure a rational person would prefer. To answer this question, one need not be able to reduce all the features to one common quantitative unit. Most of us can answer the question whether we would prefer baked ham and sweet potatoes or fried chicken and mashed potatoes for supper without a mathematical calculation by something like food utiles. Moreover, the values permit many considerations that deontologists emphasize in opposition to consequentialists, for example, comparative fairness and moral rights as determining moral error costs.

Using this method, people are likely to disagree, that is, some will prefer P_1 and others P_2. Such disagreement need not end the discussion. Argument can continue. One person might be undervaluing timeliness, and it could be pointed out how crucial that is to planning. Moreover, the various values are affected differently depending on the subject matter and context. Timeliness is more important for some decisions than for others. For example, it might be more important for a decision to hire a person than to publish an article. Nevertheless, the method will not always provide one correct decision and people, even rational people, can disagree. That is why our account is stated in terms of principles. They permit discretion3. There is scope for discretion3 in choosing particular procedures, and within the scope of discretion3 people can reasonably disagree. However, it is discretion3 and not discretion4. In most contexts, many procedures can be excluded as unacceptable, for example, flipping a coin.

The inherent purposes of burden/benefit decision procedures are truth finding and issue resolution. Obviously, people want to achieve these purposes at as little cost as possible. The purpose of truth finding primarily involves the avoidance of economic and moral error costs. The purpose of issue resolution involves process benefits making a practical acceptance of the decision more likely, although process benefits can have value independent of practical or psychological acceptance of decisions. These elements must be considered in a framework of trying to keep the direct costs of the procedure as low as reasonably possible. The fundamental decision norm for evaluating procedures, then, is to minimize the sum of economic and moral error costs and direct costs less process benefits (see also Mashaw 1983, 103 (rationality, efficiency, and process fairness)). The norm contains standards, such as costs and intelligibility, that must be weighed and balanced. It thus permits discretion3. This norm is to be applied by rational persons choosing procedures for different burden/benefit decisions in a society in which they expect to live.

Justification of Basic Principles

This fundamental norm for evaluating burden/benefit decision procedures implies that the procedural principles developed in Part I are justifiable to the extent they reduce error or direct costs or promote process benefits. As conformity to the principles usually increases direct costs, justifications will normally be by reducing error costs or producing process benefits.

The principle of impartiality is justified to avoid error costs. Biased and interested decisionmakers are less likely to reach correct decisions. As necessary to achieving accuracy, impartiality is strongly supported (see Redish and Marshall 1986, 475, 479). Although obtaining an impartial decisionmaker usually involves few direct costs, interest and bias admit of degrees and some methods to provide a more impartial decisionmaker might not be worth the direct costs. Moreover, persons can have an interest in an outcome and still determine what the proper decision should be. For example, most of us frequently recognize that we are not entitled to an income tax deduction. The exception for necessity makes allowance for situations in which direct costs are great and influence on a decision is unlikely.

Fairness is also a reason for impartiality. For example, one might object to a co-worker's uncle determining merit pay increases for both oneself and the co-worker. The co-worker might also object, because people are sometimes more critical of their relatives than nonrelatives. Even if one gets the increase one deserved and expected, the procedure appears tainted. Consequently, the process benefit of confidence in the procedure also supports a broad principle of impartiality, condemning not only partiality but the appearance of partiality. Indeed, avoidance of error costs cannot justify prohibition of the mere appearance of partiality.

An opportunity to be heard helps to avoid error costs. A person can contribute important relevant information not otherwise available. With less available information, decisions are less likely to be correct. Even without providing new or additional information, a person can present the information in a different light, which might indicate that a different decision is appropriate. Sometimes good reasons exist to believe that an opportunity to be heard will not provide any useful relevant information. In such a case, affording an opportunity to be heard will merely increase direct costs without reducing error costs, so a purely instrumental concern will not support it.

Consequently, the process benefit of participation probably provides the strongest support for affording people an opportunity to be heard. It applies even if participation does not decrease error costs. An opportunity to be heard accords the person a dignity and respect; this is especially true of an opportunity to know and rebut evidence against one. Children who are punished without an opportunity to explain often complain that parents did not have enough faith in them even to listen to their side of the story; they feel a lack of love and trust. If one believes that one was denied respect in decision making, one might contest the decision not so much to alter the outcome but to gain the attention and respect one thinks one deserves—to be taken seriously.

The process benefits of intelligibility and timeliness support some of the subprinciples of an opportunity to be heard. Intelligibility can support overall participation, for a person who participates is more likely to understand the process. It especially supports openness of hearings, for this provides persons other than the subject of decision a chance to observe and understand the process. Timeliness, of course, is a primary value in promptness and notice.

The principle of providing findings and reasons is supported to reduce error costs. The requirement of standards is necessary for there to even be errors, for without standards (including norms) decisions cannot be characterized as correct or incorrect. Among the reasons offered earlier for presentation of findings were to facilitate judicial review, more careful consideration, and a decision based on the record. Judicial review and careful consideration increase accuracy and reduce error costs. Less obviously, decisions on the record do also. Decisions not based on the record are more likely to be based on inaccurate or irrelevant information. The avoidance of incorrect decisions was one of the reasons we gave for presentation of reasons. Avoidance of arbitrariness should also be considered an element of avoiding error costs, for arbitrary decisions are beyond the pale of reasonable discretion3 and thus incorrect.

The other reasons presented in chapter 4 for presenting findings and reasons and the requirement of standards promote the process value of intelligibility. There being standards and knowing the findings and reasons enable one better to plan one's conduct to obtain benefits or avoid burdens. Even if no relevant future conduct is planned, one will better understand why the decision was made. Perhaps one will find the decision more acceptable, thus advancing psychological resolution of the issue. In any case, one often simply wants to know why something happened to one. People who escape disasters in which many others are injured often wonder why they were spared, and a similar question arises when one is struck by a disaster others avoid—"Why me, Lord?"

The justification of the various elements of formal justice is more complex. The requirements of consistency, adherence to precedent, and conformity to rules are not easily justified to avoid error costs. Consistency does not necessarily mean correctness; one can be consistently wrong. Moreover, attempts to provide consistency can increase error and direct costs (see Mashaw 1983, 87). The development of standards and rules can increase consistency, but perhaps at the cost of overgeneralizations that force cases into inappropriate categories. Moreover, use of statistical goals can also increase error and inject unfairness. For example, a teacher who always assigns 10% of a class As can increase errors, for more students in some classes do A work than in other classes.

Neither do following precedent and rules necessarily reduce errors. As discussed in considering adherence to precedent, the original decision might be incorrect. Consequently, adherence to it increases error costs. Conformity to rules does reduce error costs in one sense, but can increase them in another. If correctness is determined by the appropriate rule, then conformity to it must give correct decisions. However, in a broader sense, a rule might not be substantively justified. If it is not, then conformity to the rule increases errors as judged by appropriate substantive criteria.

Although avoidance of direct costs supports following precedents and rules, the central justification for formal justice stems from the process values of fairness, intelligibility, and timeliness. Efficiency is one reason for following precedents or rules, and it can thus make decisions more timely. Timeliness and saving direct costs provide little support for consistency, because striving for consistency, especially across a large number of decisions, often takes much time and effort. Comparative justice or fairness is a central reason for all three elements of formal justice. Consistency, adherence to precedent, and following rules also render decisions more intelligible. A pattern exists into which they can be placed and understood. This intelligibility is the basis for the predictability promoted by following precedents and rules. Finally, the argument from commitment for conformity to rules is not an instrumentalist argument, at least not a direct one. It is a variation on promise keeping, and a duty to keep promises is not justified by its consequences in particular cases.

Summary

The fundamental norm for evaluating burden/benefit decisions is to minimize the sum of economic and moral error costs and direct costs less process benefits. Efficiency is promoted by reducing errors when the gain is less than the direct costs of doing so. Because moral error costs are included, the norm does not promote pure economic efficiency. Moreover, the fundamental norm balances efficiency with process benefits that do not necessarily operate through correct outcomes of particular decisions but the process itself. Because the norm incorporates standards, it provides discretion$_3$ in choosing procedures. In choosing between procedures, the question is which one rational persons using the fundamental norm would prefer for a society in which they expected to live.

Without claiming completeness, we have suggested participation, fairness, intelligibility, timeliness, and confidence in the procedure as process values or benefits. Participation is based on the pervasive human desire to have a say in decisions that significantly affect one. Fairness requires equality of procedures applied in similar cases; it promotes comparative justice and is especially important in competitive contexts. Intelligibility involves making decisions perspicuous, especially to those persons to whom they apply. It can promote persons' ability to plan, regardless of whether a decision is favorable or unfavorable, correct or incorrect. Timeliness is making decisions within an appropriate time, not leaving affected persons hanging. Confidence in the procedure is a second order value based on people's belief that efficiency and the other process benefits are appropriately realized in the procedure. A failure of confidence can lead to demoralization and lack of voluntary compliance.

All of the factors in the fundamental norm for evaluation are relevant to justifying the principles of impartiality, opportunity to be heard, grounds for decisions, and formal justice. However, as we have seen, substance and procedure should be evaluated together. The legal requirement of procedures has greater direct costs than their ethical requirement. Consequently, for some subjects and types of decisions legally requiring procedures might not be justifiable.

CHAPTER 7

THE LIMITS OF LAW

The chief question in this chapter is when compliance with principles of procedural justice should be legally required. As noted below, both the U.S. Supreme Court and common-law courts confront a version of this issue in applying the constitution and principles of natural justice. However, our question is broader, because it also includes when legislatures should mandate compliance by statute. Indeed, we shall not consider the particular way procedural justice should be legally required—by a constitution, common law, or statutory law. However, common-law courts should generally be able to require compliance in the absence of statutory requirements unless there is a manifest legislative intent not to do so.

A general answer to this question is important for any complete moral theory of procedural justice for burden/benefit decisions. A theory that told one what procedures are appropriate but not the types of means for ensuring that they were followed would fail to indicate the importance of principles for various contexts. Moreover, it would not indicate the appropriate response to procedural injustice—whether it should be only moral condemnation or also legal correction. In the United States today, many people believe, or act as though they believe, that any moral wrong should be legally redressed. As that view is rejected by most theories, it behooves us to indicate when procedural justice should be backed by the force of law and when it should not.

The discussion focuses on reasons for and against the legal imposition of procedural justice principles. We assume that if the law should not impose procedural requirements, ethics should still do so. In some situations procedures should not even be ethically required, but that amounts to there being no requirements of procedural justice. In presenting reasons or factors counting for and against legal requirement of principles of procedural justice, we are presenting the criteria of a standard for their legal imposition. Consequently, the criteria are usually principles to be balanced against one another. Thus, discretion$_3$ is involved in determining whether principles should have legal force in particular types of situations. As with the fundamental norm given in the previous chapter, the question is whether rational persons using this standard would want procedural principles legally required for certain types of situations in a society in which they expected to live.

Amendments V and XIV(1) of the U.S. Constitution provide that neither federal nor state governments may deprive persons "of life, liberty, or property, without due process of law." Many scholars believe the original, literal meaning of this clause was fairly narrow, namely, to prohibit the government executing persons, incarcerating them, or taking their property as by fines without a legal proceeding (Graglia 1985, 818; Miller 1977, 4–11, 25; Monaghan 1977, 411; Williams 1983, 20). Others believe that it had a much broader meaning (Ely 1980, 19). Whatever the historical intent or meaning, as with other general constitutional clauses, the Supreme Court has not left it a closed issue. Current constitutional doctrine maintains that in applying the due process clauses, two questions must be answered. First, when is due process required? Second, what does it require? Although our questions are broader because not restricted to constitutional requirements, this chapter largely parallels the first question, and the next chapter the second question. Some interpretations of when governmental action deprives someone of life, liberty, or property so that due process must be provided help answer our broader question. Consequently, this chapter uses the Court's constitutional interpretation as a basis for discussion (for analysis of the constitutional issue, see Bayles 1988).

Common-law natural justice principles apply to a similar but broader class of situations. Generally, they apply when rights or legitimate expectations are affected (Flick 1984, 26; Galligan 1986, 362–63). Rights include liberty and property (Flick 1984, 27–28). Legitimate expectations cover a broad spectrum of other matters the precise limits of which have not yet been fully worked out. They seem to include many of the newer areas in which the Supreme Court is requiring due process. Consequently, common-law analysis provides a helpful supplement.

Law and ethics Before we can determine when law as well as ethics should require compliance with principles of procedural justice, we need to clarify some differences between legal and ethical requirements. Law and ethics are two methods by which societies evaluate and impose norms on their members. Here is not the place to discuss in detail the similarities and differences between law and ethics. Whether we think a norm should be legally or ethically imposed, we insist that everyone comply with it even if doing so is contrary to his or her interests, because we consider it important for social order or welfare (see also Hart 1961, 84–85). Norms are both ethically and legally imposed on persons whether or not they accept or agree with them. Even if a woman does not think abortion ethically wrong, those who do judge her action of having one wrong.

For present purposes, the primary difference between law and ethics concerns the methods used to insist on compliance. The difference is not whether we impose our judgments on others, but how we do so. Ethical requirements are imposed by appeals to conscience, attitudes of approval and disapproval, and expressions of praise and blame. We point out to people that proposed conduct would be morally right or wrong, think well or ill of them depending on whether they do comply, and often express our approval or disapproval by praise and blame. The enforcement is diffuse and informal, depending on the attitudes and behavior of individuals. Law is imposed by a centralized, formal system backed by the direct or indirect use of state coercion. Sometimes, as in criminal law, noncompliance directly results in coercive sanctions. In administrative and civil law, normally noncompliance results in judgments or directives being given. Only subsequent failure to comply with these judgments or directives results in coercive sanctions such as contempt of court.

Because the threat of direct or indirect coercion generally imposes a greater burden than the expression of praise and blame, legal enforcement requires a stronger justification than ethical enforcement. Coercion is a greater limit to freedom than blame. Although public blame can be a significant detriment to individuals, normally this results not merely from the expression of blame but other conduct on its basis, such as shunning condemned persons.

Legal enforcement involves greater direct costs to the public than ethical enforcement. The formal processes of the law incur the expense of court hearings and so forth. There are other costs as well. If rules are used, then legislative or administrative time and effort must be involved. Often a governmental enforcement bureaucracy such as police or inspectors is needed, although sometimes aggrieved individuals can file their own claims. Persons subject to laws incur expenses in ensuring that they are in compliance. Of course, decisionmakers and organizations also have to spend time and effort to comply with ethical norms. Nonetheless, compliance with legally required procedures is often more expensive, because legal advice will often be required, and frequently periodic reports must be made to governmental agencies.

Once mandated, legal procedural niceties must be complied with whether or not they are beneficial in a case. For example, in one tenure decision, a chairperson was to ascertain the views of the tenured faculty and then provide his own recommendation indicating why he agreed or disagreed with the majority. The chairperson reported that three faculty favored and three opposed tenure and that he was in favor. After the completed process resulted in a denial of tenure, it was discovered that the chairperson incorrectly counted himself among the three tenured faculty in favor; he should not have been included in the tenured faculty. Thus, the entire process was repeated, only this time with the chairperson's report saying that three faculty were opposed and two were in favor and that he agreed with the minority. Needless to say, this procedural correction did not affect the outcome. Ironically, the person was an acting chair. Had the regular chair not been on leave, he would have had to report that the decision of the tenured faculty was three in favor and two opposed, and that he agreed with the minority. The procedural correction took considerable time and effort, had no effect on the outcome, and increased enmity. This case certainly did not increase the untenured professor's respect for procedural justice.

One might reply that the difficulty here is not the legal imposition of procedural requirements, but the triviality of the requirement. Stating the chairperson's vote separately from that of the tenured faculty is a small point. Yet, even ethically one would require a chairperson forwarding a recommendation at odds with a majority of the tenured faculty to present reasons for disagreement. The point is that as the chairperson's mistake, if any, favored the candidate and did not negatively influence the outcome, ethically one would allow it. However, once a requirement is legally mandated, then all the t's must be crossed and all the i's dotted. Otherwise, the affected individual has a legal grievance. Consequently, as legal requirement of procedures involves expenses and rigidity ethical requirement does not, it should not be used without careful consideration of its benefits.

State Action

The constitutional requirement of due process is limited to government or state actions. That is, the due process clauses do not impose procedural requirements on conduct of private individuals. This limitation does not apply to statutory requirements; legislatures can require private individuals and organizations to comply with procedural justice. More importantly, the common-law principles of natural justice have regularly been imposed on private persons and organizations (Flick 1984, 32; Schauer 1976, 58–61; Hewitt 1972, 98; Verkuil 1986, 698–701).

No clear reason exists to limit the legal imposition of procedural justice principles to state actions. General arguments could be given about the appropriate limits of government intrusion into private lives and decisions, but it is unclear why these should be any stronger with respect to procedure than substance. Indeed, as procedural principles basically leave people free to pursue any substantive end, the grounds for limiting legal imposition of procedural principles is weaker than those for limiting imposition of substantive ones. Why should a private homeowners association be legally permitted to discipline its members without due process, for example, by withholding such privileges as use of the swimming pool, any more than a city might use of a public pool? Moreover, arguments against government intrusion into private lives are too general to provide much direct guidance for our purposes.

Various reasons support a principle or criterion for legally requiring procedural justice for most governmental burden/benefit decisions. One reason is that being subject to government is not voluntary (see also Scanlon 1977, 112–13 (substantive due process)). One does not have as great a choice to become a member of a state as one does a homeowners association. Yet, the question is more pointedly the particular interaction, and many interactions with government are quite voluntary, for example, applying for governmental subsidies, contracts, or employment. Still, many more interactions with government than with private entities are nonvoluntary.

A second reason is that the government claims to or should represent all residents equally. Many principles of procedural justice, such as impartiality and giving reasons, are partly justified to avoid unfairness or comparative injustice. The government should not have special friends and enemies among the citizens; it should treat all citizens impartially. In contrast, private citizens should often give some individuals preferential treatment; ethics dictates their having special concern for some persons—family and friends. Consequently, fairness and impartiality are always requirements for governmental conduct toward its citizens, but private persons may, indeed should, give some people preferential treatment.

Third, if procedural injustice by the government is legally permitted, then any attempt by government to require private persons to comply with procedural justice smacks of hypocrisy and does not seem deserving of respect. The legal requirement of procedural justice by private individuals must depend on voluntary compliance in most instances. The government cannot oversee each private burden/benefit decision made. Yet, failure of government itself to provide procedural justice in similar situations could lead to loss of confidence and demoralization effects. The government should be sure its own house is in order before it attempts to straighten others.

It might be objected that at least in many substantive areas, the government does exempt itself from legal requirements. A classic example is governmental tort immunity. The sovereign tort immunity, however, rests on unsound arguments and would be rejected by rational persons (Bayles 1987, 258–59). Moreover, when publicly exposed, many such exemptions bring public disapproval. Recently, workers in the congressional mail room were shown on national television to be working in an unsafe and unhealthful environment because Congress had exempted itself from health and safety laws. The 1988 Florida legislature raised state employees' contributions to health insurance 50%. In debate on the bill, it was forcefully pointed out that legislators and top administrators did not have to make contributions which brought significant public reaction, although the injustice has not yet been fully corrected.

Thus, sufficient reasons exist for a principle supporting the government being legally required to comply with procedural justice principles. Of course, principles of procedural justice might not apply to some governmental actions any more than they do to private ones, but if they do apply to a type of decision, then there is a strong principle for government being legally required to comply with them when it makes such decisions. Citizens subject to decisions in which the principles were violated should normally have legal redress either through administrative agencies or the courts if necessary. Of course, as state action is a principle, it must be balanced against other considerations. Consequently, sometimes the cost of legal enforcement or other considerations will outweigh even this principle. However, the principle makes it take stronger reasons for not requiring governmental compliance than private compliance. Contrarily, all else being equal, if procedures should not be legally imposed on the government, they should not be legally imposed on private persons.

Deprivations

To a large extent, the constitutional question has been when a hearing is required. Traditionally, both constitutional law and common-law natural justice distinguish between legislative and adjudicative contexts (*Londoner v. Denver*, 210 U.S. 373 (1908); *Bi-Metallic Investment Co. v. Colorado*, 239 U.S. 441 (1915); Macdonald 1980, 532–33). (The common law also distinguishes administrative contexts (Hewitt 1972, 182).) Legislative contexts address matters of policy, while adjudicative ones primarily concern the application of standards, principles, precedents, and rules to particular individuals or cases. Of course, policy issues are sometimes significantly raised in adjudicative cases. Moreover, some nonadjudicative situations are close enough to adjudication that the common law classifies them as quasi-judicial and imposes the requirements of natural justice. Although common law might no longer require a decision to be judicial or quasi-judicial before natural justice applies, it does still exclude legislative decisions (Flick 1984, 37–38).

The import of the legislative/adjudicative distinction is to require a hearing in all adjudicative cases. Nonetheless, exceptions to the general principle have been recognized. For present purposes, the most important exception was privileges. In U.S. constitutional law, if persons were being given or denied something to which they had no preexisting right, then it was a privilege and due process was not required. Rights required due process; privileges did not. A similar division has sometimes been used in natural justice analysis, although not as consistently (Schauer 1976, 62–63; Hewitt 1972, 179).

The underlying rationale, which plagues many contemporary analyses, is that if persons do not have a right to something, then they have no claim to something of which they can be deprived; therefore, due process does not apply. A slightly different rationale is that if the government is merely bestowing a gratuity—a benefit that it does not have to bestow, then it should have as much discretion as an ordinary citizen does in contributing to charity. Among the privileges were licenses (*Smith v. Liquor Control Comm'n*, 169 N.W.2d 803 (Iowa 1969) (to run liquor stores); *R. v. Gaming Bd. for Great Britain, ex parte Benaim*, [1970] 2 Q.B. 417 (C.A.)); government employment (*Bailey v. Richardson*, 341 U.S. 918 (1951)), entry of an alien immigrant to the United States (*United States ex rel. Knauff v. Shaughnessy*, 338 U.S. 537 (1950)), and government benefits such as pensions (*Lynch v. United States*, 292 U.S. 571 (1934)).

The distinction between a right and a privilege is not as clear as one might think. Very early, the Supreme Court held that a license to practice law could not be revoked without notice and a hearing (*Ex parte Robinson*, 86 U.S. 505 (1873)). What, one might ask, distinguishes a license to practice law or medicine from a license to sell liquor? It cannot be that the latter is more dangerous; for a drunk physician is more dangerous than serving alcohol to minors (Lorch 1980, 125). One suspects that the distinction rested on judges being professional peers of lawyers and physicians and not of liquor store owners. Moreover, in an industrialized, urban society, what once might have appeared as mere privileges and governmental gratuities, such as licenses to drive a car, became economic necessities (*Wignall v. Fletcher*, 303 N.Y. 435 (1952); *Bell v. Burson*, 402 U.S. 535 (1971)). Finally, classification of something as a right or privilege is a conclusion, not a premise. To classify something as a privilege is to say that procedural protections will not be applied. The central issue, however, is whether procedural protections should apply, and that requires some basis for distinguishing when they should and should not, between rights and privileges.

The due process clauses apply when persons are being deprived of life, liberty or property. Instead of focusing on the concepts of life, liberty, and property, as the Supreme Court has, we focus on the concept of deprivation which for some unknown reason the Court has largely ignored (see Bayles 1988 (advantages of deprivation analysis for constitutional issue)). The right/privilege distinction is an inapt basis for determining when deprivations occur, because one can in an ordinary sense be deprived of a privilege. A deprivation constitutes a harm, a setback of a person's interests that makes the person worse off than previously (Feinberg 1984, 33–34). Burden-imposing decisions set back interests. As discussed below, benefit-terminating decisions also often set back interests; the person is worse off than had the benefits continued. Benefit-conferring decisions advance interests; consequently, denials of benefits do not make a person worse off, they merely fail to advance the person's interests. Similarly, burden-relieving decisions advance interests, and their denial does not make one worse off. Thus, decisions to impose burdens and often to terminate benefits make persons worse off; deciding not to do so leaves persons as they were. For individual subjects of decisions, these are no-win decisions—subjects cannot be better off and might be worse off. Decisions to confer benefits and to relieve burdens advance persons' interests; deciding not to do so leaves persons in the state they were in. For individuals, these are no-lose decisions.

Still, one might contend that this distinction is without a difference. Whether one is denied a thousand dollar grant or is fined a thousand dollars, one has a thousand dollars less than had the decision been the reverse. However, there are several differences between them. First, in burden-imposing and benefit-terminating cases, the government (or other person) is taking action against one (Friendly 1975, 1295–96). Second, because they are no-lose decisions, persons ask for or seek benefit-conferring and burden-relieving decisions; they rarely ask for no-win burden-imposing and benefit-terminating decisions. Third, persons do not usually receive the same utility from benefits and burdens of the same dollar amount. Most persons' utility curves decrease much more rapidly than they rise from the point representing their current position. One reason is that people count on and allocate to current needs what they have. Further increases have not yet been taken so strongly into account. However, this reliance on current benefits is not justifiable if one knows that they might easily cease. (The preceding six paragraphs are revised from Bayles 1988, 206-07, 211-12.)

This last argument might seem to contradict the argument in chapter 4 that welfare recipients cannot use reliance to support a higher standard of proof for termination than original grant of benefits. However, the argument there was only that it was circular to rely on the higher standard of proof itself. Nonetheless, the general point is that it is unreasonable to count on current benefits if they might be lost.

Two points about reliance weaken the force of this objection. First, the argument does not apply to necessary collateral reliance. In many cases, collateral reliance is necessary to obtain the full value of benefits. For example, an applicant for an original television license has not expended the money in station equipment and broadcast tower of a renewal applicant who has operated a station for years. Although radio and television station licenses are awarded for short periods and subject to renewal, for them to be of any benefit one must invest in broadcast equipment. Thus, the utility lost when an application is denied is less than when one is terminated. Consequently, the government rarely denies applications for renewal and does so only after exhausting inquiries (see "RKO License Renewals Denied" 1987 (not final after 20 years of dispute)). More generally, one must rely on life, liberty, and property to go about the business of living. They are crucial factors in how one lives.

Second, even if reliance is not necessary to reap full advantage of benefits, many people have a strong tendency to spend current income. Thus, mortgage companies usually require monthly payments to escrow accounts for taxes and insurance, and the government withholds income and social security taxes. Even fully rational persons might recognize that they are not always rational and seek similar protections such as stronger procedural safeguards for benefit terminations. That is, at the least they will want to be sure that the standard for termination is properly applied. The common law recognizes this element of reliance by applying natural justice when legitimate expectations are affected (see Flick 1984, 33–36; see also Galligan 1986, 363).

The element of necessary reliance for living is involved in a consideration developed in varying degrees by several scholars (Williams 1983, 22–24 ff.; Terrell 1982, 901–11; Terrell 1985, 579; Scanlon 1977, 111–12). This consideration is the monopolization of specific types of benefit by the government. In some situations, such as many city utilities, the government has a monopoly. Anyone wishing electrical service in Tallahassee must obtain it from the city. If one cannot rely on continually receiving the service, one has few alternatives. Consequently, termination of the benefits, even for a brief period, can call for legal enforcement of procedural safeguards (*Memphis Light, Gas, and Water Div. v. Craft*, 436 U.S. 1 (1978) (municipal utility cancelling service)). Moreover, this argument applies to private monopolies, as of utilities, as well as to public ones.

The extent of governmental monopolization can vary. To practice law or medicine, one must be licensed by the state. For elementary and secondary education, the government does not have a complete monopoly, but anyone who wishes to opt out must still pay taxes to support the public system. Thus, most people have no practical choice to obtain these educational benefits but from the state. Termination of these benefits also calls for legal procedural safeguards (*Goss v. Lopez*, 419 U.S. 565 (1975)). Perhaps the governmental monopoly of welfare benefits, such as Aid to Families with Dependent Children and social security disability, is even weaker. Government entrance into the fields has not precluded private charity or disability insurance. However, private organizations have probably withdrawn or made other less favorable arrangements due to governmental action. For example, private employers undoubtedly provide less disability insurance because they rely on governmental coverage; even if they provide the same dollar coverage, they contribute less to it than they would were they not also contributing to social security. Even though the social security act places the burden on the applicant to show a continuing qualification for disability (42 U.S.C. § 423(d)(3)), the monopolization requires procedural justice.

The monopoly argument has been criticized as requiring an answer to an unanswerable question, namely, whether the private market would have supplied a benefit or more of a benefit had the government not become involved (Simon 1986, 751). Now there undoubtedly are cases in which the question is unanswerable, but they are not in the core areas. In countries without national health insurance, private health insurance exists. Private educational institutions existed before the government became involved, and some exist now. Similarly for welfare organizations; moreover, some evidence indicates that as government support of charitable activities decreases, private support increases. Unions do bargain for disability insurance. Perhaps were it not for social security disability, the overall benefits would be less than now, but they would likely be higher than current private benefits. Finally, if one cannot make a reasonable case for governmental monopoly precluding alternative sources of benefits, then the monopoly argument will not apply.

Governmental monopolization with another factor can even support legally requiring procedural protections in conferring benefits. This further factor is the difference between competitive and noncompetitive or eligibility-based distributions (Rubin 1984, 1161). In competitive situations, only the best are chosen to receive benefits, whereas in noncompetitive situations, everyone who meets the criteria receives benefits. Compare lawyers and air traffic controllers. Both occupations are under governmental monopolies—lawyers by licensing and traffic controllers by employment. Yet, in hiring air traffic controllers, the government is choosing the most qualified on a competitive basis. Only a limited number of openings exist. For lawyers, an unlimited number can exist. An applicant for the bar is entitled to be admitted, provided the person meets certain standards. So procedural justice should apply even to benefit conferral (*Willner v. Committee on Character and Fitness*, 373 U.S. 96 (1963); *Cord v. Gibb*, 254 S.E.2d 71 (Va. 1979)). The situation with lawyers would be different if only a limited number were permitted to join the bar thus making admission a competitive rather than eligibility-based matter, although there are good substantive grounds for opposing limiting the number of lawyers. The common law applies natural justice principles to applications for statutory occupational licenses which are granted on a noncompetitive basis (Flick 1984, 31). The preceding is not to say that no procedural safeguards should be recognized in hiring air traffic controllers, only that the stringency of the safeguards might be less. Since both involve state action, impartiality is required.

We can now complete discussion of the appropriateness of a higher burden of proof for termination of welfare benefits than original conferral of them. Because of the governmental monopoly and the noncompetitive criteria for receipt of welfare, equally good reasons exist for applying due process to, and preferring AU to ~AD errors in, original receipt as well as termination of benefits. Consequently, in light of our analysis in chapter 6, if one requires more than the preponderance of the evidence to terminate welfare benefits, one should require less than that to confer them initially. One might, however, accept the preponderance of the evidence for original conferral to avoid possible demoralization, but at the cost of comparative injustice. Alternatively, one might find that the comparative injustice outweighs the decreased error costs of a different burden of persuasion for termination. One would then use the preponderance of the evidence for both.

In effect, the choice involves balancing two process benefits—confidence and comparative justice. Rational persons might decide either way. Two suggestions will not settle the issue. First, it has been suggested that problems of justice, especially discretion$_3$ related problems, might be solved by surplus financing of welfare programs (Goodin 1988, 220–23). However, that simply makes less pressure to avoid AU errors in both cases; it does not address the choice between conferral and termination burdens of proof. Second, one might think that the choice is between comparative justice and utility (avoidance of demoralization) and that justice should always be preferred. However, the demoralization results from injustice, the injustice of those who probably do not deserve benefits on the given noncomparative grounds receiving them. So in effect, the choice is between it being seen that noncomparative justice is done, and comparative justice.

Another element is involved in many burden-imposing or benefit-terminating decisions that makes procedural justice more important than for benefit-conferring and burden-relieving decisions. Often burdens are imposed or benefits terminated because of a negative judgment of a person's character. Most obviously, criminal sanctions involve negative judgments of a person's character. So do many decisions to terminate benefits, for example, revoking professional licenses for unprofessional conduct. The Supreme Court has given some recognition to this stigmatizing aspect of decisions, although it has not permitted it to be a basis by itself for invoking due process (cf. *Wisconsin v. Constantineau*, 400 U.S. 433 (1971) with *Paul v. Davis*, 424 U.S. 693 (1976); see also Flick 1984, 30 (natural justice applies if damage to reputation possible)). A stigma is rarely involved in benefit-conferring and burden-relieving decisions, because these involve meeting some standard of good and failure to meet such a standard does not necessarily imply fault or a stigma. The failure to achieve a standard of excellence is not necessarily a bad. However, it can be. For example, a requirement to obtain many professional licenses is to be of good moral character, which basically means not to be of bad character. Consequently, failure to meet such a standard does stigmatize, because it implicitly suggests a bad character trait.

Several factors thus support a more stringent requirement of principles of procedural justice, and thus make a stronger case for their legal requirement, in burden-imposing and most benefit-terminating decisions (deprivations) than in burden-relieving and benefit-conferral ones. First, burdens are imposed and benefits terminated involuntarily. Benefits and relief from burdens are usually voluntarily sought. Second, because of necessary collateral reliance and the human disposition to rely on what one has, imposition of burdens and termination of benefits involve a greater disutility than refusals to confer benefits or relieve burdens. However, monopoly and noncomparative criteria for benefits make some benefit-conferring situations like deprivations. Third, burden-imposing and benefit-terminating decisions often impose a stigma that burden-relieving and benefit-conferring ones do not.

Importance

The importance of the interest at stake affects the extent to which the law should impose procedural justice principles (see also Galligan 1986, 361). The law should not concern itself with trivial and minimal matters. The primary reason is that only important matters can justify the usually higher direct costs of legal than ethical enforcement. If the matter in question is of little importance, then savings of error costs will not offset the greater direct costs of legal over ethical enforcement. The economic cost of an error in a decision involving a thousand dollars is only one hundredth of that in a decision involving a hundred thousand dollars. However, the loss of a thousand dollar benefit might be of greater relative importance to an affected individual than a hundred thousand dollar error to a giant corporation.

A moral error cost might be involved for the individual but not the corporation. Moral costs are involved when an aim makes one type of error worse than another. Consequently, a relevant point is whether a benefit is intended for the recipient's good (see Michelman 1977, 151; see also Galligan 1986, 364). If it is, then one prefers benefiting the person to not doing so. Failure to benefit defeats the purpose, whereas benefiting others does not. Consequently, there is a moral cost in failing to provide such benefits (~AD). Public housing and welfare are primarily intended to benefit the individual recipients. Public employment, at least outside of work programs such as the Civilian Conservation Corps, is primarily provided for the benefit of the organization. Even though the economic effect of denial on an applicant for public employment might be as significant as that on an applicant for other benefits, it does not defeat the purpose of the benefit. The loss, if any, is economic loss to the employer from not having the best person and even that does not occur in many cases. A similar consideration applies to burden-relieving decisions; for example, sometimes prisoners are released not for their sake but to relieve illegal overcrowding. Such releases differ from ordinary parole decisions which are for the inmates' relief.

The importance of a matter depends on process benefits as well as error costs. Process benefits or values must be interpreted from the perspective of the affected person. In some cases, the process benefits of participation, fairness, intelligibility, timeliness, and confidence are not as significant as in others. One might think that they are always more important to individual persons than to corporations, but that is not true. Although for purposes of process benefits one should not simply treat corporations as human persons, timeliness and fairness, for example, can be crucial for corporations. Imposing a burden on one corporation that is not imposed on other similarly situated corporations can place it at a severe competitive disadvantage. Moreover, one must not fail to pierce the corporate veil and to recognize that behind it are human beings with concerns like others. For example, employees of the unfairly treated corporation might lose their jobs.

In some situations, legal imposition of procedural justice principles might defeat the purpose of procedural justice. This possibility arises from the importance of process benefits in what have been called nonformal situations. In these situations, individuals do not look for legal justification but the personal satisfaction of being treated justly (Michelman 1977, 126–27). The person's goal is the respect and consideration that is due one as another human being and partially realized through process values. These concerns arise in informal relations between individuals. Intrusion of the law to require procedural justice will not produce the respect and consideration the person desires (Michelman 1977, 149–50). Instead, it will merely produce routinized, purposeless, and perhaps disruptive actions. This limitation might best be seen in the family. A legal requirement of procedural justice in disciplining children might well become a mere ritual and disrupt family relations. Parents would go through a ritualistic routine of asking children if they had committed an alleged misdeed, reciting the evidence that they did, and then officiously announcing a penalty. Matters would be even worse if children could appeal to courts for relief from improper procedures in being disciplined, as opposed to physical and mental abuse. This limitation on the legal imposition of procedural justice is merely another example of the inability of the law to structure the informal relations of love, friendship, and mutual respect that are central to the good life (see also Fuller 1971, 205–06, 212).

In short, because legal enforcement of procedural justice principles is usually more costly than ethical enforcement, it should not be pursued unless the increased direct costs are outweighed by error costs savings and process benefits. An important question in determining moral costs, especially in benefit-conferring and burden-relieving contexts, is whether the benefit or relief is intended for the well-being of the recipients. Process benefits also vary in different situations. In nonformal contexts, legal imposition of procedural justice will usually frustrate the respect desired from process benefits and procedural justice.

Special Standards

In *Board of Curators of the University of Missouri v. Horowitz* (435 U.S. 78 (1978)), the Supreme Court suggested another factor that limits the legal applicability of due process. This case involved a female medical student's appeal from being dropped from the medical program. Technically, the Court did not determine whether due process applied, because it found that even if it did, Ms. Horowitz had been given all the procedural protection to which she would be entitled. However, then Justice Rehnquist elaborated on the difficulties of using formal adversarial procedures to make academic evaluations. Because of the nature of the decision involved—an academic one—he found due process considerations inapplicable.

This argument is capable of at least two interpretations. The more plausible one, as an interpretation, is that the Court was focusing on whether judicial procedures are appropriate for making academic decisions. Since it did not think they were, it held that due process does not apply. This argument assumes that the adversary adjudication model of procedural justice is the only possible model for legal enforcement. If that model is inappropriate for a type of decision, then procedural justice (due process) does not apply. This assumption is considered in the next chapter.

Less plausible as an interpretation is the contention that because academic decisions are of a type courts are not well-equipped to evaluate, procedural requirements should not be legally imposed. This argument is invalid. Even if courts cannot make academic judgments, it does not follow that they cannot evaluate the procedures followed in making them. Even if decisionmakers must be left a large scope of discretion3, it does not follow that one cannot legally require procedures to be followed in making decisions. Indeed, this is precisely the position courts theoretically take with respect to decisions by administrative agencies, although many of those decisions are adjudicatory.

Nonetheless, the nature of some types of decisions make them less appropriate for legal enforcement of procedural principles. One type of decision is that requiring professional judgment. In *Horowitz* professional judgment was doubly involved. First, the judgment was one for professional education—was the student competent. Second, the competency was in another area of professional expertise—medicine. Standards of professional judgment depend on expertise and the current state of knowledge in the profession. Thus, they should be set by professionals (Bayles 1989, 193).

However, it might be objected, we just indicated the difference between prescribing the standards of professional judgment and the procedures for reaching such judgments. Moreover, courts are regularly involved in evaluating professional judgments in malpractice litigation. The first point is only partially correct. If professionals set the substantive standards, then they must also have discretion$_3$ in determining the types of tests for professional expertise. In education, the types of tests to be given are perhaps clearer, but one can still debate objective tests versus essay exams, clinical practice, and so forth. Nevertheless, this does not prevent the requirement of some principles of procedural justice, for example, impartiality. The *Horowitz* Court implicitly recognized its ability to evaluate academic procedures within some range, because it held that even if due process applied, all necessary procedural protections were provided. However, courts have traditionally permitted great scope of discretion$_3$ in academic dismissals and intervened only for bad faith or arbitrariness (Latourette and King 1988, 220). Indeed, the Supreme Court subsequently got the matter about right in holding that a court should not overturn an academic decision "unless it is such a substantial departure from accepted academic norms as to demonstrate that the person or committee responsible did not actually exercise professional judgment" (*Regents of the Univ. of Mich. v. Ewing*, 474 U.S. 214, 225 (1985)).

The answer to the second point is that the standards legally imposed in malpractice litigation are second order ones—"Was the professional careless?" Whether a professional was careless depends on whether he or she conformed to professional standards. Malpractice thus depends on professional standards set by professionals with professional testimony as to whether they were met. Similarly, dismissals of students for disciplinary as opposed to academic reasons is subject to due process (see Latourette and King 1988, 215–20).

Nonetheless, in student dismissals, it may sometimes be difficult to distinguish areas of professional expertise from others (see Latourette and King 1988, 227–29 (academic or disciplinary reasons)). Consider the following example (suggested by Barry Hoffmaster). A graduate student flunks her Ph.D. exam for the third time, and academic regulations only allow a student to take the exam three times. She contends that she is entitled to an exemption from the rule; she claims that she did poorly because she had recently been sexually assaulted. The graduate director summarily rejects her request for an exception. Does the issue fall within professional expertise? Is the matter procedural or substantive? If the question is whether a recent sexual assault should provide an exemption from the three attempts rule, it is substantive. Although the three attempts rule itself seems to fall within professional expertise, perhaps based on past experience of students who tried more than three times, the exemption is not obviously an academic matter of faculty expertise. If the question is whether the student should be entitled to appeal the graduate director's decision, then it is clearly procedural. Moreover, it is not within the domain of professional expertise; it is a question of procedural justice.

Legally imposed procedures are also inappropriate when the standards are the subjective ones of the decisionmaker. These standards are set by the decisionmaker to achieve the decisionmaker's ends. The ends need not be the fulfillment of the decisionmaker's desires, but the decisionmaker is not subject to any independent standards in determining how to achieve those ends. In short, the decisionmaker has discretion$_4$. An example of subjective standards is presidential appointment or dismissal of aides. A president's goals or ends are presumably not satisfaction of his or her desires but the operation of the executive branch to promote the commonweal. As Navy Secretary William Ball said, "There is only one criteria [*sic*] by which chiefs of staff are judged: whether they have the confidence of the president" ("Baker Successor" 1988).

If the substantive standard for a decision is within a decisionmaker's discretion$_4$, then legally imposed procedural safeguards become futile. In the end, no basis exists for claiming a decision is arbitrary and capricious unless no standard is used (a whim) or it is quite unreasonable. If the standard is plausibly appropriate for an end the decisionmaker sincerely has, a decision is not arbitrary if it applies the standard. Even impartiality (except perhaps for race, sex, and age which is to deny discretion$_4$) cannot be a requirement, because a decisionmaker's liking or trusting a person might be an adequate standard. No matter what procedures are required—opportunity to rebut evidence and so forth—the decision will stand. Granted, requiring a decisionmaker to review carefully the "evidence" or factors causing like or dislike of performance might alter the decision, but the potential benefits do not outweigh the costs. Even process benefits are unlikely, for if the criterion is the decisionmaker's approval, the subject is most likely seeking personal respect.

That is, the decision context is probably one of the nonformal types considered in the previous section.

Alternative Protections

The availability of other forms of protection is another factor relevant to legally requiring procedures. In *Ingraham v. Wright* (430 U.S. 651 (1977)), the Supreme Court held that due process does not require notice and an opportunity to be heard before physical discipline of school children. Among the reasons were the low incidence of abuse and the availability of other remedies under Florida law, such as a tort action against the disciplinarian. The Court's claim of a low incidence of abuse is questionable. According to personal information, eight years after the Court's decision, in one small Florida town during a one week period three students reported to the hospital emergency room for treatment as a result of physical disciplinary actions. Moreover, in practice, a civil tort action is not as readily available as the Court suggests. One must question the judgment of a Court that requires notice and a hearing for short disciplinary suspensions from school (*Goss v. Lopez*, 419 U.S. 565 (1975)) but not for physical discipline.

Nevertheless, the concept of an alternative remedy is certainly meritorious as a limit to imposition of procedural principles. In unionized private employment, the contract customarily specifies procedures for grievances and terminations. Providing such features is usually a high priority of newly unionized workers. If the procedural protections are thought inadequate, then employees can negotiate a contract with better ones. Of course, procedures are still being legally enforced, but they are privately agreed to and not the result of public law. A single individual negotiating with a large organization cannot realistically negotiate procedural protections, but companies are beginning to provide fair and effective grievance procedures for nonunion employees (see Westin and Feliu 1988, esp. chap. 3).

The position of public employees is somewhat different. Although often represented by a union, many features of their contracts are determined by public law and not subject to negotiation. One might contend that legislation governing employment is itself the result of a process similar to negotiation (see Wright 1987, 530–41). Governmental employee unions and administrators often operate as interest groups, and the resulting legislation is a form of compromise between these competing groups. Yet, it cannot be denied that other considerations often intrude, and public employees sometimes lack the potent bargaining weapon of a strike. However, the strong reason for treating government employment differently from private employment is state action. Most government jobs are not governmental monopolies, and public employment is not for the benefit of the employee.

The central issue is the extent to which individual choice and liberty are to be respected. Individual choice is involved because persons on their own or through their union representatives might bargain some procedural safeguards for other benefits such as layoff provisions, severance benefits, and so on (Wright 1987, 547). Indeed, it might be improper to view the matter as waiving or trading rights (but see Terrell 1987a, 375). Whether one has a right to a procedure might depend on the result of the bargain. Even if grounds exist independent of the contract for people having procedural rights, they should be free to make voluntary, informed waivers in exchange for other things they value more. Few constitutional rights are imposed against a voluntary, informed waiver and these are substantive, not procedural (see also Flick 1984, 32 (natural justice can be excluded by clear, voluntary choice)). Even in criminal cases, various procedural rights such as to have a lawyer present and not to incriminate oneself and to a trial by jury can be voluntarily waived, the issue has been when such waivers are voluntary (see *Miranda v. Arizona*, 384 U.S. 436 (1966); *Brewer v. Williams*, 430 U.S. 378 (1976); *Rhode Island v. Innis*, 446 U.S. 291 (1979); *North Carolina v. Alford*, 400 U.S. 25 (1970)).

In contract situations, there are two reasons against imposing procedural principles beyond what the contract requires. First, if procedures are unwaivable, then employees lose a bargaining chip. Second, what is gained in procedure might be lost indirectly. For example, tenured professors have very secure jobs. Part of the price of that security is perhaps the longest probationary time there is—six years rather than a more usual six months, say, for nurses.

Waiver and the employment contract do have limits. Usual contract defenses should apply. Two points are implicit in the requirement of informed, voluntary agreement. First, unconscionability might apply in some cases. Second, to ensure that the agreement is informed, one might require that it be explicitly called to the attention of a prospective employee (Terrell 1987a, 384). Still, some waivers might be completely forbidden much as some other contract terms are not subject to private alteration (Terrell 1987a, 379–81; see also

Bayles 1987, 175–77). However, the judgment must be an ex ante one; what a reasonable or rational person might legitimately have waived at the time of contracting, not what the person would have done after the problem occurred (Wright 1987, 547–48).

On a similar basis, an alternative protection always exists in private, voluntary, noncontractual relationships. One has full choice to deal with the other party or not. For example, formal grievance procedures are not needed for volunteer guardians ad litem. If one disagrees with the policies and conditions of one's volunteer work, one can always find another place to do useful volunteer work. Moreover, most of these situations will be nonformal ones where legal imposition would not achieve process benefits desired.

Summary

Principles of procedural justice need not always be imposed by law. Sometimes procedural justice should be only a matter of ethics. Several factors or criteria are involved in a standard for determining whether principles of procedural justice should be legally required. A special criterion or principle supports legally requiring procedural justice by the government, because citizens are not voluntarily subject to it, it should treat all citizens equally, and failure to do so can create demoralization effects if it tries to impose procedural justice on others for similar situations.

A second criterion or principle is whether the decision involves a deprivation, that is, will make the individual worse off. If it will, the case for legal enforcement is stronger. Deprivations are not sought by individuals, they often involve a greater amount of utility than comparable failures to benefit, and collateral reliance on their not occurring is often necessary. Governmental and other monopolization of benefits make reliance necessary. When monopolized benefits are awarded on a noncompetitive basis, then there is support for procedural protections even in benefit conferral. Deprivations also sometimes stigmatize an individual, because they involve negative evaluations of character. This factor primarily applies to burden-imposing and benefit-terminating decisions, but it can apply to some failures to benefit.

Another factor to consider in legal enforcement is the importance of the interest affected vis-à-vis the costs of enforcement. The importance must include process benefits as well as both the economic and moral costs of errors.

The more important the interest affected, the greater error costs will be. In determining moral costs of errors in benefit-conferring situations, a significant consideration is whether the benefit is primarily intended for the well-being of recipients or has other purposes. To the extent it is the latter, then moral costs are less or nonexistent. Legal enforcement is particularly unlikely to attain process benefits in nonformal contexts where the process benefits depend on the respect of the other person.

Two other factors are relevant to legal enforcement. One is the nature of the standards involved in decisions. If professional standards are involved, then the law is not capable of providing adequate first order standards of evaluation. At best, it can require second order standards requiring compliance with standards and procedures common in the profession. Thus, the law should permit considerable scope of discretion$_3$ in establishing the procedures. If the standards are the subjective preferences of the decisionmaker, then legal enforcement is inappropriate because the minimal benefits are not worth the costs. A second factor is the availability of alternative means of protection, for example, by contractual bargaining and waiver or simply ceasing a voluntary activity.

As our analysis provides only a multifactor standard, it leaves discretion$_3$ in determining when the law should require principles. However, as with the fundamental norm for procedural justice, there are various grounds for arguing for or against legal requirement of procedures. Each of the factors was supported by various reasons, which might or might not be present in particular contexts. Consequently, the weight of any factor in a particular context is not simply a matter of gut reaction. In the end, appeal is made to when rational persons using the standard would want legal requirement of principles of procedural justice for a society in which they expected to live.

We have now established a fundamental norm for determining principles of procedural justice. We have also developed a multifactor standard for legally requiring compliance with those principles. More generally, this standard establishes when there is a stronger or weaker case for requirements of procedural justice, when it is more or less important. To complete the theory, we need to provide some guidance as to which procedural principles apply in different contexts.

CHAPTER 8

ALTERNATIVE DECISION-MAKING MODELS

Whether enforced by law and ethics or ethics alone, not all procedural principles pertain to all contexts. Even when the U.S. Supreme Court has been sure that due process applies, it has wrestled with what due process requires. It has not held that all the principles of the adversary adjudication model apply in all types of situations. The same issue arises for a moral theory of procedural justice: In what situations do the various principles of procedural justice apply?

The central thesis of this chapter is that which procedural principles are appropriate depends on the appropriate model of decision making. All the principles and subprinciples of impartiality, opportunity to be heard, grounds for decisions, and formal justice were developed from the adversary adjudication model of decision making (see Galligan 1986, 339 (natural justice from adjudication)). As suggested various places earlier, this model might not be appropriate for all situations. Consequently, we must ask: Is adversary adjudication always the morally preferable model for burden/benefit decisions? What alternative models are there and what procedural principles are appropriate to each? If no model is always preferable, what considerations help determine which is best for different situations?

We begin by evaluating the adversary adjudication model by the fundamental norm for procedure. After that, we explain and evaluate several alternative models and consider which of the previous principles of procedural justice apply to each. The final section provides criteria for determining which model best applies to various types of situations. As the models make relevant various procedural principles developed in Part I, by applying different models to different situations one also determines which procedural principles apply. Interestingly, the criteria for the application of decision-making models are closely related to the factors elucidated in the previous chapter for determining when principles of procedural justice should be legally required.

The Limits of Adversary Adjudication

The four general principles of impartiality, opportunity to be heard, grounds for decisions, and formal justice are readily realized in the adversary adjudication model of decision making. As outlined in chapter 1, the model involves particular parties presenting information and arguments to a third party who then decides the issue on the basis of reasons referring to substantive norms and the information supplied by the parties at the hearing. Thus, the third party decisionmaker is impartial, a hearing is held in which parties have an opportunity to be heard, the decisionmaker provides findings and reasons based on substantive standards or norms and complies with formal justice.

The adversary model should be evaluated by its ability to resolve issues so as to avoid disputes; to determine the truth; and to minimize the sum of error costs, direct costs, and process benefits. An important study concluded that adversary adjudication produces more satisfaction with unfavorable decisions than alternatives, especially inquisitorial or investigatory adjudication (Thibaut and Walker 1975, 74, 80, 91). However, this study was in a dispute resolution context, not a burden/benefit context. In dispute resolution, two parties are in conflict. As used in this chapter, a conflict exists when two parties assert inconsistent positions on an issue. In a burden/benefit context, one party is being evaluated by a standard or norm; often no conflict exists. For example, a motorist files a claim for damages to his or her car from a limb falling on it, and the claims adjustor has not initially asserted that the claim is invalid. No conflict exists unless or until the claims adjustor denies the claim. Even then, there might not be a conflict, for example, if the adjustor accepts the claim but for less than the motorist asked and the motorist accepts that amount. The aim in many burden/benefit contexts is not to resolve a dispute but to decide in such a way as to avoid a one. Consequently, the study's evidence of dispute resolution is not directly applicable to many burden/benefit decision situations, although we later use aspects of the broad study to determine which decisionmaking models are appropriate for various situations.

Good reasons exist to believe that adversary adjudication fosters disputes rather than minimizes them. It structures decisions as between opposing parties. For example, an application for social security benefits involves the Social Security Administration's evaluation of the qualifications of the applicant; at least initially, the applicant and administration need not be opposed (Mashaw 1983, 81). Use of the adversary adjudication model would immediately pit the claimant against the Social Security Administration. Although good lawyers usually try to advise clients so as to avoid disputes and to settle disputes by negotiation, not all of them do so. Trained to be partisan advocates for the interests of their clients, some of them often exacerbate discord and tensions (Frankel 1980, 114). This was notoriously true in fault-based divorce. Couples were often parting amicably with a reasonable division of assets until they met with their lawyers. Even in no-fault divorce, many lawyers create antagonism and enmity by encouraging their clients to seek a larger share of the assets, at the same time running up legal fees. The adversarial process is an especially poor method for handling issues between parties who must continue to deal with each other after the dispute—between employers/employees, landlords/tenants, spouses, neighbors, and others. Consequently, adversary adjudication cannot be touted as necessarily an ideal model for issue resolution and dispute avoidance for all burden/benefit decisions.

Is the adversarial process efficacious at truth finding? Truth finding and reducing error costs go together, because determining the truth reduces errors. Correctly determining factual matters will not eliminate all errors, because mistakes can still be made about standards or norms and their application to facts. Proponents of the adversarial method claim it is effective at truth finding. For example, Lon Fuller argued strenuously that in an investigatory adjudication, to evaluate the facts an investigator must form a theory early; whereas adversary presentations permit an adjudicator to wait and form a theory only after hearing arguments from different perspectives (Fuller 1978, 382–83). The early formation of a theory is likely to bias the decisionmaker and thus lead to less accurate decisions. Moreover, one psychological study claims to support Fuller's thesis about adversary presentations counteracting a decisionmaker's bias (Thibaut and Walker 1975, 49). However, the bias set up in the study was not exactly that Fuller had in mind, but a bias from having seen several cases in which the decision was adverse to persons similar to the present one. Fuller's concern was not bias from previous cases but from early formation of hypotheses to understand the fact situation.

The formation of a theory or hypothesis to evaluate facts need not bias an investigatory adjudicator any more than a scientific investigator. Indeed, close parallels exist between the two methods. Scientists set up hypotheses and then seek evidence to confirm or refute them. Legal cases are presented with theories, for example, the plaintiff claims the defendant negligently injured him or her. Given the burden of proof, one can formulate the hypothesis that the defendant did not negligently injure the plaintiff and then seek evidence to refute it. Similarly, a welfare claims processor can use the hypothesis that the claimant is not entitled to welfare and then seek evidence to rebut or confirm it.

The central claim in behalf of the adversarial method's truth finding is that the parties have an incentive to discover and produce evidence in their favor and to dispute opposing evidence. The open competition is likely to produce the truth. However, another psychological study indicated that client-oriented attorney's were inclined to seek evidence more thoroughly than non-client-oriented attorney's only when most of the evidence was unfavorable to their client (Thibaut and Walker 1975, 38). As such attorneys present only the favorable evidence, the evidence presented will be skewed. Side A, which the evidence supports, will present five items; while side B will also present five items. However, perhaps only 25% of the total evidence supports side B. The decisionmaker is then presented with a skewed sample.

Many resources are spent by a party trying to mislead the decisionmaker (Tullock 1980, 96). One party's claim is incorrect, yet all that party's efforts are bent toward supporting its claim and getting the decisionmaker to reject the truthful claim. Moreover, many aspects of the adversarial process obscure rather than promote the truth. Lawyers often try to discredit witnesses whom they know are telling the truth, and many criminal lawyers put their clients on the stand even when they know their clients are committing perjury.

Consequently, the adversarial process, at least as it has been practiced in the United States, is not especially good at discovering facts. Indeed, in this regard, even strong advocates of adversary adjudication concede that it is not as good as alternatives (Thibaut and Walker 1978, 541). As a prominent trial judge has remarked, "[W]e have allowed ourselves too often to sacrifice truth to other values that are inferior, or even illusory" (Frankel 1980, 12).

One must distinguish between true findings and "true" or correct decisions. When the question is not finding distinct facts—was the money paid?—but the construction to put on them—was it a legitimate business expense?—the adversarial process is better. Here competing interpretations and evaluations are possible, and adversary presentations of views are often helpful (Frankel 1980, 9). Before making such decisions, one wants to hear the strongest possible arguments on both sides. For such normative evaluations, the adversarial process is good (Thibaut and Walker 1978, 541–2).

One must also consider the direct costs of adversary adjudication. The traditional adversarial process probably involves greater direct costs than a less adversarial or nonadversarial process, because of the inefficient direction of resources by parties both prior to and at a hearing (Tullock 1980, 97). Other aspects also increase direct costs. For example, in an adversarial procedure, all the evidence and witnesses must be presented at one continuous hearing. Each side has an opportunity to present all its evidence (except for rebuttal) in one continuous process. Alternative procedures can allow for the accumulation of evidence at various discrete times and in any order.

Finally, the adversarial process must be evaluated by its ability to provide process benefits. The principle of intelligibility is not especially relevant. Other procedures can also be understandable and provide intelligible decisions. Nor is there any reason to believe timeliness is better fostered by adversary adjudication than other procedures. Indeed, the law is not noted for its speedy resolution of matters.

Participation and fairness are the two process benefits that many advocates of the adversarial process think especially support it. Party control (participation) and perceived fairness (confidence) are closely related. Parties desire to present their own positions, their sides of the story, as they see them. Only by doing so do they feel that their concerns have been presented fairly. The general conclusion of a major psychological study of procedural justice was that party control, which is the primary defining characteristic of adversary adjudication, is the best predictor of people's preference for and perception of the fairness of procedures (Thibaut and Walker 1975, 121). Participation and control can promote a sense of fairness by increasing understanding of the substantive norms and decision process and by assuring parties that proper efforts are being made on their behalf (Mashaw 1983, 140).

Although these are significant reasons that one can rationally accept, they are not overwhelming arguments for adversary adjudication. One can easily overemphasize the satisfaction of parties with their participation (see Simon 1978, 94–99). It is optimistic to think that most persons who have been a party to a legal case are satisfied with the fairness of the legal system. Moreover, many persons are only concerned with the outcome—will they receive money or have to pay. People who receive a decision in their favor are as satisfied with one procedure as another (Thibaut and Walker 1975, 91). Nor do people get to have their say; as they see it, their lawyers cant mumbo jumbo irrelevant to the issue, and because of their lack of expertise, they might have little control over the presentation.

Confidence in the process or perceived fairness is not the same as actual fairness. Various factors can prevent full-fledged fairness in adversarial procedures. Perhaps the most important are the different financial strengths of the parties and their experience with the process (see Galanter 1979; Fiss 1984, 1076–77). Other features, such as differential abilities to question witnesses and the greater effectiveness of oral testimony and cross-examination in presenting weaknesses rather than strengths of evidence, also prevent complete equality (Mashaw 1983, 89). Although a formal equality exists in adversary adjudication, it is often overwhelmed by substantive inequality.

One might contend, however, that the fairness of adversary adjudication resides in its formal justice of treating like cases alike and its defense of rights (Terrell 1987b). However, other decision-making models can use standards or norms to produce consistency. Indeed, as we shall see, one model—bureaucratic investigation—relies heavily on nondiscretionary decision rules. Furthermore, rights are not always at stake in burden/benefit decisions. For examples, students do not have rights to an A grade or faculty to merit salary increases. If there is a rule or standard by which they qualify, then one might claim they have a right to such and such a grade or salary increase. But that simply amounts to saying the grade or salary increase would be the correct decision given the standard or norm. In any case, at least in the first instance, other decision-making processes might be as likely to get the decision correct and thus vindicate rights. They do not simply pursue a negotiated compromise.

Consequently, adversary adjudcation is not a perfect model of burden/benefit decision making. By forcing issues into an adversarial dispute, it can foster rather than avoid disputes. It is not an ideal system for determining facts, although it is distinctly better for fostering evaluations. The method has several features contributing to high direct costs, and the claims for its realization of process benefits can easily be exaggerated.

Alternative Models

Given the deficiencies of the adversary adjudication model for burden/benefit decision making, it is important to examine alternative decision-making models. (For other classifications of models, from which I have liberally borrowed, see Mashaw 1981b; Mashaw 1983, 23–34; and Macdonald 1981. Galligan's models (1986, 114–17) primarily vary to include rule or policy making, while those here are all for decisions about individuals.) Four aspects of each model are developed: (1) a description of the decision-making process, (2) a statement of its general features, (3) an indication of the relevance or incorporation of various procedural principles in it, and (4) a brief general evaluation.

Decision-making models can be characterized by five features. One feature is the usual goal of the method of decision making. A second is the value primarily realized by the decisions. A third feature is the usual subject matter of judgment or decision—what the decisions are about. The type of standards or norms used in making such decisions is a fourth feature. (In this context, 'standard' should be taken to include norms.) A closely related and final feature, especially relevant for our purposes, is whether and what kind of discretion a decisionmaker has. Obviously, the discretion depends on the standards involved.

Adversary adjudication At this point, the adversary adjudication model has been adequately described, and we have seen how the procedural principles discussed in the early chapters apply to it and have evaluated it. However, we have not indicated the general features that will be presented for the other models. Adversary adjudication has as its primary goal the resolution of conflicts. The legal system, in which adversary adjudication finds its primary home, is often characterized by this goal. The value advanced by adversary adjudication is individualized justice. Decisions are to take into account the particularities of individual situations. The primary subject matter of adversary adjudication is faulty conduct. The common law has traditionally involved judgments of fault—violation of a contract, commission of a crime or tort. Granted, various no-fault principles have entered the law—strict liability in torts and no-fault divorces (see Simon 1983, 1250–51). However, the judicial process is not especially relevant to an uncontested no-fault divorce, which seems more a clerical matter than a judicial one. In making judgments of fault, the norms used are "moral" ones. The concept of moral involved here is not necessarily an ethical one; objective standards of negligence do not indicate ethical fault. However, the norms are for judging people's conduct as right or wrong which sometimes reflects on their character. In this general sense, they are moral as opposed to standards for measuring people's height and weight.

Finally, because the standards require evaluation and often use multifactor tests to produce individualized justice, discretion3 is often involved in applying them in particular cases.

Bureaucratic investigation Another model can be called bureaucratic investigation. On this model, the decisionmaker has primary responsibility for developing the evidence and finding facts for the decision. Often individuals are required to provide information, but the decisionmaker is not restricted to that information. Usually only one person is being judged at a time. This model is exemplified in many situations in society, such as loan officers determining eligibility for a loan or credit card, customs officials determining whether duty is owed, college officials determining eligibility for graduation, and so on.

The goal of bureaucratic investigation is to implement a purpose or policy set by others. The goal is more means-ends related than in adversary adjudication. The underlying values are certainty or regularity of classification and thus consistency over time. If every case can be properly classified, then certainty and regularity will result. For example, a student knows that a certain number of credit hours are necessary for graduation, and all students who graduate have at least that number of credit hours. The subject matter or object of decision is finding facts and properly classifying a case. A customs officer tries to find out what goods were bought abroad and their dollar value. If it is less than $300 or whatever, then no duty is owed. The norms applied are those of the organization the goals of which are being implemented. To provide for certainty and regularity, the norms must be precise and cover all cases. Nondiscretionary decision rules are common. Consequently, little or no room is left for discretion3 (see Simon 1983, 1201–04).

The bureaucratic model largely characterizes the continental inquisitorial criminal system (see Damaška 1979). The system is highly bureaucratic with specially trained judges, strict rules for decisions, and significant hierarchical control. The hierarchical control is necessary to ensure that various decisionmakers all properly apply the norms. The hierarchical system also places control in a few persons at the top of the pyramid with authority to set the goals and standards. For control to be exercised, complete files or records need to be kept.

That continental inquisitorial law is based on the bureaucratic investigation model indicates that many of the procedural principles apply in the model. First, impartiality applies, but it does not include the separation of functions.

The decisionmaker is the primary investigator, and a prosecutorial function can be irrelevant. Although the continental criminal system does have prosecutors, in many other contexts the notion is inapplicable because the situation is not presented as a conflict. There need not be a ban on ex parte communications, especially when there are not two contesting parties. Second, most of the principles of an opportunity to be heard can apply—prompt, open hearing with notice, presentation of oral and written evidence with assistance of counsel, a record of proceedings, and an opportunity to appeal. However, the principle of discovery cannot pertain, because there is usually no opposing party and the decisionmaker conducts the inquiry. Third, the various principles pertaining to grounds for decisions can apply—presentation of findings and reasons, judicial review, and burden of proof. However, the burden of production does not apply in any significant sense, although one might have to produce some evidence to support a claim to initiate an inquiry. The burden of persuasion is solely an instruction to the decisionmaker about the weight of evidence necessary for a decision; it has little role as setting a task for a party to amass so much evidence. Fourth, the elements of formal justice can apply. Rule following dominates; consistency primarily applies as consistent application of rules or objective standards. Precedents can be used, although the continental inquisitorial system denies that precedents are followed; correct application of rules is more important than following precedent.

While most of the principles of procedural justice can apply, a number of them that can apply are not necessary. Hearings need not be open or actually held, if by 'hearing' one means an opportunity for oral testimony. Indeed, the focus is usually on written evidence (see Simon 1983, 1205–06 (documentation in bureaucratic welfare eligibility determinations)). Counsel need not be permitted; whether counsel is appropriate will partly depend on the situation. Judicial review is not always appropriate, although some form of review is essential to ensure regularity of decision making. We already noted that precedents need not be used.

How does bureaucratic investigation meet the criteria of evaluation? It is less likely than adversary adjudication to encourage disputes, because it does not structure decisions as conflicts between parties. The extent to which it otherwise prevents disputes generally depends on its providing process benefits. As a method of finding facts, it is probably preferable to adversary adjudication. The decisionmaker has access to all the facts, not just those parties decide to present. Thus, if 25% of the evidence supports side B and 75% side A, the decisionmaker will have access to, say, twenty items of information, five supporting B and fifteen supporting A rather than five supporting each as in adversary adjudication. One might think the decisionmaker less motivated than adversaries to discover evidence, but recall that client-oriented attorneys were more motivated than non-client-oriented ones only when their case was especially weak (Thibaut and Walker 1975, 38). However, whether overall accuracy is promoted depends on the subject matter. Recall that rules are only appropriate when factual features are quite reliably correlated with appropriate decision outcomes, and that rules are almost always suboptimal. The weaker the correlations, the less optimal the outcomes, that is, the greater the error costs. Moreover, quality control assurance may focus on mere paper errors, that is, errors in documentation but not substance (see Simon 1983, 1208). However, the direct costs of bureaucratic investigation are often less than those of adversary adjudication. It avoids the misallocation of resources of adversary adjudication, and objective nondiscretionary rules are more easily applied.

The process benefits can generally be obtained in bureaucratic investigation. Participation is less than with adversary adjudication, because parties do not have control over the presentation of their views. However, they can and usually are given the opportunity to present what information they have. When two parties are involved, each can be given equal opportunities. The process can be intelligible, although many bureaucratic decision processes are not. Indeed, as bureaucratic investigation seeks to use clear, objective criteria, the reasons for decisions are likely to be more intelligible than with adversary adjudication. Bureaucratic investigation can be a faster method than adversary adjudication and thus more timely. If the above benefits are provided, people can and do have confidence in the process.

Directorship A third decision-making model is directorship or managerial direction (see also Fuller 1969, 207–08; Fuller 1971, 200; Fuller and Eisenberg 1972, 89–90). Directorial decisions direct and coordinate efforts to achieve ends. These are decisions of those at the top of a bureaucratic hierarchy, although they can occur in nonorganizational situations. Directorial burden/benefit decisions often concern the relationships between the director and a subordinate, not those between subordinates and others. Such decision making often requires considerable flexibility. Like bureaucratic investigation, the decisionmaker often gathers the evidence and information or has someone else do it in an investigatory manner. The exemplar is a business entrepreneur deciding who to hire or fire, assigning offices or tasks to staff, and giving pay raises.

The goal of the directorial model is furthering the director's ends. These ends need not be selfish ones; for example, the chief executive officer of a corporation might have ends of increasing profit, or, if it is a nonprofit corporation, furthering its ends such as quality research. The underlying value is the decisionmaker's satisfaction. The subject matter is organizing activities and allocating resources to achieve the director's ends. Although the subject is means-ends oriented, the ends are not externally given as in bureaucratic investigation. The standards are the subjective ones of the decisionmaker. They are subjective in the sense that the decisionmaker can always change desires or ends; others cannot prescribe them for the director. However, like any desires or ends they might be reasonable or unreasonable, and the ends can be objective states of affairs. For example, a director's end might be maximizing profit, which can be objectively determined. Nonetheless, because a director might modify an end, for example, employ a relative at a higher salary than required to hire an equally competent nonrelative, the ends are not confining. In effect, as a director has $discretion_2$ concerning ends, he or she also has $discretion_4$ concerning standards and judgments.

This sketch is of the ideal type; in practice decisionmakers come more or less close to it. Generally, a continuum exists between bureaucratic investigation and directorship. As one peels off more and more characteristics of bureaucratic investigation, one comes closer and closer to directorship. Most people are not purely in positions of one type or another. Rather, some of their decision situations exemplify directorship and others are closer to bureaucratic investigation.

In its ideal type, none of the principles of procedural justice except personal consistency need apply in directorship. Indeed, in discussing the limitations of consistency in chapter 5, we noted that when the decisionmaker has $discretion_4$ concerning the standard for decision comparative justice is easily satisfied. This is not to say that other principles of procedural justice cannot be applied in the model, but they need not be. Whether a director is impartial, an opportunity to be heard is allowed, findings and reasons are given, and precedents and rules are followed depends on the circumstances and the director's voluntary agreement. For example, a director might be responsible for determining salary increases for subordinate employees. The director does not necessarily have a conflicting interest unless he or she owns the company, and the director certainly need not be biased. The director can request that employees submit all information pertinent to the decision; this need not but can involve an oral presentation. Reasons for decisions can be presented to employees, records kept, and requests for reconsideration allowed. Announced rules and principles for decision making might exist, but they are for the efficient achievement of the director's goals, so a departure from them in particular cases for more effective achievement of those goals is understandable and expectable. A crucial consideration is apt to be how an allocation of funds for salary increases can best promote the interests of the organization, and this consideration can vary from year to year as the needs of the organization change, thus making rules and precedents less useful. To the extent decisions become confined by announced rules and other norms, the process moves toward bureaucratic investigation.

Directorial decision making is generally undesirable because it involves decisions affecting other people without any set substantive standards or procedural principles. Of course, few process values are realized. Individuals have no participation, the decisions might be quite unintelligible and unfair, so there is not likely to be much confidence. However, decisions can be quite timely. The lack of process benefits might increase disputes, but it probably does not do so although psychological dissatisfaction will exist. Given the director's position, no point exists in disputing a decision. Nonetheless, if those subject to a director's decisions have the same ends and the director generally makes reasonable decisions, they might not be very dissatisfied.

Interestingly, more can be said for directorship than one might expect. First, personal autonomy has usually been considered a good reason for it in charitable giving. Moreover, recall that the presence of $discretion_4$ does not mean that decisions cannot be criticized as misguided and so forth. One might well condemn a person who gave funds to the Rockefellers, but there would be no procedural injustice involved. However, autonomy might not be a sufficient justification for permitting $discretion_4$ in allocating burdens. Second, directorship has low error and direct costs. That it has low direct costs is obvious; the procedures are minimal. That error costs are likely to be few is less obvious. Recall that error costs are those of mistaken decisions. In directorship, an error exists only when a decision does not best further a director's ends. If a director employs a less competent person whom the director likes better, no error has been made! Working with people he or she likes is also one of the director's goals, so the decision provides more satisfaction (value) than employing the less liked but more competent person. So long as the director is aware of the factors involved in the decision and accepts the trade-off, no error occurs. Errors can, of course, still occur, but they are mistaken choices of means to a director's complex of goals, for example hiring X rather than Y thinking one would like working with X better, when in fact one would like working with Y better.

Professional service A fourth model is that of professional service. Physicians' decisions about treatment of patients and teachers making decisions about students exemplify this model. Clients present professionals with particular problems. Professionals investigate the problems, determine their nature, and recommend courses of action. Although a person's problems might involve conflict with others—a legal problem or psychological conflict, the issue is not presented as a conflict. The professional does not resolve the conflict between the two persons but aids the client. In the case of lawyers, that can mean waging conflicts for clients.

In marked contrast to directorship, the goal of professional service is to improve the individual's well-being, not that of the decisionmaker. The corresponding value is individual welfare. The subject matter of judgment is the individual's needs, desires, or skills and predictions (prognoses, projections) about what will satisfy or improve them. Physicians and educators, like decisionmakers in adversary adjudication, often evaluate individuals. However, they are not concerned with fault, but with skills and abilities. Unlike the standards for bureaucratic decisionmakers, the standards are not established by a superior in a hierarchy, but by professional peers. Because professional standards leave scope for professional judgment, decisionmakers have discretion3.

More procedural principles are appropriate in this model than the directorial model but fewer than in bureaucratic investigation. Ideally, professionals are impartial and unbiased, although a fee for service payment system tends to import a conflict of interest—professionals can profit by performing unnecessary services. The investigative function is an essential part of professional activity, but because a direct conflict is not involved, the prosecutorial function is irrelevant. Moreover, ex parte communications are not only appropriate but often essential, for example, laboratory reports. Most of the subprinciples of an opportunity to be heard do not apply or are rejected. For example, the principles of notice and discovery do not make much sense. Principles of openness, counsel, and rebutting evidence are rejected. Most discussions with professionals concern private matters; it would be quite inappropriate for them to be open to the public. Although professionals obtain evidence, written or oral, from clients, the idea of rebutting evidence is at best incongruous, although on some matters a professional will want an explanation.

Presentation of findings and reasons should apply to professional decisions. Generally, professionals must have the informed consent of clients to act in their behalf, and that cannot be obtained save by presenting findings and reasons for actions. Although informed consent was originally applied to the physician/patient relationship, the same general idea applies to a lawyer or accountant acting in behalf of a client—filing a legal action or contesting an IRS decision. Burden of proof and judicial review are inappropriate. Getting a second opinion is analogous to judicial review, but it is not usually an element of professional decision-making. The extent to which formal justice applies varies between professions and exactly how one construes following precedents and rules. Consistency, of course, applies to all the decisions. Physicians, for example, do not follow precedents, but they do follow professional rules of good practice. Lawyers, of course, should always use precedents and rules in evaluating a client's situation. They do not, however, treat a client's problem the way they did a similar one of a previous client merely because it is a precedent—suppose the previous client lost the case.

The professional service model is probably the best at dispute minimization. One must distinguish issue resolution for professional decisions pertaining to clients from that pertaining to clients vis-à-vis others. Only the former are properly relevant to evaluating the model, although it is probably the best for the later also. While the rates of malpractice cases and complaints against professionals have increased greatly in recent years, compared to the number of professional/client interactions they are miniscule. The reason for the model's efficacy at dispute minimization is that the goal and value are the client's well-being and welfare. A professional is thus working in the client's interest and if consent is obtained, the client agrees with the decisions.

Professional service is also quite good at truth finding and minimizing error costs. With the guarantee of confidentiality, clients are willing to disclose much more information than in the other models. The two primary sources of errors are professional carelessness or incompetence and the inherent difficulty of making correct judgments. Carelessness and incompetence are probably not greater than with other decisionmakers, but the subject matter and standards create more errors than in bureaucratic investigation. However, direct costs are usually greater than in directorship or even bureaucratic investigation. The personnel costs and often the equipment used (medical and dental technology) are high.

Process benefits can be realized in professional service, but many complaints against professionals indicate that they often are not. Fairness is hard to judge, because professionals claim that each case requires individualized decisions. Many people suspect, however, that the rich or those with more interesting or lucrative problems receive disproportionate attention (see also Bayles 1989, 34–35, 95). Participation is limited, because much of the investigation requires professional expertise. Still, informed consent is intended to involve client participation and understanding or intelligibility. Actual practice in many professions often does not meet these conditions. Timeliness is certainly possible, but it's lack is one of the most common complaints about lawyers. Despite it all, people probably have more confidence in professional service than in other methods.

Negotiation The negotiation model is not really one for burden/benefit decisions as we have defined them. It is included as the last model because it is relevant at the borders of problems we discuss. For example, in the previous chapter we suggested that principles of procedural justice need not be independently imposed by law if alternative protections are available and that often these protections can be obtained in collective bargaining agreements. A description of negotiation is hardly necessary, as almost everyone is familiar with the process. Two parties make offers and counteroffers of exchanges until both agree to a proposal or break off negotiations.

The goal of negotiation is agreement. The value involved is mutual voluntary acceptance of relations between the parties. The subject matter of decision is satisfactory interpersonal relations; that is, whether one is bargaining over wages and hours, compensation for an accident, or the sale of a bicycle, the issue is whether the interaction is satisfactory. The standards are the personal desires and preferences of the parties. Consequently, neither party is bound by external standards, so each has discretion[4]. In negotiating a settlement of a dispute, there can be external standards in the background. That is, the parties know that if they cannot settle it themselves, it will be settled in court by adversary adjudication in which certain legal norms will be applied. However, parties can exceed those standards if they wish. For example, in negotiating a divorce settlement, a party can be more generous than the law would require.

Few principles of procedural justice apply to negotiation. None of the particular principles of impartiality apply. A party will have a conflict of interest, can be biased, investigate the situation, prosecute his or her case against the other, and receive information (such as independent evaluations) without the other party present. Only a few subprinciples of an opportunity to be heard apply. Basically, the only requirement is that parties be able to present any evidence they desire, including rebuttal, in written or oral form. Of course, the other party can simply ignore or deny it, but that will not further that party's goal of reaching an agreement. Parties can usually be represented by counsel, although that is strictly up to them. The other principles of an opportunity to be heard should not be applied. Nor do the principles of grounds for decisions appropriately pertain. Findings and reasons for agreeing need not be given, and no burden of proof applies. In some cases, however, judicial review of negotiations is possible. Formal justice does not apply, except insofar as personal consistency is a requirement of rationality. One certainly need not agree because one agreed to a similar deal in the past, nor are there any rules to follow. Procedural justice in negotiation primarily consists in the absence of force and fraud and unconscionability, which are basically requirements for the agreement to be voluntary.

The negotiation model fares well by the standards of evaluation. Because based on voluntary agreement of both parties, it minimizes disputes. Truth finding is a difficult concept to apply to it. In one way, truth finding involves discovering those facts that a person believes relevant to agreeing to a proposal. In that regard, it works well, although people can agree to proposals because of mistaken beliefs; if mistakes are due to fraud, grounds exist for voiding the agreement. In another way, truth finding involves making the best deal one can. In this respect, many agreements are not the best possible. However, it would normally be improper to attribute error costs to such agreements, because the agreements were satisfactory. Direct costs can be high, because often the process takes considerable effort and time. Thus, if there are objective standards and time pressure, people prefer third party decisionmakers (Thibaut and

Walker 1975, 15). This also indicates that timeliness may not be a process benefit realized in negotiation. Except perhaps when others negotiate in one's behalf, participation and intelligibility are probably greater in negotiation than any other model.

Fairness and error costs can be a problem in one type of negotiation, namely, settlement of disputes against a background of standards and norms (see Fiss 1984; Terrell 1987b). If there are such standards for settling a dispute, then error costs pertain when negotiated settlements do not give the results correct application of the standards would yield. Moreover, if the standards indicate that one party should win and the other lose, a negotiated settlement is almost certainly going to give the party that would win less than he or she could obtain by winning. Moreover, fairness is often absent in two ways. First, one party can have greater bargaining power than another (which is possible in all negotiation). Second, as formal justice does not apply, a settlement will not establish a precedent for future cases. Thus different individuals negotiating over the same matter with a given person might not receive comparative justice.

The preceding discussion of these models is summarized in tables 8.1 and 8.2. The table of principles in models is condensed and only provides the general idea. In particular, the 'M' designation means the principle applies in some situations or to a limited extent. Principles can even be applied in some cases marked 'N'. The 'N' designation is used when a principle cannot be required independent of the voluntary agreement of the decisionmaker. For example, it is applied to directors following rules although they might commit themselves to rules.

Choice of Models

With the outline of the various models for burden/benefit decision making and their obvious actual use in society, it becomes implausible to claim that any one is appropriate for all situations. Consequently, it is necessary to try to indicate types of situations for which a model is most appropriate. In the following discussion it is important to bear in mind that the models are ideal types. We have already suggested how directorship can blend into bureaucratic investigation. Other combinations are also possible. Many decision-making procedures are a blend of the different models, although this can involve tensions and stress (see Mashaw 1983, 34–46; Mashaw 1981b, 190–201). Consequently, the best

TABLE 8.1
Features of Decision-Making Models

MODEL	GOAL	VALUE	SUBJECT	STANDARD	DISCRETION
Adversary adjudication	conflict resolution	individualized justice	faulty conduct	moral	discretion$_3$
Bureaucratic investigation	policy implementation	certainty & regularity	factual classification	organizational	little or no discretion
Directorship	decision-maker's ends	personal satisfaction	contribution to ends	personal	discretion$_4$
Professional service	individual well-being	client welfare	needs & skills	professional	discretion$_3$
Negotiation	agreement	voluntary acceptance	party satisfaction	personal	discretion$_4$

TABLE 8.2
Procedural Principles in Decison-Making Models

PRINCIPLE	AA	BI	D	PS	N
Impartiality					
Interest	Y	Y	N	Y	N
Bias	Y	Y	N	Y	N
Independence	Y	Y	N	Y	N
Investigation	Y	N	N	N	N
Prosecution	Y	Y	N	DNA	N
Ex parte	Y	N	N	N	N
Opportunity to be heard					
Open	Y	M	N	N	N
Promptness	Y	Y	N	Y	N
Notice	Y	Y	N	DNA	DNA
Discovery	Y	M	N	DNA	N
Written evidence	Y	Y	N	M	M
Oral evidence	Y	M	N	M	M
Rebut evidence	Y	Y	N	N	Y
Counsel	Y	M	N	N	M
Record	Y	Y	N	Y	N
Appeals	Y	Y	N	M	N
Grounds					
Findings	Y	Y	N	Y	DNA
Reasons	Y	Y	N	Y	DNA
Burden of proof	Y	M	N	DNA	DNA
Judicial review	Y	M	N	M	M
Formal justice					
Consistency	Y	Y	Y	Y	Y
Precedents	Y	M	N	N	N
Rules	Y	Y	N	M	N

AA=adversary adjudication; BI=bureaucratic investigation; D=directorship; PS=professional service; N=negotiation; Y=yes usually required; M=may be required; N=not required; DNA=does not apply.

that can be attained are factors indicating which model should be dominant in a type of situation.

John Thibaut and Laurens Walker have identified four factors that affect preferences for dispute resolution procedures (Thibaut and Walker 1975, 7–8; Thibaut and Walker 1978). The first factor is whether the conflict is cognitive or of interest. By a conflict of interest (or value), they mean a situation in which judgments of justice or moral evaluation are dominant (see also Stevenson 1963, chap. 1). The underlying conception is the legal process judging fault and deciding between claims of right. The other three factors are the time available for reaching a decision, the existence of a standard for determining a claim, and outcome correspondence—whether an outcome can be mutually beneficial. The last factor requires some clarification. In some conflict situations, both parties can gain and the conflict is over how much each will gain; these are correspondent outcomes. In other situations, both parties cannot gain; what one gains the other must lose; or both will lose and the question is how much. These are noncorrespondent situations. This distinction is similar to our previous distinction between no-lose and no-win decisions.

Thibaut and Walker (1975, 15) found that the strongest preference for a third party decisionmaker exists when there is a standard, time pressure, and the outcome is noncorrespondent. Along with other evidence they obtained about party satisfaction with fairness, they concluded that the adversary adjudication model was the best. This led them to recommend the adversary adjudication model for new areas of due process such as welfare determinations (Thibaut and Walker 1975, 123). In a subsequent article, they implicitly qualified this general conclusion by limiting it to situations involving conflict of interest. They argued that "autocratic" procedure (similar to bureaucratic investigation) is preferable for cognitive conflicts (Thibaut and Walker 1978, 547–52).

The Thibaut and Walker criteria are only for conflict resolution procedures. As we have frequently noted, many burden/benefit decisions do not present themselves as conflicts. Thus, their factors need revision to take this difference into account. The following three factors can be taken as primary in determining the choice of decision-making models for burden/benefit decisions: (1) whether the issue is presented as a conflict or dispute, (2) whether the individual stands only to gain (no-lose) or only to lose (no-win), and (3) the nature of the standards and the subject matter involved which affect discretion.

Two models are only for situations of conflict or disagreement, namely, adversary adjudication and negotiation. Without two opposed parties, both are impossible. Although one can structure decisions to create opposed parties—one for an individual and one against—doing so increases disputes rather than minimizes them. Given the aim of issue resolution including dispute minimization, so structuring decisions is inadvisable. Consequently, unless an issue presents itself as a conflict or disagreement, adversary adjudication and negotiation are contraindicated.

Whether a decision is posed as a conflict is closely related to whether individuals stand to gain or lose. Burden-imposing and most benefit-terminating decisions confront individuals as losing (no-win) propositions. Persons do not request such decisions and view the situation as a conflict between them and the person or organization considering imposing a burden or terminating a benefit. Technically, a decisionmaker considering imposing a burden has not necessarily asserted a position, so there would not be a conflict as we earlier defined it. However, the subject of the decision is opposed to any imposition of a burden and thus the positions are inconsistent—possibly impose burden versus not impose a burden.

In contrast, in benefit-conferring and burden-relieving decisions individuals stand to gain and at worst maintain the status quo (no-lose situations). They often seek such decisions. No other party need stand to lose. A benefactory agency need not and usually does not view the conferral of a benefit as contrary to its interest (see Mashaw 1983, 81). One might contend that with a limited budget its concern for balancing the budget creates opposition, but that does not imply opposition to conferring benefits in deserving cases, only a stricter standard for being deserving. A somewhat different aspect appears if an employee asks for a salary increase. If the decisionmaker is also the owner, then the decisionmaker can view an increase as a potential burden and the situation as a conflict. An owner need not see the matter that way; he or she can consider salary increases to be incentives to further productivity and increased morale. Decisions in which individuals stand to gain can also present themselves as conflicts if they are competitive. Several applicants for a television station license or job promotion are in conflict with one another. Thus, whether individuals stand to gain or lose is not the same as whether a conflict is present.

The third factor, the nature of the standards and subject matter, is closely related to Thibaut and Walker's distinction between cognitive and interest conflict, but it is not the same. They divide the subject matter somewhat differently and do not emphasize the type of standards to be used. If norms are clear and admit of objective and precise application (nondiscretionary rules), then the bureaucratic investigation model is most appropriate. If the standards are the subjective satisfactions of the decisionmakers, then the directorial or negotiation model is most appropriate. The professional service and adversary adjudication models are intermediate in this respect. As standards become more subjective or less precise, certain models become less appropriate. The combinations of subject matter and standards imply different degrees of discretion—none, discretion$_3$, or discretion$_4$.

We can now briefly note how these factors apply to the different decisionmaking models. The adversary adjudication model is appropriate only if the decision presents itself as a conflict. Because of the greater significance of deprivations (as discussed in the previous chapter) and adversary adjudication's greater procedural protections, it is more appropriate when the decision confronts the individual as a losing proposition. Finally, it is more appropriate as the standards are imprecise and permit discretion$_3$. In particular, it is especially good when "moral" judgments of faulty conduct or character are involved. Adversary adjudication is also often appropriate for appeals from decisions denying benefits or relief from burdens. Once individuals are denied benefits or burden relief, they see themselves as in conflict with the individual or organization denying them (see Mashaw 1983, 94).

The bureaucratic investigation model is most appropriate for nonconflict, no-lose situations with objective standards permitting precise application. The model can appropriately apply to some conflict situations. For example, Thibaut and Walker found the "autocratic" process, which largely corresponds to our bureaucratic investigation model, most preferred in correspondent situations with standards and need for a quick decision (Thibaut and Walker 1975, 15). Thus, the bureaucratic model appears appropriate for competitive benefit situations with precise standards. For example, compare a decision about granting a television station license with judging the fattest man at the county fair. A decision about television licenses involves imprecise standards about the public interest and judgments of the character or disposition of owners to program in the public interest. These "moral" standards allow scope for discretion$_3$. Adversary adjudication is perhaps most appropriate. In contrast, who is the heaviest man is capable of objective and precise determination, so the bureaucratic model applies. Finally, the bureaucratic model might also be appropriate for no-win decisions in which individuals stand to lose only a small amount. The matter is not important enough to justify the usually greater direct costs of adversary adjudication over bureaucratic investigation. The Social Security Administration basically follows an investigatory model, and it has been suggested as perhaps appropriate for mass justice cases such as social security and welfare (Friendly 1975, 1289–91; but see Simon 1983 (advocating professional service for welfare determinations)).

The major determinant of the appropriateness of the directorial model is the standards involved. If the standard depends on the decisionmaker's discretion$_4$, then whether a decision confronts an individual as a conflict and a no-win or a no-lose situation becomes of very minor importance. (However, we have questioned the wisdom of permitting such discretion$_4$ when burdens are imposed.) The criterion is the satisfaction of a single decisionmaker; when two parties are involved, negotiation becomes dominant. The clearest case might be that of presidential appointments of aides discussed in the previous chapter. The primary standard is presidential satisfaction with the candidate. As previously discussed, legally imposed procedural principles are inappropriate. Ethically, one could require the president to at least solicit information from a person and to explain reasons, especially for dismissal. A third party could conclude that dismissal of an aide was not in good faith, that it was not dissatisfaction with the performance but some other factor, such as racial discrimination, that was involved. Nonetheless, to the degree that the standard is based on a subjective determination of satisfactoriness, the directorial model is most appropriate.

The professional service model is most appropriate when there is no conflict, the decision is a no-lose one, and professional standards or norms are used. As discussed, professionals do not usually resolve conflicts between a client and another person, although they might be assisting clients to obtain favorable resolutions to conflicts. (Joint marital counseling is an exception.) As the goal of professional service is client well-being, it primarily involves conferral of benefits. Professionals do often impose burdens on clients, for example, teachers giving examinations and dentists extracting teeth. Because these burdens are part of the means to an overall benefit and clients have usually consented, no conflict is involved. The chief difference between the appropriateness of the professional and bureaucratic models is the standards and subject matter. When standards require professional expertise and professional judgment ($discretion_3$), the bureaucratic model is inappropriate. Judgments of clients' skills and abilities, for example, ability to do calculus, can be objective, but professional expertise is required to test those skills and abilities.

TABLE 8.3
Appropriate Models for Situations

CONFLICT	GAIN/LOSE	DISCRETION	MODEL
C	G	~D	BI
C	G	D_3	AA
C	G	D_4	N
C	L	~D	BI
C	L	D_3	AA
C	L	D_4	N/D
~C	G	~D	BI
~C	G	D_3	PS
~C	G	D_4	D

C=conflict; ~C=no conflict; G=stand only to gain (no-lose); L=stand only to lose (no-win); ~D=no discretion; D_3=$discretion_3$; D_4=$discretion_4$; BI=bureaucratic investigation; AA=adversary adjudication; N=negotiation; PS=professional service; and D=directorship

Finally, the negotiation model is appropriate when there is conflict or lack of agreement and the standard is the personal satisfaction of the conflicting parties. Without an objective standard, third parties cannot make an appropriate decision, and all the other models involve third party decisionmakers. This is one reason why arbitration is rarely used to conclude contracts, except when only one or a few issues subject to objective standards remain, for example, a fair wage given market conditions. Negotiation can also be appropriate when several issues are contested, for example, several tax deductions claimed by a taxpayer. It will not work when one party has no leeway to vary elements; for example, when there is dispute over an applicant's eligibility, social security cannot agree to pay a lesser amount (see also Mashaw 1983, 94). The negotiation model is not necessarily limited to situations without objective standards. If there is adequate time and the benefit or burden can vary, conflicting parties can perhaps negotiate an agreement. Most legal cases are settled by negotiation rather than adjudication. An individual can even come to agree to a burden-imposing decision. However, we noted that error costs are greater and fairness likely to be less in such negotiation than other types of negotiation. Thus, its advantages over adversary adjudication are less clear.

Table 8.3 roughly summarizes the preceding discussion of situations in which models appropriately apply. No-win, nonconflict situations are not represented. We have argued that such situations do not exist, because no-win situations present to individuals as conflicts. Basically, bureaucratic investigation is appropriate whenever objective standards permit little or no discretion. Adversary adjudication is appropriate for conflict situations involving discretion$_3$. Negotiation pertains to conflict situations involving discretion$_4$. In nonconflict situations involving discretion$_3$, professional service is appropriate. In nonconflict situations involving discretion$_4$, directorship is appropriate. The anomalous case is no-win, conflict situations involving discretion$_4$. In some situations the standard is not the satisfaction of both persons but only of the decisionmaker. Thus, the appropriate model is directorship or negotiation depending on whether the standard is the satisfaction of one or both parties.

Summary

This chapter has completed our theory of procedural justice for burden/benefit decisions by indicating when various principles of procedural justice apply. Different sets of principles are relevant depending on the type of decision-making process involved. Thus, by elaborating different models of decision making and indicating when each model is appropriate, we determine which procedural principles apply. Of course, the application of a procedural principle does not automatically determine that a particular procedure be used. Other principles might appy and have to be balanced, and different specific procedures can satisfy a principle to a greater or lesser degree. For example, notice might be oral or written or in a newspaper. Particular arrangements must be evaluated by the fundamental norm and appropriate principles as those rational persons would accept for a society in which they expected to be subject to them.

Lon Fuller claimed that the distinguishing feature of various forms of social ordering, roughly corresponding to our decision-making models, is the mode of participation in them (Fuller 1978, 363; see also Galligan 1986, 340–44).

We have not used any one feature to distinguish models or to determine when each is appropriate. If one feature is dominant in our analysis, it is the joint one of subject matter and standard reflected in the scope of discretion. Nonetheless, an adequate conception of models and their appropriateness requires attention to a variety of features including discretion, the presence of conflict, and whether individuals stand only to gain or lose.

The usual legal model of procedural justice is adversary adjudication. In part, this model dominates because of lawyers' familiarity with it. It cannot be supported as always the best model. It can create rather than avoid disputes, is not an effective process for determining factual matters, and often has greater costs than alternative procedures. The process benefits of adversary adjudication are often overestimated.

Other possible models of burden/benefit decision making include bureaucratic investigation, directorship, professional service, and negotiation. These models, along with adversary adjudication, are distinguishable by their goals, implicit value, subject matter, standards, and discretion. Adversary adjudication seeks to resolve conflicts and provide individualized justice on the basis of "moral" standards permitting discretion$_3$ in judging faulty conduct. Bureaucratic investigation seeks to implement policy and provide certainty and regularity using objective and precisely applicable organizational norms and standards permitting little if any discretion$_3$. Directorship seeks to achieve the decisionmaker's ends and satisfaction by decisions contributing to the achievement of those ends as determined by the decisionmaker's subjective evaluation and discretion$_4$. Professional service seeks individual clients' well-being and welfare by assessing their needs and abilities using professional standards requiring professional judgment. Finally, negotiation seeks voluntary agreement based on the personal standards and satisfaction of parties which allows them discretion$_4$.

The principles of procedural justice developed earlier in the book are not all appropriate for each of the different models. Thus, in determining which model is appropriate for different situations, one is also largely determining which principles can or might apply to the situation. Three factors or considerations are primary in determining the appropriateness of a model for a situation. The first factor is whether the decision presents itself to the affected individual as a conflict. If it does not, then adversary adjudication and negotiation are usually inappropriate. The second factor is whether the individual stands only to gain or only to lose. Even if there is conflict, the bureaucratic model is more appropriate than that of adversary adjudication if objective and precise standards exist and individuals will gain or suffer small losses. The third factor is the subject matter and standards as they affect discretion. If purely personal or subjective standards are involved, then directorship or negotiation is appropriate depending on whether conflict and the satisfaction of one or more persons are involved.

Finally, the factors supporting legal imposition of procedural justice principles and the use of adversary adjudication tend to coalesce. In particular, legal imposition is more appropriate when a decision might deprive an individual—set back the individual's interests—and alternatives such as negotiation are not available. These tend to be situations in which adversary adjudication is more appropriate, because the decision confronts the individual as a conflict and a loss is involved. Even when objective standards exist and the bureaucratic model is appropriate, its inclusion of most principles obscures the difference between it and adversary adjudication. Moreover, there is a stronger reason for legal enforcement when the state seeks to act. These are precisely the types of situations in which the due process clauses of the U.S. Constitution apply—the government deprives an individual of life, liberty, or property. Consequently, it is not surprising that in the United States the adversary adjudication model has been dominant. By the above analysis, it should be.

PART III

APPLICATIONS

CHAPTER 9

PROFESSIONAL DISCIPLINE

Part III illustrates and applies the principles and theory from Parts I and II. The purpose is to show that the theory provides a basis for analysis and criticism. This involves several elements. The criteria for legally requiring procedural principles are applied to determine whether the law should intervene. Our criteria for determining which decision-making model should apply will be used to determine the appropriate model and thus which principles pertain. The fundamental norm will be used to help analyze particular problems, and appeal will be made to procedures rational persons using these standards and norms would accept for a society in which they expected to live.

Discipline of licensed professionals presents one type of burden/benefit decision and is analyzed in this chapter. Procedures for professional discipline are well developed and primarily fit the adversary adjudication model. Application of the theory to this topic is relatively straightforward and practice generally conforms to the theory. Considerable description is provided to confirm this claim. Professional disciplining is thus a good introductory illustration of the theory.

The final chapter on employment decisions involves more difficult and controversial issues. Different decision-making models are appropriate for different types of employment decisions, so different procedural principles are relevant to them. Moreover, as actual practice is quite varied, prescriptive implications of the theory are more evident. Obviously, a full analysis of this complex and important topic would require a much longer discussion. The point here is not to provide a full analysis of procedural justice in employment decisions, only to show that our theory can be useful in helping to sort out the issues and guide resolution of them.

The issue in professional discipline is whether an individual has violated norms of professional conduct. The procedures for discipline of licensed professionals vary from state to state and often between professions. Despite the variety of procedures used, it is useful to describe a typical system. It is usually a four part process: (1) investigation into probable cause, (2) hearing, (3) review by a board, and (4) final determination by a state agency or court.

Possible sanctions include a private reprimand or admonition, a public reprimand, probation, and suspension or revocation of license. Often the process is controlled by a state administrative procedure act.

The process usually begins with a complaint filed with a committee of a state or local professional organization, such as a county medical or dental society. A local committee, frequently with the assistance of an investigator from the state organization, investigates the complaint to determine whether there is probable cause to believe that a violation of professional regulations has occurred. Although a hearing is usually held, this part is predominantly investigatory. If the committee determines that probable cause exists, then it so reports and a more formal hearing is held. The same committee that conducted the first hearing might conduct the second.

After the second hearing, the committee reports its findings and recommendations to a state board which reviews them. Because the process is considered part of an agency decision, the board usually has full powers to review and alter findings, conclusions, and proposed sanctions. Either the board makes the final decision or its findings and recommendations are conveyed to a state agency head or other body. The authority to discipline derives from legislation that might designate the highest authority on professional discipline to be a board of a professional organization, a separately appointed one, or an administrative department of the state government. The primary exception is the legal profession. Courts have always maintained the right to control who practices before them. (Many regulatory administrative agencies, such as the Securities and Exchange Commission, also possess this power.) Consequently, the judiciary has an inherent power to control practice before it, and this has been extended to the whole legal profession (ABA 1979, Standard 2.1). For lawyers, the highest appellate court thus makes the final decision. Of course, courts also possess standard powers of judicial review for disciplinary decisions of other agencies.

This full process is normally abbreviated if a recommendation is for no or minor discipline such as a private reprimand. At any point a recommendation is made for no discipline, the process usually stops. Sometimes the agency is not considered a party to the process and so is not permitted to appeal (see Morris 1984, 124, 132). This roughly corresponds to the no double jeopardy principle in criminal law. If at some point in the process a recommendation is made for minor discipline and the professional accepts it, then the discipline is carried out.

Although this chapter focuses on state licensed professionals, this is not the only context for professional discipline and many licensed occupations are not normally classified as professions. Indeed, the legal, health, and public teaching professions are the main licensed professions. Engineers, professors, and many other professionals need not be licensed, but professional societies can censure, suspend, or expel members. The process is remarkably similar to that for state licenses. A special committee or the board of the organization has final authority for disciplinary matters (see, for example, IEEE 1980). After a complaint is received, an individual or committee investigates, often holding a hearing, to determine whether there is probable cause to believe that a violation occurred. If there is, a formal hearing is held by a committee or the board. If a committee conducts the hearing, often the society's board reviews its findings and recommendations. In short, the same four step process often exists with perhaps omission of agency or court determination.

Law and Adjudication

The principles developed in chapter 7 present a clear and strong case for legally imposing procedural principles in disciplining licensed professionals, especially by suspension or revocation of licenses. Those principles are state action, deprivation, importance of the decision, use of special standards, and availability of alternative protections. First, such discipline involves state action. As professionals are licensed under state law, even if the discipline is conducted by a board of a professional organization, the state is simply using it to implement state policies. Officials authorized by state law are acting against a professional.

Second, discipline involves deprivation. It sets back a professional's interests. Most crucially, if a license is suspended or revoked, a professional loses the opportunity to practice the profession and thus usually his or her livelihood. (In some occupations, states merely give certification which is not required to practice the occupation. In such cases, the effect on the professional is significantly less.) Professionals necessarily rely on their licenses in their careers. If a license is required to practice a profession, a strong state monopoly exists with eligibility (noncompetitive) criteria. Even if the penalty is a reprimand, there is a stigma and loss of reputation that can affect a professional's ability to attract clients and thus earn a living. Although a private reprimand might not affect clients and income, it still affects the professional's self-respect and reputation among those who know of it. Thus, all the elements of our analysis of deprivation apply.

Third, important interests of the professional—wealth and reputation—are at stake. Although a professional does not have a vested property interest in a license because the state cannot make irrevocable contracts affecting the public welfare, he or she has an important liberty interest—the liberty to engage in an occupation (Morris 1986, 790, 798). As early as 1889, the U.S. Supreme Court recognized a qualified right of citizens to pursue any profession (*Dent v. West Virginia*, 129 U.S. 114 (1889)). This right has force with respect to original licensing. However, it does not necessarily make disciplining nonviolators (AU errors) morally worse than not disciplining violators (~AD errors), that is, give a moral cost reason to avoid disciplining the innocent more than letting the guilty go.

In chapter 7 we noted that the moral importance of an individual's interest is nonexistent or counts for less if a benefit was not primarily conferred for the individual's advantage. If the benefit is intended for someone else's advantage, then the individual has no moral claim and there are no moral error costs. That is precisely the situation with professionals. Although professional organizations usually seek required state licensing to practice the profession for the economic benefits of restricted competition (Gellhorn 1976, 11), that is not an acceptable justification. A rational layperson would not accept the state restricting access to an occupation merely to increase the salaries of its practitioners. Instead, an acceptable justification must rest on the benefits to professionals' clients and the public—protection from unethical or incompetent practice (Morris 1984, 10; ABA 1979, Standard 1.1). The state has no more interest in the income of a professional than of a gas station attendant. Some procedures for professional discipline seem to ignore this point, focusing on the harm to the professional with insufficient regard to the well-being of clients. Nonetheless, the economic error costs at stake suffice to outweigh the direct costs of legal enforcement.

Finally, the two chief reasons against legal imposition of procedural principles do not apply. First, a professional has no other means of protecting his or her interests, such as a negotiated contract or a civil suit. Granted, professionals might sue for defamation people who report them for unprofessional conduct. However, as discussed below, persons should generally have immunity from such suits. Second, although sometimes special standards are involved, those who judge professional conduct are capable of applying them. The issues are usually moral ones that laypersons are quite capable of judging—stealing from clients, unfair practice, and so forth. Incompetence does usually involve professional standards and thus sometimes expertise to evaluate it, but hearings and recommendations are normally conducted and made by other members of the profession. Judges or administrators are capable of reviewing a record to determine whether procedures were followed and judgments were within the limits of discretion3.

The case for legal imposition of procedures for discipline by professional societies is weaker. State action is not involved. Often no monopoly exists; for example, most engineers have several societies relevant to their practice. Although a deprivation with stigma is involved, the setback to interests is not as great as a loss of license. Moreover, as membership is voluntary, a professional has contractually agreed to the procedures so alternative protections are available. Nevertheless, common law outside the United States has traditionally required many professional societies to conform to the principles of natural justice (see Flick 1984, 29, 32). One might explain this on the ground that often the societies did have near monopoly status and though not legally required, membership was crucially important in pursuing a professional career. Moreover, natural justice does not require all the detailed principles developed in Part I.

The weaker case for legal imposition of procedural principles in professional societies can be handled in two different ways. First, our theory basically implies that for those in which membership is not very important, only ethical enforcement is appropriate. The ethical sense of members and refusal to accept unethical procedures often suffices for enforcement. Second, as membership becomes more important, say, due to a near monopoly or public reliance on membership in employing professionals, one can impose the principles of impartiality, opportunity to be heard, grounds for decisions, and formal justice more strongly. For example, some but not all of the elements of an opportunity to be heard can be legally required. In effect, this is the approach of natural justice—legally requiring the basics of impartiality and opportunity to be heard. How much should be required involves application of the fundamental norm to determine whether the reduction of error costs and increased process benefits outweigh the increased direct costs of legal enforcement.

The criteria developed in the last chapter for determining which decision-making model is appropriate for situations support use of adversary adjudication for the central decision concerning professional discipline. First, the issue presents itself to the professional as a conflict or dispute. The issue is one of imposing a burden (reprimand) or terminating a benefit (suspension or revocation of a license) with necessary collateral reliance. Second, for the professional it is a no-win situation. Third, the standards and subject matter for decision involve discretion3. The subject matter is violation of a code of ethics; so the norms, or at least many of them, are moral ones in a stronger sense than in many legal rules. The choice of sanctions clearly involves a decision among permissible alternatives. Finally, adequate time usually exists for an adversary hearing. This is the model generally used. In some situations (discussed below), suspension by bureaucratic investigation might be appropriate pending the outcome of an adversary adjudication.

The professional and bureaucratic models of decision making should and do have a role in professional licensing and discipline. The original granting of a license involves conferring a benefit, no conflict, and judgment of skills and abilities as well as character which call for the professional service model. However, the process is not purely professional, because the goal is set by the organization and the value is not the applicant's well-being but that of the public. The process for licensing should thus combine the professional and bureaucratic models. Practice generally conforms to such a combination. One has bureaucratic investigation by professionals. As professional expertise is involved, courts usually defer to the expertise of the licensing authority (Morris 1984, 137–38).

The bureaucratic investigatory model is also at least acceptable for determining whether there is probable cause to believe that a professional has violated a standard of conduct. Although there is conflict, it is not strong as no determination is yet being made to impose a sanction. A finding of probable cause to hold a hearing is not a major loss. However, the standards are no more precise than for the subsequent decision, even though the level of evidence needed is less. Once formal charges are made, a stronger conflict situation with greater possible loss exists and adversary adjudication should be used. Again, practice generally conforms to these points.

Impartiality

The adversary adjudication model makes all the subprinciples of impartiality—independence, no conflicting interest, bias, or commingling of functions—applicable. We briefly review how these subprinciples pertain. The total or preponderant membership of disciplinary committees being members of the profession can raise issues of impartiality. Except for some final decisions by administrative agencies, the disciplinary process is usually conducted by members of the same profession. In some states, nonprofessionals serve on disciplinary committees. For example, in Florida, at least one third of the members of bar grievance committees must be nonlawyers (Integration Rule of the Fla. Bar, Art. XI, R. 11.03(2)(c); see also ABA 1979, Standards 3.4 and 3.6).

As discussed in chapter 2, the professional membership of disciplinary committees can create indirect conflicts of interest and possible bias. In *Gibson v. Berryhill* (411 U.S. 564 (1973)), the independent Alabama optometrists were not permitted to hear charges of unprofessional conduct against employed optometrists, who were indirectly prohibited from serving on the disciplinary board. Another example, although decided on nondelegation grounds, is *Allen v. California Bd. of Barber Examiners* (25 Cal. App. 3d 1014, 102 Cal. Rptr. 368 (Cal. Ct. App. 1972)). In this case, the board had revoked barbers' licenses for providing services at below minimum fees. The power to regulate a competitor's business practices, the court claimed, requires stringent standards to guide the exercise of discretion. The underlying issue was the conflict of interest between members of the profession in regulating prices. In short, barbers could protect their business and income by prohibiting severe competition, so the board was not impartial.

A more subtle influence might be operative. Professional licenses have probably most frequently been revoked for conviction of a crime or violation of economic rules. Criminal convictions are public and not easily ignored. Economic rules are those like fair competition (advertising, minimum prices, and so on) that can affect the economic well-being of other professionals. Professionals have self-interested reasons to report and sanction others whose conduct might adversely affect professional income.

The pattern of conduct for which sanctions are imposed suggests an inherent partiality in disciplinary committees composed of members of the profession (for detailed discussion, see Bayles 1989, 191–94). The bias favors professionals against clients but operates against professionals for conduct economically detrimental to other members of the profession. If such a pattern of partiality plausibly exists, then impartiality supports increasing the nonprofessionals on disciplinary committees to a majority. The justification for licensing is protection of the public, not the economic well-being of professionals. Even if no partiality is operative, professional dominance of disciplinary committees might create the appearance of injustice and decrease public confidence in the justice of the system. The result can be demoralization and cynicism about professionals. Consequently, rational persons would prefer laypersons on disciplinary committees, perhaps comprising half the membership.

Another general concern is with the separation of functions. As discussed in chapter 2, commingling investigatory and adjudicatory functions need not prevent impartiality (see *Withrow v. Larkin*, 421 U.S. 35 (1975)). In many situations, the same local committee investigates whether probable cause exists, and if it so finds, holds an adversary hearing. We earlier claimed that it is not necessary to separate investigation from decision making, especially when the investigation is really a determination of probable cause. However, full investigation can be quite close to denying impartiality. For example, if members of the board investigate a professional and testify against the person, the risk of unfairness is great (*Rogers v. Texas Optometry Bd.* (609 S.W.2d 248, 250 (Texas 1980)). The direct costs of excluding people who investigate generally or for probable cause from serving on hearing committees are few. As excluding them can decrease error costs and increase the process benefit of confidence, they should normally be excluded. For example, Florida law excludes members of the professional board who sat on inquiry panels from participating when the board reviews the panels' results (Fla. Stat. § 455.225(5) (1985); see also ABA 1979, Standards 8.11 commentary and 8.12 commentary).

In adversary adjudication, strong reasons exist to separate the prosecutorial and adjudicatory functions. It is not necessary to prohibit both functions being conducted by one agency, for example, a state licensing board, but personnel performing the different functions in a particular case should be isolated from one another (see Morris 1984, 88, 90, 99; ABA 1979, Standard 3.2). It is a denial of impartiality for the same person to perform both functions in the same case; yet, at least in the past some states have permitted this. At least at one time, California rules, for example, did not permit alleged bias or prejudice as a reason for disqualifying members of the Board of Governors of the State Bar from participating in a disciplinary decision (7 Cal. Jur. 3d *Attorneys at Law* § 120 (1973)). This precludes a challenge even if a member has acted as prosecutor in obtaining the facts (*Golden v. State Bar*, 213 Cal. 237, 2 P.2d 325 (1931)). According to our theory, this mixture of functions should be legally prohibited. A prosecutor tries to build as strong a case as possible against the defendant, and the resulting mind-set is too great to expect the ordinary person to overcome and render an impartial judgment (Morris 1986, 801).

A better practice, and one often followed when disciplinary procedures are under a state administrative procedure act, is for an independent hearing officer to conduct the hearing to receive evidence (Morris 1986, 802; see, for example, Fla. Stat. § 455.225(4) (1985)). This provides full protection from the commingling of functions, even investigatory ones. However, as the hearing officer's report is still usually acted on by a board composed of members of the profession, it does not eliminate the problems of possible partiality discussed above.

To ensure the independence of investigatory or hearing committees and appointed boards, members should not be removable at will (ABA 1979, Standards 3.4 and 3.6). They need not have the life tenure of federal judges; indeed, as service is often voluntary, few people would agree to serve were membership for life. Furthermore, not even federal judges are unremovable. But some assurance of independence is important, so they should only be removable for cause.

Opportunity to Be Heard

The full set of subprinciples of an opportunity to be heard also apply with the adversary adjudication model. Before considering some issues that they raise, we briefly consider not fully applying them in summary suspensions. We then consider a few issues of timeliness, openness, and presentation of evidence.

Summary suspension A full adversary hearing should be and is always held before a final decision to suspend or revoke a license. Sometimes suspensions are imposed pending a hearing. The basic rationale for so doing is the necessity to act quickly to protect the public (Morris 1986, 799; Morris 1984, 113; Davis 1972, 172; Davis 1977, 287; ABA 1979, Standard 6.5; Flick 1984, 40). As the purpose of licensing is protection of the public, if that protection is significantly jeopardized, then it overrides some protections for professionals. There can be significant error costs in permitting an unethical or incompetent professional to continue to practice. For example, Illinois law provides for suspension of physicians' licenses without a hearing if "a physicians's [*sic*] continuation in practice would constitute an immediate danger to the public" (Ill. Ann. Stat. ch. 111 § 4441 (Smith-Hurd 1978)). Proceedings must also be instituted at the time of the suspension.

A frequent basis of suspension without a hearing is a criminal conviction. Usually it is not necessary that the crime relate to the practice of a profession (Morris 1984, 40), but that should be necessary. For example, conviction of a nurse for willful violation of tax laws would rarely reflect on suitability to practice nursing, but it would often do so for lawyers and accountants, especially those involved in tax practice. It is arguable that any criminal conviction should suffice for lawyers, because as officers of the court they are supposed to uphold the law. Nonetheless, for lawyers, as opposed to other professions, the crime is often required to be one involving "moral turpitude," that is, showing some defect of character.

Although often described as automatic suspension, some review is usually involved. One reason for review is to determine whether the criminal conviction does reflect on qualifications to practice the profession. For example, the automatic suspension of a lawyer in Ohio involves a review within ninety days by the Board of Commissioners on Grievances and Discipline to determine whether the offense involves moral turpitude. The Board's action is not final, it only recommends to the Supreme Court which makes the final decision (Sup. Ct. Rules for the Government of the Bar of Ohio, Gov. R. V(8)). Consequently, there can be considerable delay between conviction and suspension. The issue is not whether the professional committed the act, but whether it reflects adversely on the person's qualifications for practicing the profession and the appropriate penalty (ABA 1979, Standard 9.4 commentary). As these are more matters of rule interpretation than fact, the absence of a full adversary hearing is not highly detrimental.

The Florida Bar has a more expeditious procedure for suspension following conviction for a felony (Integration Rule of the Florida Bar, Art. XI, R. 11.07; see also ABA 1979, Standard 9.1). The court entering such a judgment must immediately notify the clerk of the supreme court and the executive director of the state bar. Suspension automatically follows in eleven days unless within that time the lawyer files with the Supreme Court a petition to modify or terminate the suspension. If the lawyer makes a timely petition, suspension is delayed until the court acts. If the petition is late, the suspension continues until modified or terminated by the court.

The choice between the slower Ohio procedure and the faster Florida procedure primarily depends on a judgment of the error costs involved. The Ohio method has a perhaps narrower standard for suspension—a crime involving moral turpitude, although the Florida grounds are only felony convictions. The central issue is whether it is preferable to err on the side of suspensions or failure to suspend. This, in turn, depends on a preference for protecting potential clients and the administration of justice or protecting professionals. The Florida system arguably provides more protection to clients and the administration of justice than the Ohio system. Consequently, at least for lawyers, rational persons would prefer the Florida system for a society in which they expected to live; one who commits a felony cannot be trusted as an officer of the court to uphold the law. The only exceptions would be any felonies that required only negligence. For other professions, fewer felony convictions are arguably related to the practice of the profession. Even for them, immediate notification of the board with a requirement that it act within thirty days is certainly plausible and one that rational persons would prefer as the possible error costs to the public of permitting an unqualified professional to continue to practice outweigh those to professionals.

Timeliness Notice of charges against a professional should be given prior to the inquiry into probable cause, and in practice adequate notice is required for adversary hearings (Morris 1984, 109). Proceedings should not be delayed any longer than necessary for a fair hearing. An innocent professional deserves to be cleared as soon as reasonably possible. Promptness is especially important if a professional's license has been suspended pending an adversary hearing (Morris 1984, 61). Although guilty professionals might be interested in delaying proceedings as long as possible, the concern for timeliness is not based solely on their interests. The public's interests support removal of incompetent or corrupt professionals as soon as possible (Morris 1984, 16). The Ohio Bar, for example, requires that investigations be completed in sixty days, and that decisions about dispositions of complaints be rendered within another thirty days (Sup. Ct. Rules for the Government of the Bar of Ohio, Gov. R. V (4)).

Any increased direct costs of similar time limitations for all professions are surely outweighed by the reduced error costs of mistaken suspensions.

Another issue is delay in bringing charges and proceedings against professionals. General statutes of limitations do not apply to professional disciplinary proceedings (Morris 1984, 55; see ABA 1979, Standard 4.6). The public's strong interest in protection militates against permitting a defense of delay in starting proceedings (see Morris 1984, 58). Nevertheless, an equitable doctrine of laches can be used as a defense if the professional is harmed or prejudiced by the delay (Morris 1984, 56). The harm must be more than the mere passage of time. These rules appear to be a reasonable balancing of the competing interests and related error costs of the public in protection and professionals in not being harmed. Indeed, they do little more than spell out the principles underlying statutes of limitation; the difference is that statutes of limitation draw bright lines to avoid having to make difficult balancing decisions in individual cases.

A major issue of timeliness is the postponement of procedures pending the outcome of court proceedings. Sometimes disciplinary proceedings are suspended pending the outcome of criminal or civil court cases. In Oklahoma, a revocation of a professional's license for conviction of a crime cannot occur until all legal rights of appeal have been exhausted, which can be years after the original trial (see *State v. Birdwell*, 592 P.2d 520 (Okla. 1979); see also ABA 1979, Standard 9.2 commentary). When proceedings are delayed and are confidential (see below), the public can unknowingly be subject to the practices of an incompetent or corrupt professional for years. Of course, the public is protected if the professional is suspended pending the outcome of appeals.

An asymmetry exists between criminal conviction and nonconviction. A conviction should be sufficient to establish the commission of a disciplinary offense, but a failure to convict does not establish that no disciplinary offense occurred. There are two reasons for this. First, the standard of persuasion in criminal cases is beyond a reasonable doubt, but a lower standard exists for disciplinary matters (see below). Fulfillment of the higher standard automatically fulfills the lower. But failure of proof beyond a reasonable doubt does not imply that a lower burden of persuasion has not been met. Second, the substantive standards for disciplinary action can be and should be broader than for criminal convictions. Conduct can suffice for revocation of a license without constituting a criminal offense. For example, incompetence is often a basis for revocation of a license but is not criminal.

Consequently, as there are different grounds and standards of proof for disciplinary and criminal decisions, disciplinary proceedings should not usually be delayed pending the outcome of court cases. This approach is the more modern one (see Integration Rule of the Fla. Bar, Art. XI, R. 11.04(2)(c); Rules of Procedure of the State Bar of Cal., R. 19.1(a)). Reasons do exist for making some exceptions and postponing proceedings. For example, if court decisions might expedite or aid proceedings or the disciplinary proceedings might prejudice the case, then postponement might be appropriate, although there are countervailing reasons as well (see Rules of Procedure of the State Bar of Cal., R. 19.1(b), for a good statement of appropriate considerations).

Openness The openness of disciplinary proceedings is a difficult issue. In looking at it, we see how careful consideration of the reasons for and against openness can indicate how rational persons would balance factors. The prevailing practice is for strict confidentiality of preliminary investigations and inquiries into probable cause, more openness about hearings, and a presumption of making public final decisions to impose discipline. Besides the reasons for open public proceedings presented in chapter 3, other reasons support openness of disciplinary proceedings. One reason is the process benefit of confidence. Professional disciplinary proceedings might appear (and perhaps actual be) improper. If potential clients have reasons to suspect that professions do not adequately police themselves, the confidentiality of proceedings probably increases such suspicions and contributes to a further loss of confidence. Potential clients also have an interest in not contracting with possibly incompetent or unscrupulous professionals. Reasonable potential clients might not want to engage a professional even if there is only a strong suspicion of misconduct, particularly if the alleged misconduct pertains to misuse of client funds or other conduct directly detrimental to clients. The confidentiality of proceedings prevents clients taking such factors into account.

Nonetheless, good reasons exist for keeping confidential preliminary investigations and probable cause proceedings. Privacy can be especially important for accused professionals. A good name or reputation is an important attribute for most professionals. Completely unfounded charges can be made against them by irate former clients or others, but such charges need to be investigated. Were investigations made public, a professional's reputation could be severely damaged despite a subsequent complete exoneration—no probable cause for an adversary hearing. Consequently, so long as those proceedings are expeditiously completed, the protection of professionals outweighs the public interest in openness. A contrary policy would subject professionals to damaging but groundless attack.

A reasonable quid pro quo for this protection of confidentiality is protection of complainants from suit for bringing complaints and witnesses for their testimony. Illinois, for example, provides immunity for all good faith reports against physicians (Ill. Ann. Stat. ch. 111 § 4452 (Smith-Hurd 1978); see also ABA 1979, Standard 8.37). California has a similar provision for reports to the Medical Quality Review Committee, except that it apparently applies only to other physicians and surgeons and permits the admission of reports in defamation actions alleging the statements to be false and malicious (36 Cal. Jur. 3d *Healing Arts and Institutions* § 120 (1977)). Complainant and witness immunity are important, for without them more error costs are likely from unreported violations and failure to obtain accurate facts.

At the hearing stage, the grounds for open proceedings are stronger. The purpose of confidentiality is still usually to protect the professional's reputation, because often adversary hearings can be public at the professional's request (see, for example, Sup. Ct. Rules for the Government of the Bar of Ohio, R. V 21(a)). If hearings are normally open, a professional probably cannot insist on confidentiality to protect the professional/client privilege (Morris 1984, 106). Because there has been a finding of probable cause, the public's interest in knowledge of possible wrongdoing by the professional is increased. Moreover, the standards of proof required for discipline are often higher than the balance of probabilities. That is, a professional might not be disciplined even though the preponderance of the evidence is that he or she committed a disciplinary offense. It is entirely reasonable for potential clients to avoid such professionals, yet with closed hearings a finding of "innocence" almost always keeps the records confidential.

Except in unusual circumstances, the reasons for open disciplinary hearings outweigh those for confidentiality (ABA 1979, Standard 8.25 and commentary). It is one thing not to revoke a professional's license without strong reasons, but quite another to prevent potential clients having access to information about possible incompetence or unprofessional practice so that they can make their own decisions about which ones to engage. Moreover, failure to discipline is not proof of innocence, only of insufficient evidence, and cautious clients might not wish to take chances. The private nature of matters often arising in determinations of incompetence, such as mental illness or addiction, provide stronger grounds for confidentiality (see ABA 1979, Standard 12.3). But these concerns are not present in all cases concerning competence, so at most an exception should be made for hearings involving mental illness or drug dependence.

It follows that the case for confidentiality after final determination to impose discipline (or remove for incompetence) falls before that for disclosure. Not only should the fact of discipline be public, but the grounds for discipline should also be public. The public is better informed of the protections afforded by professional discipline, and other professionals are advised of the type of conduct deemed impermissible. Such information is usually available. If removal of a license is based on health reasons (including drug dependence), then the specific reasons need not be made public.

One anomaly, especially with lawyers, concerns private reprimands. A public reprimand is part of a court record or bar proceedings. A private reprimand, however, is communicated only to the professional. California law holds that even private reprimands do not require complete confidentiality; if an attorney merits condemnation, then the public has an interest in knowing (*Chronicle Publishing Co. v. Superior Court*, 54 Cal. 2d 548, 7 Cal. Rptr. 109, 354 P.2d 637 (1960)). In contrast, Florida law preserves confidentiality of private reprimands (4 Fla. Jur. 2d *Attorneys at Law* § 94 (1978)). However, Florida has precise criteria for misconduct for which a private reprimand is inappropriate (Integration Rule of the Fla. Bar, Art. XI, R. 11.04(6)(c)(ii)). If misconduct does not prejudice client interests and it is not the case that the professional should have known that the conduct violated standards, then confidentiality can be justified. One can view the reprimand as primarily practice advice. Even then, the advice might be useful to other lawyers, so it is worthwhile publishing the case without identifying information for their enlightenment. If one lawyer engages in questionable practices, others probably do too.

Presentation of evidence Only a couple of issues need to be examined concerning the presentation of evidence. As preliminary or probable cause investigations are made by bureaucratic investigation, our theory does not require all features of a full adversary hearing. But as we saw in the previous chapter, most of the principles of presentation of evidence apply to bureaucratic investigation, and the recent trend appears to be to include more of them. Generally, an accused professional has a right to be present, to present evidence, to have counsel, call witness, and so on (see Integration Rule of the Fla. Bar, Art. XI, R. 11.04(3)). The main exception pertains to the full jury trial rules of evidence, which need not be followed (Integration Rule of the Fla. Bar, Art. XI, R. 11.04(2)(b)). When investigations and probable cause determinations are conducted according to an administrative procedure act, the rights of an accused may be less.

Because a formal disciplinary hearing is adversary adjudication, most of the features of a civil trial should and do apply. Florida law, for example, simply prescribes that the rules of civil procedure apply to bar disciplinary hearings except as specifically modified (Integration Rule of the Fla. Bar, Art. XI, R. 11.06(3)(a); see ABA 1979, Standards 8.29 through 8.36). These principles include counsel and confrontation and cross-examination of adverse witnesses (Morris 1984, 71). However, the right to counsel is that of civil proceedings, not criminal ones, so counsel need not be provided. As the rights are those of civil and not criminal proceedings, people do not have to be advised of them (Morris 1984, 102–03). Our theory supports not having to provide counsel, because no moral costs attach to incorrect decisions to discipline (although they do in some civil cases).

One area of disagreement is the application of technical rules of evidence. Ohio, for example, requires adherence to civil rules of evidence in all bar disciplinary hearings (Sup. Ct. Rules for the Government of the Bar of Ohio, R. V(35)), but technical rules and the hearsay rule apparently do not apply in Illinois (*In Re Heirich*, 10 Ill. 2d 357, 140 N.E.2d 825 (1956)) and California may be unclear (7 Cal. Jur. 3d *Attorneys at Law* § 108 (1973)). These examples pertain to discipline of lawyers, who have traditionally been the most legally protected professionals, no doubt due to their knowing how to use the legal system to obtain the protections and the subtle bias of their fellow practitioners on the bench. Before other licensing boards, strict rules of evidence are not usually followed (Morris 1984, 116; Morris 1986, 803). As there are fairly strong arguments against the traditional technical rules of evidence, not following them is not a defect (Bayles 1987, 55–58); indeed, if the criticisms are sound, not following them can be a benefit.

Nevertheless, revoking professional licenses on grounds of hearsay evidence alone is questionable and not usually permitted (Morris 1984, 119). Indeed, one commentator supports the residuum rule for revocation (Morris 1984, 120). Recall that this rule requires some evidence that would be legally admissible. However, if evidence would be admissible in a court of law over objection or legally inadmissible evidence is admitted without objection, then it should be weighed like any other evidence. Reasonable people can disagree over these fine points; our theory cannot eliminate all disagreements.

Findings, Reasons, and Formal Justice

The adversary adjudication model requires application of all the subprinciples of standards, statement of findings and reasons, burden of proof, and judicial review. Generally, all disciplinary proceedings—bureaucratic investigations of probable cause and adversary adjudication hearings—involve a statement of findings and recommendations. One reason is that one or more further steps are necessary before a final decision is made, so findings and recommendations must be prepared for the next higher level. Recommendations are not the same as reasons, but as recommendations are to be reviewed by higher authorities, they need supporting reasons. Two issues deserve analysis.

One is the burden of persuasion. Theoretically, the burden of production should fall on the person making a claim, and the burden of persuasion should be a preponderance of the evidence unless evidentiary problems or moral costs justify shifting the burden or setting a higher standard. In professional disciplinary decisions, the burden is thus on the state to establish the basis for revocation (see Morris 1984, 114). As discussed in chapter 6, if there is a moral aim or purpose jeopardized by an error of one type but not another, then the burden of persuasion should be higher.

By analogy, one might claim that the same burden of persuasion should apply in professional disciplinary actions as in criminal cases. Both involve sanctions for wrongful conduct and should involve a presumption of innocence. However, there are reasons against the criminal law standard of proof beyond a reasonable doubt. First, as we have already seen, there is no moral cost to one type of error over another. Licenses are not for the benefit of professionals but the public. Consequently, there is no reason to prefer errors affecting one more than the other. Second, there are no peculiar evidentiary problems and the economic error costs for professionals are not greater than those for the public. Although perhaps often devastating, the loss of a license to practice a profession is not as great a loss of liberty as incarceration. Nor is the sanction the same as a fine (ABA 1979, Standard 6.14 (prohibiting fines); professionals are not deprived of money they currently have. Instead, they are forbidden to obtain future income by practicing that profession. Earning as much or more in other ways is permitted. Yet the continued practice of unethical or incompetent professionals can be a greater risk to the public than most common criminals. Because professionals normally deal with several members of the public each day but criminals at most prey on a few each day, more members of the public are likely to be exposed to professional misconduct than that of the ordinary criminal.

Consequently, the burden of persuasion should be less than beyond a reasonable doubt. Indeed, there does not seem to be any reason for it to be greater than the preponderance of the evidence. This is often the case; disbarment in Ohio, for example, is on the preponderance of the evidence (6 O. Jur. 3d *Attorneys at Law* § 79 (1981)). However, some states use a higher standard; Illinois uses clear and convincing evidence (Ill. Sup. Ct. R. 753(c)(6); see also ABA 1979, Standard 8.40).

Another issue concerns the scope of review. As noted in chapter 3, appeals or review do not increase accuracy unless the reviewer is less likely than the original decisionmaker to be mistaken; without that condition, direct costs are increased without any decrease in error costs. Chances of accuracy are increased if a reviewer does not reconsider all aspects but only checks for significant errors beyond the scope of reasonable discretion3. In short, if a reviewer conducts a de novo inquiry, the benefits of checking the decision at the previous level (reduced error costs) are often lost (Davis 1969, 142). As process benefits do not seem to be greatly enhanced by a broad scope of review, they alone do not support much increase in direct costs.

Unfortunately, this point is often flouted or practically ignored in disciplining professionals. Most administrative reviews are considered part of the administrative decision-making process, so reconsideration of all findings, conclusions, and recommendations is possible (see MSA § 4-216(d)). Even after a hearing and review by the Board of Commissioners on Grievances and Discipline, the Supreme Court of Ohio retains final judgment even on facts (6 O. Jur. 3d *Attorneys at Law* § 79 (1981)); and in California the Board of

Governors of the State Bar may set aside a grievance committee recommendation and hear the case de novo (7 Ca. Jur. 3d *Attorneys at Law* § 130 (1973) citing Cal. Business and Practice Code § 6043). Similarly, a court reviewing action of a healing art licensing board may substitute its own evaluation of the evidence (36 Cal. Jur. 3d *Healing Arts and Institutions* § 115 (1977)).

A preferable procedure is that of the Florida Bar. In Supreme Court review of disciplinary decisions by lower courts or trial by a referee, the burden is on a party seeking to show that the report is erroneous, unlawful, or unjustified (Integration Rule of the Fla. Bar, Art. XI, R. 11.09(3)(e)). This essentially limits the scope of review, although it still permits some overturning of findings of fact on the basis of the record. Moreover, reviewing authorities should perhaps be prohibited from increasing penalties, for example, from suspension to revocation. This limit is analogous to the principle of double jeopardy in criminal cases.

Generally, discipline of professionals is subject to the usual legal standards of formal justice for administrative decision making. That is, decisions must be consistent or a good explanation given, precedents must be adhered to unless a justification is given for not doing so, and agency rules must be followed. For the bar, courts will follow their standard practice, which might involve a more rigid adherence to precedent than in administrative agencies.

Nevertheless, consistency in the punishment given is difficult to achieve. In chapter 4 we considered the Supreme Court's struggle to narrow the scope of discretion3 in death penalty cases yet permit individualized justice. Similar problems beset professional discipline. Rarely does a precise schedule of punishments for the variable fact situations exist, and even if it did, it might jeopardize the adversary adjudication model's goal of individualized justice. As individualized justice requires sensitivity to the fact situations in particular cases, it is difficult for a reviewing authority to second guess the judgment of those persons who actually hear testimony. In this process of tailoring punishment to fit the wrong, precedents are not very useful. Again, the ideal of individualized justice requires taking into account those aspects of a case that might not have been present in previous ones. Still, as we have seen, Florida has precise criteria for lawyer conduct that cannot be sanctioned with a private reprimand. Moreover, several states now have complex sentencing guidelines for criminal cases. Even if nondiscretionary sentencing rules are inappropriate, more uniformity and consistency than exists might be achieved.

Recall that in the death penalty cases the Supreme Court considered one aspect of narrowing discretion to be precise legislative definitions of crimes for which the death penalty can be imposed. The same point arises in professional discipline; a person should not be disciplined for conduct that was not clearly prohibited by professional standards and rules. Professionals must have notice of prohibited conduct. A person of ordinary intelligence must be able to determine what the rule requires or prohibits (Morris 1984, 23). However, courts have been generous in construing terms such as unprofessional conduct, immoral conduct, and unfair practice to permit license revocation (see Morris 1984, 76–87). Although more laxity is permissible in professional discipline than imposing the death penalty because the interests involved are less important, they should be as precise as reasonably possible.

Summary

This chapter has tested our theory against procedures for professional discipline. Generally, current practice conforms to what the theory requires. The implications and conformity are most clear for the legal imposition of procedural principles and use of the adversary adjudication model for professional disciplinary decisions. Legal imposition is justified by our criteria because professional discipline involves state action, deprives persons of government monopolized benefits on which they necessarily rely thereby imposing a stigma, and the importance for the individual makes error costs significant enough to support the costs of legal enforcement. However, moral error costs are not involved, because professional licenses are for the benefit of the public, not professionals. Our theoretical criteria against legal imposition—alternative means of protection and inability to judge by special standards—do not apply.

Our theoretical criteria call for the predominant use of adversary adjudication to make disciplinary decisions. The issue presents the professional as a conflict; the professional stands only to lose; a standard for evaluation involving a moral judgment exists; and there is usually time for such a procedure. Even though the standards are not precise, bureaucratic investigation may be used in the preliminary stage of determining probable cause since the conflict is less and a negative decision is not final and so is less important.

As the adversary adjudication model applies, so do all the subprinciples of impartiality, opportunity to be heard, grounds for decisions, and formal justice.

The principle of impartiality requires absence of conflicting interest or bias, independence, and separation of functions. Because professionals are judged by other members of the profession, the possibility of indirect conflicts of interest between segments of a profession exists. An appearance of bias favoring professionals against clients and disfavoring them when their conduct threatens professional economic well-being also exists. Consequently, probably no more than half the members of disciplinary boards should belong to the profession. In practice, persons involved in investigatory decisions of probable cause often participate in determinations of actual guilt. As eliminating this commingling of functions would not greatly increase direct costs and could decrease error costs and increase confidence, it should be eliminated. Moreover, no one with a prosecutorial role in a case should be, and is not permitted to be, involved in decision making.

Most or all of the subprinciples of an opportunity to be heard also apply. However, to protect the public, suspension of a license pending an investigation and final determination can be justified. Suspension following conviction of a crime reflecting adversely on a professional's qualifications for practicing the profession is also justifiable; sometimes, however, the process takes longer than appropriate, placing the public at a continuing and unjustifiable risk. Disciplinary proceedings should provide adequate notice and be concluded as quickly as possible without jeopardizing rights to be heard. Promptness is especially important when professionals are suspended pending results. Delay in the start of an investigation and proceedings should not, absent a showing of harm or prejudice, be a defense. Rarely should disciplinary proceedings be postponed pending the results of court cases, although competing reasons need to be balanced in some cases.

The principle of openness must be applied with a concern for the importance of privacy to the professional involved. A reasonable balance is struck by confidentiality of probable cause investigations but open hearings. A quid pro quo for confidentiality of investigations is immunity from civil suits for complainants and witnesses. In hearings, the requirements of the full adversary adjudication model should apply—right to counsel, to present evidence, to call witnesses, to confront and cross-examine adverse witnesses, and so forth. Relaxing the technical rules of legal evidence is proper, since some of the rules are of questionable soundness.

The adversary adjudication model also implies that the subprinciples of grounds and formal justice apply. Findings and recommendations should be made at each phase of the disciplinary process. In revoking or suspending a license, as no moral costs or evidentiary problems are involved, the burden of persuasion should be the preponderance of the evidence. Review of hearings should not be of a de novo type, because the possible reduced error costs and process benefits do not outweigh much increase in direct costs. Findings and recommendations should be accepted unless they are beyond the boundaries of reasonable discretion[3].

The usual legal requirements of consistency, adherence to precedent, and conformity to rules should apply. Because of the concern for individualized justice, consistency is difficult to achieve in determinations of the appropriate sanction, but more could probably be done to achieve consistency than is. Discipline should not be rendered unless clear and intelligible standards and rules prohibited the conduct.

Thus, our theoretical principles reasonably apply to professional discipline. While practice largely conforms to them, they do indicate some areas in which it might be reformed. Throughout, the concerns with issue resolution, truth finding, economic and moral error costs, and process benefits have been relevant to particular issues. Nonetheless, as admitted at the beginning, professional discipline is the easy context. Employment decisions provide a stronger challenge.

CHAPTER 10

EMPLOYMENT DECISIONS

Any attempt to discuss the justice of employment decisions in one chapter suggests superficiality. Two features hopefully save this chapter from this fault. First, the topic is restricted to procedures independent of any contractual requirements such as grievance procedures; substantive issues are not discussed. The theoretical reason for ignoring procedural requirements in collective contracts is that our concern is with what is morally required independent of voluntary agreement. If a procedure can be shown to be independently morally required, that provides a good reason for including it in a contract and for criticizing contracts that do not include it. The practical reason is that most employees are not covered by collective bargaining or individual employment contracts (Snoeyenbos and Roberts 1983, 248). Most individual employment contracts are silent on procedures, and the law implies relatively few conditions. Moreover, no individual employment contracts and few collective bargaining contracts cover procedural issues of the hiring process.

Second, the purpose of this chapter is to illustrate and test the principles and theoretical framework developed in Parts I and II. Employment decisions are especially valuable for this purpose, because they involve a variety of types of benefit-conferring and benefit-terminating decisions. The theory supports different procedures depending on the types of decisions and circumstances. The aim is to show that it provides an adequate framework for analyzing specific situations.

There are at least four distinct types of employment decisions, although the procedures appropriate for them overlap. First are decisions to employ persons. Second are decisions to promote persons or to provide merit salary increases. Discipline and demotion decisions are a third type. Decisions to terminate employment by layoff or dismissal are a fourth type. Reassignments and transfers are probably another type but are not discussed.

Hiring

Decisions to hire someone are normally competitive benefit-conferring ones. Hiring decisions confer benefits—employment—on those hired. Although a new employee might resign a previous position, it is the prospective employee's, not the prospective employer's, decision to do so. The employer does not impose a burden or terminate the previous beneficial employment, only offers alternative beneficial employment. The context is usually competitive; that is, more persons than are needed are available for positions and employers choose those they consider best qualified. If labor is quite scarce, then employers can be competing with one another, but even then applicants usually compete for top rating for the best jobs.

An employer's steps in hiring are often specified as job analysis, job description, job specification, recruitment, testing, and interviewing (see Snoeyenbos and Almeder 1983, 197). We assume that the job analysis, description, and specification are done correctly, as these are mostly substantive matters. Moreover, we assume that the criteria are validly related to job performance; this includes the validity of tests and interviews as predictors of job performance. We do not claim that these assumptions are true or even usually true; they are made simply to avoid substantive issues. Thus, the focus in this section is on recruitment procedures.

One can usefully distinguish two types of employment positions by the criteria for them. Some criteria provide an ordinal scale so that applicants can be ranked from better to less well qualified, with perhaps a cut-off below which people are unqualified. These can be called scale criteria and positions. For example, the criteria for academic positions are of this sort. A necessary condition might be possession of a Ph.D. in the relevant field, but other criteria such as publications, teaching ability, and research potential can be fulfilled to varying degrees.

Other positions, such as unskilled labor, have a set of criteria establishing only a cut-off point so that everyone above that is equally qualified for the job. The criteria for these positions can be called nonscale criteria and the positions nonscale ones. If there are more applicants than nonscale positions, the context is competitive but one cannot distinguish on the basis of competence. Instead, some other principle such as first come, first hired, is needed. Such a procedure has been used in union hall hiring, as for dockworkers. If there are insufficient applicants for positions, then applicants are not really competing, even though employers are not necessarily committed to hiring all who apply and meet the criteria.

The appropriate model for hiring decisions is along the directorial-bureaucratic continuum. The decision does not confront an applicant as a dispute with the prospective employer, which rules out the adversary adjudication and negotiation models. Of course, negotiation is often involved in establishing the terms of employment, but that does not occur until the employer has decided to make an offer. Although evaluation of skills and abilities and professional personnel officers can be involved, the purpose is to benefit the employer, not the employee. Thus, the professional service model is not appropriately dominant. However, it can have a subordinate role, especially for filling many scale positions. Professional personnel officers often use professional expertise in trying to assure that people and positions are suitable to one another. Consequently, as the situation is a nonconflict, no-lose one for individuals and not for their benefit, our criteria for appropriate models indicates that bureaucratic investigation or directorship is appropriate.

Whether the directorial or bureaucratic model is most appropriate depends on the scope for discretion, but usually the process is somewhere along the continuum between the two ideal types. The significant factor determining which model should dominate is the standards to be used. The decisions are directorial to the extent the employer's satisfaction is the basis. The general criterion is the ability to contribute most to the director's ends. Even this criterion is not always required, because the decision need not even be based on a judgment of overall contribution. If owners of small businesses wish to hire their children even though more qualified people are available, that is within their discretion$_4$. It may be poor business management to do so, but it is not procedurally unjust (contra Werhane 1984, 110–11). Whether standards should be required of such employer's is basically a substantive matter. As noted in chapter 8, it is not easy to justify discretion$_4$ concerning standards, especially for allocating burdens. However, traditionally autonomy as freedom of property and contract and the fact that benefits, not burdens are being allocated, has been thought to do so. Our point is merely that if no or very few substantive standards for decision are prescribed, then the directorial model is appropriate.

In large organizations, various criteria have been established for hiring employees. The more specific and objective these criteria are, the more appropriate the bureaucratic model. Generally, nonscale criteria provide more objective criteria and make a bureaucratic model more appropriate. Scale criteria can also be objective, but the comparative ranking of applicants on the basis of several criteria usually leaves considerable scope for discretion3.

The grounds for ethically requiring procedures in hiring depend on how close the decision should be to the bureaucratic or directorial model. As we saw in chapter 8, only consistency can always be required of pure directorial decisions, but bureaucratic decisions can involve many procedural safeguards. Given that hiring is for the benefit of the employer, the full procedural protections of the bureaucratic model are not required. Applicants have no claim to the benefits and usually suffer no moral harm in not being employed. The primary error costs for employers are economic ones and must be balanced with their direct costs. Economic error costs accrue to an employer who could have hired a more qualified person. The direct costs are those of seeking out and screening applicants. An employer must balance the costs of greater recruitment efforts with the chances of obtaining better qualified applicants. For employers, procedural decisions are purely a matter of economic rationality.

From the perspective of applicants or potential applicants, some considerations support procedural features. Although as noted above moral error costs are rarely involved, economic error costs fall on better qualified persons who do not obtain a position. Of course, the economic costs to these persons are offset by the gains to those who obtain them. Also, if a poorly qualified person is hired and suffers great job dissatisfaction, then both the individual and the employer suffer error costs. In the employee's case, however, the benefits of salary and so forth might offset the disadvantages.

More importantly for applicants, process benefits are relevant. Participation is relevant to having an opportunity to present one's qualifications. Comparative procedural unfairness exists if procedures give some applicants a better chance than others independent of their substantive qualifications. (As we are assuming that tests of qualifications are accurate, we need not consider the various questions about biases of different testing methods.) Also, people often want to understand why they did not get a job, even if it is merely being told there was a better qualified applicant. Thus, intelligibility pertains. Timeliness can also be relevant. If prospective employers spend weeks or months trying to reach a decision, potential employees might have to postpone other important decisions. And, of course, confidence can be relevant; if potential employees come to believe the process is unjust, they might not apply again for positions which they might obtain because best qualified for them.

Combining the economic rationality grounds for employers and the process benefits grounds for prospective employees, certain minimal procedural requirements pertain to hiring decisions. Minimal elements of an opportunity to be heard should be provided. Notice amounts to informing a reasonable pool of possible applicants of an available position. What constitutes a reasonable pool of potential applicants varies with the context. On the one hand, advertising a secretarial position in a local newspaper is likely to reach both all those likely to apply and sufficient persons to provide a well qualified applicant. People in distant cities are unlikely to move for such a position. Anyone who would consider doing so should recognize the practice of local advertising and attempt to find out about such jobs, for example, by subscribing to the local newspaper. On the other hand, for academic appointments, the market is national in scope but limited to a relatively small number of persons. Consequently, advertising through professional associations and journals is normally adequate. In short, the benefit/cost concerns of employers generally overlap the interests of potential employees.

An opportunity to present evidence amounts to permitting applicants to submit relevant material. The interests of prospective employers and employees again usually overlap. Employers have good reasons to obtain information that will help them make better decisions, and applicants have little or no interest in spending time and money submitting irrelevant information. Unfortunately, not everyone is rational. For ease of comparison of candidates, employers often ask that applications be made on special forms, and perhaps that only limited information be provided for initial screening. Applicants have an interest in avoiding the effort of filling out special application forms by using previously prepared materials. They also think that sending more material than requested improves their chances. Sometimes sending extra material can backfire by creating unnecessary work for employing officers who then become disposed against the applicant.

Whether an opportunity for orally presenting information is provided depends on the context. Often employers reserve interviews and testing for a short list of candidates. Interviews are more costly than written information, so it is cost effective to limit them to top candidates. In some situations, especially for low-skilled jobs and in small businesses, hiring is done almost completely on the basis of interviews and oral evidence. The fairness of tests and interviews primarily pertains to their validity, which is a substantive matter.

However, interview procedures themselves can be unfair, for example, a half-dozen or more persons rapidly throwing questions at a candidate.

A central procedural issue in hiring is impartiality. If a hiring decision is near the pure directorial model, impartiality is not required. The aim is the satisfaction of the director's subjective ends which might include providing employment for relatives or other discriminatory factors, such as not liking to work with fat people. The more usual form of partiality is to make employment decisions on grounds such as race, sex, age, or the religious or political views of applicants. If the decision is nearer bureaucratic investigation, in particular, if the aim is to fill the position with the person who can provide the best job performance, then impartiality is central. It benefits prospective employers by avoiding errors and benefits applicants by supporting comparative fairness between applicants.

Without impartiality, notice and an opportunity to present information are largely worthless. Sometimes partiality is built into the process from the beginning. For example, an academic department might identify a person it wishes to hire and then tailor the job description to fit that person. Whether such a practice in fact promotes the best interests of the department is questionable, because another person might better contribute to the department's purposes, but that person is likely to be passed over. From the viewpoint of other applicants, the whole process becomes a fraud. No position is actually available, yet they are encouraged to spend time and money applying. This procedure undermines confidence in the academic employment market and is especially demoralizing to younger academics.

Notice of rejection (findings) might not be necessary (though desirable) for most applicants, but it should certainly be provided to those who have been explicitly or implicitly told that they are among the final contenders for a position. Applicants have no basis for expecting to be hired and so should not rely on it. Final contenders have been given some reason to expect employment (although the chances might still be low) and so might more reasonably postpone other decisions pending the outcome of their application. Unless the direct costs of doing so are high, employers should normally notify all applicants. The MSA suggests that its summary procedure is appropriate for employment decisions (MSA § 4-502(3)(iv)). Under that procedure, each "party" is entitled to notification of the agency's action or order (MSA § 4-503(d)). In hiring, presumably all applicants are "parties" and are entitled to notice that a position has been filled. Such a notice should not be required when a person did not apply for a specific position but, say, any opening that might arise for which the person is qualified.

The grounds for hiring decisions are usually implicit in the job description. Some considerations cannot be stated clearly. For example, in interviewing secretaries, I have found it helpful to give them a typing test. The purpose of the test is less to determine typing skills than an ineffable quality of "taking charge." Some applicants go directly to the task, insert paper, and type, while others invent irrelevant questions and fiddle with the typewriter, paper, seat, and anything else they can find. This characteristic cannot be clearly stated in a job description. Whatever the criteria, unsuccessful applicants can assume that they were found not to meet the qualifications as well as another applicant. Consequently, a detailed statement of reasons for not employing a person is usually unnecessary. If the person hired had an extra qualification, for example, a degree in library science that would be helpful in the job, this information should be conveyed to unsuccessful candidates. Doing so makes the decision more intelligible to a rejected applicant and is likely to lessen feelings of inadequacy that inevitably follow rejection.

Consistency, adherence to precedent, and conformity to rules have limited applicability to hiring decisions. Consistency, as a requirement of rationality, applies. Thus, if one applicant is ranked higher for possessing some quality, its possession by other applicants should also be deemed an asset. If a number of similar positions are being filled at one time, then consistency also applies across all of them. Consistency has limited import for positions filled sequentially, for one can always change one's mind about job tasks or what characteristics are most important for a person filling the position. For similar reasons, adherence to precedent is virtually irrelevant (see Davis 1972, 100). Hiring a second applicant because similar to a previous one whose job performance was unsatisfactory would be silly. Conformity to rules does pertain; employers should follow their procedural and substantive rules for filling positions. However, they can change the rules. Inconsistency and failure to follow rules often signify partiality.

Application of the criteria for legal enforcement of procedural principles developed in chapter 7 indicates few grounds for doing so. First, state action provides a reason only for government employment. Second, as hiring decisions are benefit-conferring, no deprivation occurs in failures to hire. As prospective employees are not receiving benefits, necessary reliance cannot occur. Few nongovernmental jobs are monopolized. Nor is there a stigma in not being hired; being judged less capable than another person does not imply one is not capable, and usually the qualities involved are not moral ones. Third, although the decisions involve important matters—persons' employment, the heavy error costs incurred by employers provides them a strong incentive to avoid errors when the direct costs are less than the error costs. Legal requirements will thus probably not help much to reduce error costs and can significantly raise direct costs. As the primary purpose of employing someone is the benefit of the employer and judgments of such benefit can involve subjective standards, especially decisionmaker satisfaction or scale criteria, courts cannot accurately second guess employers' judgments. Thus, much discretion must be left employers; and the burden of persuasion would fall on unsuccessful applicants. As Justice Stevens has said, courts are "not the proper forum in which to review the multitude of personnel decisions that are made daily" (*Bishop v. Wood*, 426 U.S. 341, 349 (1976)).

The major legal imposition has been to prohibit discrimination on grounds of race, sex, and so on. A discussion of discrimination and affirmative action would lead us too far astray from our topic. Many nondiscrimination requirements are procedural, not substantive, even though substantive rights are the central concern. Failure to hire on discriminatory grounds does involve moral costs and thus provides a stronger reason for legal enforcement. Affirmative action involves an uneasy tension between substantive and procedural requirements. Employers can set the criteria for positions as they wish, provided they are not racial or other prohibited characteristics, but they are required to advertise widely and to consider applicants seriously regardless of race, sex, and so forth. A complication occurs when goals are set for hiring members of a group. When positions involve nonscale criteria, one can more easily set and legally enforce requirements that a certain percentage of new hires belong to a given group.

Merit and Promotion

Merit salary increase and promotion decisions are also competitive benefit-conferring ones. Indeed, in some organizations, promotions are treated like initial employment decisions. Promotion requires an opening for which a current employee applies, but current employees are preferred to nonemployees. The situation is a competitive one, because usually the receipt of a promotion or merit increase depends on one's performance in comparison to that of other employees. If everyone receives the same size of increase, it is not a merit increase. Sometimes so-called merit salary increase decisions can become benefit-terminating ones that make a person worse off. This occurs when it is assumed that people will receive merit increases unless they do especially poorly. The baseline becomes an expectation of an increase, so its denial is the equivalent of terminating a benefit.

Basically the same reasons for the appropriateness of the directorial and bureaucratic models for hiring decisions—nonconflict, no-lose, and nonprofessional standards—apply to promotion and merit decisions and need not be repeated. Two factors support somewhat stronger procedural protections for promotion and merit decisions. The underlying purpose of merit increases and promotions is to enhance the efficiency and productivity of the organization by providing employees incentives. Perceived injustice in the process can significantly reduce confidence in the employer and damage employee morale. These consequences can be almost as bad for the employer as the employee. Merit increases and sometimes promotions are to reward people for past services. To the extent they are thus intended to benefit the recipient, moral costs are involved in incorrect denials justifying greater direct costs for procedural protections.

Decisionmakers should be impartial between employees. That the decisionmaker works for the organization is not relevant to partiality. The competition is not between employer and employee but employee and employee. However, merit criteria may partly depend on employer interests. Thus, an employer can decide that increasing sales is more important than cutting costs and thus reward employees increasing sales more than those cutting costs. The same reasons that support impartiality in initial hiring support it in merit increases and do not require further comment.

Other procedural principles, particularly the opportunity to be heard and the grounds for decisions, have more force in merit and promotion decisions than initial hiring decisions. Errors are more easily detected and process benefits are more likely. Detecting mistaken hiring decisions is difficult, because one side of the comparison is hypothetical. If a new hire is unsatisfactory, a mistake still need not have been made, for the other applicants might have been even less satisfactory. If the new hire's performance is satisfactory, one will never know whether another applicant might have done even better. With merit decisions, comparisons are between actual performances. Further, on-the-job evaluations can affect a person's self-concept and worth more than initial decisions. It is one's job, and being judged a good plumber, bookkeeper, or engineer is a basis for pride. Lower evaluations do not stigmatize, but higher ones enhance self-respect. The process benefits of participation, fairness, and intelligibility are more significant because they affect ongoing relations with an employer.

The three main subprinciples of an opportunity to be heard usually appropriate for merit and promotion decisions are notice, presentation of evidence, and appeals. The requirement of notice depends on an opportunity to present evidence to support one's case for a merit increase or promotion. If that opportunity does not exist, if merit increases and promotions come out-of-the-blue, then notice serves no purpose. As applicants for positions should have notice and an opportunity to present evidence, so should employees for merit and promotion decisions. Everyone should have sufficient notice to gather and prepare relevant evidence and an opportunity to present it to the decisionmaker. In some situations, a special opportunity for presentation of evidence might be less important. If the decisionmaker has closely supervised the employee during the period, then additional information might be unnecessary. For example, a nurse supervisor who has been on the floor with three or four nurses for the past year probably has more information than needed. Even here, though, employees can derive process benefits from presenting their strong points, and having all the main information collected together might reduce errors due to oversight or forgetfulness.

Usually an employee's immediate supervisor makes an initial recommendation or report concerning merit increases or promotion. The closer the relationship between supervisor and employee, the more important becomes a right of appeal. The relationship can often breed favoritism or antagonism toward subordinates (see also Davis 1969, 144–45). A greater distance from the employee can produce a more objective view. Thus, an opportunity for an appeal is important. Appeals might not be permitted when promotions are treated like applications for new positions any more than appeals are permitted for decisions not to hire.

One common academic practice perhaps to minimize favoritism and the need for appeals is to have a committee from the unit advise the supervisor. The most obvious objection to this practice is the conflict of interest often involved. If a pool of merit money is awarded to a department to be divided among its members, then an increase for one person proportionately decreases the increases for others—including committee members. The procedure can, perhaps, prevent otherwise unchecked favoritism by a department chairperson, but so can many other procedures, even simple publicity of merit evaluations. It is certainly no alternative to the possibility of appeal.

If appeals are permitted, employees need to know the grounds for decisions and some documentary evidence is needed. Preferably, employees should be permitted to see and to respond to evaluations and recommendations before final decisions. Such a practice is likely to reduce appeals, perhaps by substituting negotiation for bureaucratic decision making. However, negotiation can reduce comparative fairness if decisionmakers grant greater merit increases simply to avoid appeals making them look bad to their superiors. Evaluations need not provide specific findings, such as being late with two of eight reports, although the more detail the more guidance employees have for improvement. Moreover, decisions need not, perhaps cannot, be limited to evidence on the record. Particularly when supervisors have close contact with employees, much information is gathered throughout the evaluation period. To deny the use of this information is both practically impossible and as likely to increase errors as to decrease them. Such information is closely akin to judicial or administrative notice, except that a supervisor has access to pertinent information concerning the specific parties—adjudicative rather than legislative facts. Still, some documentary evidence is needed for appeals, and employees should be permitted to see and respond to evaluations and recommendations, preferably before a final decision by the first assessor.

The burden of persuasion for merit or promotion should be on the employee. The baseline assumption is no merit increase or a minimal one if practically everyone gets something. To place the burden of persuasion on the employer to show that an employee does not deserve a merit increase changes merit increases into standard ones—everyone gets three percent unless seriously deficient. To assume even average merit increases converts below average ones into deprivations.

Consistency, adherence to precedent, and conformity to rules pertain to merit and promotion decisions much as they do to initial employment decisions. Consistency among those being evaluated at one time follows from rationality and impartiality. Adherence to precedent does not apply. Given the competitive nature of merit and most promotions, to argue for adherence to precedent is like arguing that because a 4.10 minute time won a race last year, it should do so this year. Even when promotions are noncompetitive, as supposedly for promotion of professors, over time the standards can change. The general criteria (publications) need not change, but their stringency can (the necessary quantity and quality). If criteria could not be altered, an organization could not seek to improve the quality of its personnel except by entry and probationary decisions. The negative side is that some people find their careers stymied; their expectations of promotion in a less competent organization have been frustrated by an improving organization with increasing standards. But no one has a right that an organization remain mediocre so that he or she can be promoted. Furthermore, any rules promulgated by the organization for merit or promotion decisions should be followed. As in any instance of promulgating rules, a commitment is made to follow them. As always, the organization can change the rules.

Except when specified by collective bargaining, the grounds for legally requiring procedures for merit and promotion decisions are even weaker than those for initial hiring. State action is limited to government employment. No deprivation occurs; necessary reliance is not applicable; and no stigma is involved. In a sense the employer has a monopoly over merit increases and promotions; a nonemployer cannot give them. However, that is a logical feature of merit increases and promotions—they can only come from employers. Changing employers for a higher rank or salary might be possible. Because the dollar amount involved is much less than the base salary, economic error costs are less than in hiring; organizations have self-interested reasons to avoid errors; and the direct costs of legal enforcement would be even higher than for initial hiring—more people are considered for merit increases than are hired each year. Moreover, the criteria for merit and promotion are perhaps more discretionary than those for employment. The question is whether an employee has performed to the satisfaction of the employer, not merely whether a person has credentials indicating that he or she should be able to perform satisfactorily.

Discipline and Demotion

Demotion and disciplinary decisions are noncompetitive benefit-terminating ones. They are normally deprivations, because an employee will lose salary, work, or some other good that could normally be expected. The baseline is continued receipt of the benefits, so their termination makes persons worse-off. Some "demotions" are not deprivations, for example, if a person receives a probationary promotion and is determined not to perform satisfactorily. As the promotion is probationary, the person has no claim to its continuance, so its removal is not a deprivation. Hence, such decisions are best not thought of as demotions but as decisions not to promote. Although discipline and demotion decisions involve deprivations, they are not burden-imposing. Employers can only withhold benefits, they cannot deprive employees of goods they did not or do not provide or of past ones provided to employees.

Disciplinary decisions are always noncompetitive; it is not as though someone has to be disciplined and the question is who. As with professional discipline, it is for improper conduct such as violating safety rules. Demotions are usually not competitive, although in some circumstances they can be. An organization or a unit might need to reduce the number of employees in a higher job classification and the issue then be which employees should be reduced to a lower classification. Finally, some organizations, such as the military, use demotion as a disciplinary sanction while others do not.

As with professional discipline, possible demotion or discipline confronts the employee as a conflict. For the employee, it is a no-win decision. In disciplinary decisions, a moral judgment is involved. The employee is alleged to have engaged in conduct that is wrong by the employer's norms. Nondisciplinary decisions to demote do not necessarily have this aspect of moral judgment; unsatisfactory performance of a job is not necessarily a stigmatizing fault. Indeed, fault, as the Peter Principle indicates, might lie with those who promoted an employee beyond his or her level of competence.

Consequently, although employers perhaps tend to view such decisions, especially demotions, as directorial, an adversary adjudication or bureaucratic investigation model is more appropriate. Adversary adjudication is most appropriate for disciplinary decisions, because stigmatizing moral judgment is involved; while bureaucratic investigation is perhaps preferable for demotion decisions, because they are more likely concerned with policy implementation and perhaps judgments of personal satisfaction. However, either model should be modified toward the other, unless demotions fall toward the directorial end of the directorial-bureaucratic continuum. Potential economic and moral error costs in minor discipline do not justify a full-fledged adversary adjudication. Thus, the MSA recommends its administrative hearing procedure, which is an abbreviated adversary adjudication, for disciplinary actions against employees that do not involve more than ten day suspensions (MSA § 4-401(2)(iv)). Bureaucratic investigation with many procedural safeguards overlaps mitigated adversary adjudication. Private companies use a variety of less formal procedures often combining elements of various models.

Given the adjudicatory or investigatory nature of the decision, impartiality becomes crucial. Most disciplinary decisions are initiated by immediate superiors and follow a bureaucratic investigation procedure. A supervisor inquires into the alleged facts and either takes action or recommends it. The fact that the superior works for the organization taking action does not by itself show lack of impartiality. An investigatory function is not incompatible with impartiality, and enforcement of an employer's rules creates no more partiality than does the fact that judges enforce laws. However, suggestions of conflict of interest or bias can easily enter. For example, in *Arnett v. Kennedy* (416 U.S. 134 (1974)), Kennedy had publicly accused his superior of taking a bribe, yet the superior made the initial investigation and decision. The conflict of interest and possibility of bias is manifest. Although *Kennedy* was a case of terminating employment, the same lack of impartiality would exist were the issue merely one of disciplinary action. More common is subtle bias or conflict of interest, for example, a supervisor who simply dislikes an employee or wishes to shift the blame for something.

The simple solution to this problem is to have another person investigate an incident whenever an employee claims a supervisor lacks impartiality. Although not all such claims are well founded, the procedure normally has low direct costs and avoids even the appearance of partiality. Even from a self-interested management perspective, the appearance of partiality and loss of confidence can have a negative effect on employee morale and thus be worth the small effort to have someone else conduct an initial investigation. Nor does the possibility of appeal to an impartial decisionmaker solve the problem, because the evidence and material in the file will be tainted by the original investigation.

The number and strength of procedural safeguards in a disciplinary process should vary, at least in part, with the severity of the possible sanction. The greater the sanction, the greater the possible error costs, and thus the larger the direct costs that can be justified. Discipline, as opposed to demotion, probably involves moral as well as economic error costs. The minimal elements of an opportunity to be heard that should be afforded are notice, an opportunity to present evidence, to rebut adverse evidence, and an opportunity to appeal. Reduction of error costs and the process benefits of participation and fairness all support an opportunity to present evidence, and of course it is not meaningful without some notice of the alleged infraction. Disciplinary and demotion decisions involve specific claims that can result in deprivation, so the individual should have an opportunity to rebut adverse evidence.

Some organizations primarily conduct informal oral inquiries, for example, a superior calls an employee into the office to discuss the matter. Others are inclined to proceed primarily or exclusively by written evidence. Generally, it is best to permit an employee to present material orally or in writing. As discussed in chapter 3, some employees in low level positions might not be capable of adequately preparing a good written version of their evidence. In a society with a substantial functional illiteracy rate, one should not demand only written evidence of employees, no matter their abilities. Of course, some organizations might employ only college graduates, in which case written evidence might be reasonable, although even college graduates vary in their facility and ease at oral and written expression. The opportunity to rebut evidence need not involve confrontation and cross-examination of witnesses, only an opportunity to reply to or explain alleged misconduct or unsatisfactory performance. For demotions, usually the supervisor is making the claims of unsatisfactory performance, so an opportunity to explain or excuse it does provide confrontation with the chief critic.

For sanctions beyond a reprimand or minor docking of pay, an appeal mechanism is appropriate. From an employer's perspective, an appeal mechanism can help prevent arbitrariness or vindictiveness by supervisors and improve employee morale by increasing confidence in justice being done. Employees have greater assurance that adequate consideration has been given and that they are not being victimized. Of course, an opportunity to appeal will not eliminate all employee feelings of ill-treatment, but it can reduce them. An appeal might simply be to the supervisor's superior, or better (at least when major sanctions are involved) to a committee that includes someone from a position comparable to the employee's.

An employee should receive a statement of findings and reasons, and the burden of persuasion should be on the superior or employer to show that discipline is appropriate. Disciplinary action without a statement of reasons appears arbitrary and unjustified. Moreover, if appeals are permitted, it is preferable for the initial decisionmaker to at least provide a short written statement of the matter. Although one might prefer the informality of an oral statement, people are likely to recall details incorrectly shortly after such a conference. A brief written report is likely to be necessary for the employee's file anyway. It is little trouble to provide the employee a copy, even if the employee can examine his or her personnel file. As the superior is proposing to take action against the employee, the burden of persuasion falls on the superior (employer). Any employer that assumed its employees had acted improperly would have disastrous employee relations.

Some organizations explicitly state that disciplinary decisions are not to be taken as precedents, because all cases are unique. This contention is inadequate. It applies as much to court cases as to employer discipline. One should distinguish a certain type of conduct deserving discipline from the appropriate sanction. If Arthur's falling asleep during working hours is judged to constitute an infraction deserving discipline, there is no reason not to take that as precedent for similar behavior by Barbara. However, the sanctions might well differ, for example, if Arthur is a new employee who had been out drinking the night before and Barbara is an old employee with many years of excellent service and has been staying up late evenings caring for her elderly, invalid mother. Fitting the punishment to the wrong, as we saw in considering the death penalty and professional discipline, involves individualized justice which is not easily captured in precedents and objective bureaucratic classifications. Still, some guidelines about appropriate punishment are possible. If an organization has clear rules indicating conduct for which discipline will be imposed, for example, consuming alcohol on the job, precedents are not needed.

Nondisciplinary demotion differs from discipline in a few important respects. First, it is not usually for a specific action or actions. Instead, it is for generally unsatisfactory job performance and will normally involve a multifactor standard. Consequently, the bureaucratic decision model with variations toward the directorial rather than adversary adjudication model is preferable.

Employees often but not always know when their performance is unsatisfactory. Nevertheless, notice of unsatisfactory performance should occur in regular evaluations or special discussions or evaluations. Failure to notify of unsatisfactory performance is like a vague rule; persons do not have an opportunity to comply because they do not know what is required. The opportunity to correct deficient performance partially replaces an opportunity to present evidence. An opportunity to rebut evidence, to explain why apparently deficient performance is not in fact deficient or a person's fault, is still important. Moreover, sometimes a person must continually earn a position by satisfactory job performance. There need be no presumption of continued satisfactory performance or right to continue in a position, although usually an employer's explicit or implicit rules or policies so indicate. If no such presumption exists, then there is no right to continue in a position and no moral error costs in improper demotions.

Finally, unlike initial hiring, merit, and promotion decisions, disciplinary and demotion decisions involve deprivations, and at least disciplinary decisions are stigmatizing. Thus, the deprivation basis for legal imposition of procedural principles applies, and of course state action applies to government employment. Nevertheless, the basis for legal requirement of procedures is not overwhelming. For discipline short of termination, the importance of the interest is not great enough to involve substantial error costs. Direct costs of legal enforcement would be substantial. There could be some gain in fairness. Participation and intelligibility might also be increased provided employers complied with the law and the case did not have to be litigated. With litigation, participation comes substantially after the decision, legal processes and decisions might not be more intelligible than the original ones, and timeliness would certainly be less. Most likely, employees would at best achieve vindication. Standards for satisfactory job performance can involve broad discretion3. Employers would still be able to establish what constitutes an infraction and have great discretion3 in imposing sanctions. Moreover, at least union employees have alternative forms of protection—the collective bargaining agreement. This reason against legal enforcement is much less plausible for the majority of nonunion workers, for individuals can rarely bargain with a large employer over disciplinary and demotion procedures. Thus, it is not implausible to require legally minimal elements of impartiality, notice, and an opportunity to present evidence even in nongovernment employment.

Termination

At-will and probationary Employer decisions to terminate a person's employment can be either benefit-terminating or refusals to confer benefits. Termination of at-will and probationary employees is a failure to confer a benefit. The primary significance of at-will and probationary employment is that employees are not assured of continued employment; employment is at the employer's will. As people can legitimately expect continuation of employment only if certain conditions continue to be met, the baseline is nonemployment and cessation of employment does not make them worse off. If persons can only be terminated for cause, then they can legitimately expect continuation of employment unless certain events occur. The baseline is then employment, and termination is a benefit-terminating decision.

The purpose of probationary appointment is to determine an employee's competence on the job. The criteria are not quite the same as for original appointment, for the latter criteria primarily pertain to a person's abilities and character traits that are likely to result in good job performance. These characteristics might not be manifested in actual job performance. Moreover, more subjective features are often relevant to actual job performance, such as compatibility with other employees (Snoeyenbos and Roberts 1983, 252 (incompatibility major reason for firing managers)). Sometimes even highly qualified persons do not fit well in a particular work environment, and the result can be tensions, lack of productivity, and so forth.

Many, perhaps most, jobs are at-will. At-will and probationary employment make a decision-making model toward the directorship end of the continuum between it and bureaucratic investigation appropriate for termination decisions. Whether most employment should be at-will is a substantive issue not pursued here. Although at-will employment does not justify many procedural principles, it is not thereby a denial of due process (contra Werhane 1984, 107–13), simply less process is due.

Termination of at-will and probationary employment does not invoke procedural principles any more than a decision not to hire. Consequently, no more procedural requirements apply to termination of at-will or probationary employment than for original hiring (see also Bayles 1988, 213–15; *Bishop v. Wood*, 426 U.S. 341 (1976); Flick 1984, 29 (natural justice inapplicable)). Persons should be provided an impartial performance evaluation. Notice amounts to an indication of unsatisfactory performance, and an opportunity to be heard is satisfied by informal discussion of problems and an opportunity to correct them. These elementary procedures promote process benefits of participation, fairness, and intelligibility. An employee can participate in the decision to the extent of offering explanations for specific instances of unsatisfactory performance and know what deficiencies are the basis for termination. Providing such information during the probationary period, rather than only at the end, provides employees an opportunity to correct matters and can thereby save employers the costs of searching for and training new employees. Timeliness requires notifying employees as soon as a judgment is made.

Because of the lack of legally required procedures and substantive grounds for termination, in recent years employers have been aggressively trying to ensure that the employment relation is at-will (see Westin and Feliu 1988, 248–50). At-will clauses are being placed on job application forms and in employee handbooks. Hiring officials are advised not to make any promises of continued employment. At-will clauses are even being placed in fixed-term contracts which have traditionally permitted termination only for cause. One of the most contentious actions has been to ask current employees to sign at-will clauses, perhaps changing their status ("Employment-at-Will Clauses" 1988).

For cause Decisions about terminating employees who can only be dismissed for cause are benefit-terminating ones. Two different types of cause for termination can be distinguished. One type of cause is business necessity, for example, insufficient sales requiring the elimination of one or more positions. This type can be called position termination. The second type is due to some inadequacy of the employee such as unsatisfactory job performance, loss of ability to perform the job (for example, heart disease in an airline pilot), or violation of a significant disciplinary rule. Terminations of this type can be called employee terminations. The reasons for employee-terminating decisions divide into two categories corresponding to the difference between those for disciplinary and nondisciplinary demotions. That is, one involves moral judgment of fault in violating employer norms, whereas the other involves judgments of satisfactory performance.

Employee terminations are noncompetitive benefit-terminating decisions about individual employees. The same considerations of error costs and process benefits that apply to disciplinary and demotion decisions apply to them with even more force, because the subject matter is more important. Economic error costs are greater, because loss of a job is more important than a one day or week suspension. Being fired from a position usually reduces a person's chances of finding comparable employment. Because the person has a right to the position except for cause, moral costs attach to incorrect terminations. Consequently, all the procedures provided for disciplinary decisions should apply even more strongly. Specifically, an impartial person should make the decision providing the employee notice, an opportunity to present evidence, an opportunity to rebut adverse evidence, a statement of findings and reasons, and an appeal or opportunity for reconsideration. Consistency should also apply; if the performances of Conrad and Deborah are equal, then both should be let go or retained, unless some strong management reason exists for not dismissing both, for example, the inability to operate properly without at least one person even if not fully competent.

Legal enforcement of these procedures is justifiable even for nongovernment employment. A significant deprivation occurs, the person has necessarily relied on retaining the position in the absence of cause, and disciplinary dismissals stigmatize. The matter is important enough to justify the costs of legal enforcement, and courts are capable of overseeing the judgments. Violation of rules is precisely the sort of judgment courts often make. Unsatisfactory job performance does involve standards allowing considerable scope for discretion$_3$, and judges often will not be able to examine that aspect closely. Nevertheless, they can reasonably judge whether appropriate procedures were followed. Alternative protections are plausible only for employees under a collective bargaining agreement.

One might contend that the cost of courts evaluating all employee terminations would be excessive, and we already rejected legal enforcement of discipline and demotion procedures on those grounds. However, the error costs of incorrect terminations are significantly greater than those of minor discipline and demotion. Furthermore, courts should allow employers a large scope for discretion$_3$ in making employee-terminating decisions, at least for unsatisfactory job performance. Consequently, one would expect few legal appeals, although the number has been growing significantly in recent years (Westin and Feliu 1988, 2). Also, employee-terminating decisions are already subject to legal enforcement. An incorrect termination violates substantive contractual rights of even nonunion employees, and they can sue on the contract. If the law can be invoked to protect the substantive contractual rights, it is appropriate for the law also to require procedures that reduce the risk of errors. In short, besides directly protecting the substantive right not to be dismissed except for cause, the law and courts should enforce procedures to help ensure that erroneous violations of substantive rights do not occur. If employers then conformed to those procedures, fewer claims of substantive violation are likely to be brought in court (see Westin and Feliu 1988, 16–17 (companies with procedures estimate lower wrongful discharge suits)). Indeed, just procedures for termination decisions might preclude subsequent legal action by former employees (see Westin and Feliu 1988, 271–73).

Position-terminating decisions do not directly invoke procedural protections. Decisions to create or eliminate positions are directorial decisions par excellence. The decisions are not based on evaluations of individuals but on economic and organizational efficiency considerations. Barring some contractual commitment, an employee does not have a claim that his or her position be continued. One must distinguish evaluating an employee by a standard and evaluating the benefits of an employee's position, whoever occupies it. Even though the latter have implications for the allocations of burdens and benefits to individuals, they do not involve evaluating individuals against some standard. Consequently, position-terminating decisions are not burden/benefit decisions of the sort considered in this book. Thus, principles for burden/benefit decisions do not apply. Arguments for notice of plant closings and so forth must then have some other basis.

Nonetheless, position-terminating decisions can lead to employee-terminating ones. For example, if it is decided to terminate 10% of the positions in a job classification, decisions must be made as to which persons to let go. Here the employee-terminating decision is a competitive or comparative one. Usually, various factors, including competence, length of service, and so forth, are considered in deciding who should be laid off. Collective bargaining agreements often cover these matters in detail. When they do, the bureaucratic investigation model is appropriate. It should, however, allow for appeals. Even if decisions are made solely on the basis of seniority, some employees might wish to challenge findings, for example, the effect of a leave of absence on seniority.

When criteria for employee terminations due to termination of positions are not spelled out, the situation is more complex. One might analogize the decision to an initial hiring one, treating all the employees in the classification as applicants for a limited number of positions. Alternatively, one might compare the decision to a merit increase one, only instead of a salary increase, continued employment is the benefit. Finally, one might object that loss of employment is a deprivation, not a mere failure to receive a benefit. Consequently, the decision should be treated as analogous to demotion or termination for unsatisfactory performance.

The merit evaluation analogy is the most appropriate and appears to be the approach most employers use. The initial hiring analogy is inappropriate, because as the people have been employed, the standards and evidence for making judgments differ significantly. At the least, one must shift to an analogy with termination of probationary employees. The analogy with employee termination for unsatisfactory performance is inappropriate, because performance has been at least satisfactory. Moreover, as the baseline has become no employment, the decision is closer to termination of at-will or probationary employees. In some respects, common practice does not correspond to the merit evaluation model. Often employees do not have notice and an opportunity to present evidence; employers make their decisions simply on the basis of past evaluations of performance. Also, appeal procedures, other than simply complaining to one's superior, do not appear common.

An employee might want to challenge a position-terminating decision as a disguise for terminating him or her. For example, in 1970 the City University of New York received a very small budget even though "open enrollment" was to be implemented that fall and everyone knew that a supplemental budget would have to be provided to allow for increased enrollment. Nevertheless, at least one college terminated all or most nontenured positions. A few months later when the supplemental budget was approved, many similar positions were created. Many terminated employees were rehired, but the college used the opportunity not to rehire certain faculty it did not want. Technically, there was no choice in terminating the positions, because the college could not continue unfunded positions. However, it used their abolition to avoid direct employee-terminating decisions.

More contentious cases arise when only one or two positions are eliminated, for then decisions come close to terminating specific employees. Although an employee should be able to challenge such a decision, an employer need only show that credible business reasons exist for the decision, not that there is cause for terminating the employee. Perhaps the only useful appeal is to courts for contractual violations, because impartiality within the organization might always be suspect.

Summary

Initial hiring decisions are competitive benefit-conferring decisions. Because they are nonconflict, no-lose decisions not for the applicant's benefit, the appropriate decision-making model is the directorial or bureaucratic one depending on the objectivity and precision of the standards. Few procedural protections are due. The chief procedural requirement is impartiality in evaluating applicants. Corresponding to an opportunity to be heard are notice of an opening and an opportunity to apply. Findings should be provided at least applicants on a short list and preferably all of them. Presumably the grounds for not hiring are not fulfilling the requirements for the position as well as another applicant, so no detailed statement of reasons is usually needed. Generally, the self-interest of employers and of potential employees support the same procedures. Except to prevent discrimination on grounds of race, sex, and so forth, legal imposition of procedures is not generally appropriate for nongovernment employers due to the lack of deprivation, absence of stigma, the importance of the interest in comparison to the high direct costs, the scope for discretions permitted by the standards, and the interest of employers basically coinciding with what is appropriate.

Merit and promotion decisions are also competitive benefit-conferring ones. Again, as the context is a nonconflict, no-lose one not usually involving professional standards, the appropriate models are bureaucratic investigation or directorship. Because more evidence is available permitting a better detection of errors, the grounds for procedural protections are stronger than for initial hiring. The appropriate procedures are an impartial decisionmaker, notice, an opportunity to present evidence, a statement of reasons (evaluation), an opportunity to appeal, and consistency. The burden of persuasion falls on the employee. Although ethically more procedural safeguards should be provided than for initial hiring, the basis for their legal requirement is not significantly stronger.

Demotion and disciplinary decisions are noncompetitive benefit-terminating ones. Disciplinary decisions involve a moral judgment, but nondisciplinary decisions to demote do not. Consequently, as the situation is a conflict, no-win one with discretion3, the adversary adjudication model should dominate for disciplinary decisions. The bureaucratic investigatory model is appropriate for demotion decisions because they are more concerned with policy implementation and perhaps involve judgments of personal satisfaction (moving them toward directorship). The procedural safeguards of impartiality, notice, opportunity to present oral or written evidence, opportunity to rebut adverse evidence, appeals, statement of findings and reasons, consistency, adherence to precedent, and following of rules should be provided in disciplinary decisions. The formality or stringency of these elements should be greater the greater the proposed sanction. Demotion decisions should provide the same safeguards, except that adherence to precedent and conformity to rules are usually not appropriate or applicable. In both types of decisions, the burden of persuasion usually falls on the employer. The reasons for legal imposition of these safeguards are stronger than for the previous types of decisions. Disciplinary and demotion decisions confront employees as disputes, involve deprivations, stigmatize (disciplinary decisions), and employers might not be sufficiently motivated by self-interest to avoid error costs. Nevertheless, as the importance of the interest is relatively small, it is hard to justify the significant direct costs of legal enforcement. At most, impartiality, notice, and an opportunity to present one's side should be legally required.

Termination decisions should be divided into those to terminate at-will or probationary employees, to terminate permanent employees for cause, and to terminate positions. Decisions to terminate at-will and probationary employees do not involve deprivations, because there is no legitimate expectation of continued employment. They are similar to initial hiring decisions except for greater evidence and somewhat different standards. The appropriate procedures are notice of unsatisfactory performance, an opportunity to explain or improve, and a statement of reasons. Position-terminating decisions are not burden/benefit decisions applying standards to individuals, so the procedural principles for burden/benefit decisions do not apply to them. They are directorial decisions. They can require subsequent comparative decisions that should be treated analogously to merit increase decisions.

Employee-terminating decisions are noncompetitive benefit-terminating decisions. They can be distinguished into types corresponding to disciplinary and nondisciplinary demotion decisions. Similarly, the appropriate models are adversary adjudication for the former, and bureaucratic investigation for the latter. Moral costs attach to incorrect dismissals, because individuals have a right to continue in the position absent good cause for dismissal. The fullest set of procedural protections are appropriate for disciplinary terminations, including an impartial decisionmaker, notice, an opportunity to present and rebut evidence, a record, appeals, a statement of findings and reasons, consistency, adherence to precedent, and conformity to rules. Except for adherence to precedent and conformity to rules, these safeguards should also be provided for nondisciplinary employee-terminating decisions. Finally, legal enforcement of some procedural safeguards is appropriate. In nongovernment employment, although state action does not apply, the decisions are deprivations with stigmatization in disciplinary dismissals, and the importance of the interests create significant economic and moral error costs to offset the high costs of enforcement. Employees without a collective bargaining agreement do not have plausible alternative protections. Moreover, under contract law, courts must protect the substantive right not to be terminated except for cause, so it is not unreasonable also to require procedural safeguards that would reduce substantive errors.

Employment decisions can thus be benefit-conferring or benefit-terminating. The appropriate procedural models vary depending on the type of decision and its context. The appropriate procedural protections increase as one goes from initial hiring decisions to merit and promotion decisions to demotion and disciplinary decisions to employee-terminating decisions. Similarly, the case for legal enforcement of procedural principles increases. Our theory provides a framework for analyzing appropriate procedures for all these situations. Although some of the decisions properly involve a blend of procedural models, none of them requires a radically different format. Consequently, our theoretical analysis is adequate for employment decisions as well as professional discipline. Although other situations might exist in which our theoretical analysis is inadequate, it has met two significant tests of adequacy.

Just procedures can be as important, and sometimes more important, than substantive rights. To be entitled to a job and dismissal only for cause can be useless if, as in *Arnett v. Kennedy* (416 U.S. 134 (1974)), the procedure for determination of cause permits a biased person to make the decision. However, procedural justice is not simply instrumental to the protection of substantive interests. Process benefits support procedures even if the procedures do not lead to more accurate outcomes. A focus on just procedures will not eliminate all injustice, but it will provide a balance to the disproportionate emphasis on substantive rights, help make those rights more secure, and increase treatment of persons as worthy of respect.

WORKS CITED

Abraham, Henry. 1975. *The Judicial Process.* 3rd edn. New York: Oxford University Press.

Alexander, Lawrence. 1987. "The Relationship Between Procedural Due Process and Substantive Constitutional Rights." *University of Florida Law Review* 39: 323–43.

American Bar Association. 1972. *Code of Judicial Conduct.* N.p.: American Bar Association.

_____. 1979. "Standards for Lawyer Discipline and Disability Proceedings." In *Selected Standards on Professional Responsibility*, edited by Thomas D. Morgan and Ronald D. Rotunda, 367–409. Mineola, N.Y.: Foundation Press, 1987.

Atiyah, P. S. 1983. *Law and Modern Society.* Oxford: Oxford University Press.

Baier, Kurt. 1965. *The Moral Point of View: A Rational Basis of Ethics.* Abridged edn. New York: Random House.

"Baker Successor Brings Experience to New Role." 1988. *Tallahassee Democrat*, 16 June, p. 10A.

Barry, Brian. 1965. *Political Argument.* London: Routledge & Kegan Paul.

Bayles, Michael D. 1977. "Participation: An Overvalued, Impractical Ideal." In *Equality and Freedom: International and Comparative Jurisprudence*, edited by Gray Dorsey, 351–57. Dobbs Ferry, N.Y.: Oceana Publications.

_____. 1978. *Principles of Legislation: The Uses of Political Authority.* Detroit: Wayne State University Press.

_____. 1987. *Principles of Law: A Normative Analysis.* Dordrecht: D. Reidel Publishing Co.

_____. 1988. "Procedural Due Process." In *Philosophical Dimensions of the Constitution*, edited by Dianna T. Meyers and Kenneth Kipnis, 206–21. Boulder, Colo.: Westview Press.

_____. 1989. *Professional Ethics.* 2d edn. Belmont, Calif.: Wadsworth Publishing Co.

Brandt, Richard B. 1979. *A Theory of the Good and the Right.* Oxford: Clarendon Press.

_____. 1985. "A Motivational Theory of Excuses in the Criminal Law." In *Criminal Justice: Nomos XXVII*, edited by J. Roland Pennock and John W. Chapman, 165–98. New York: New York University Press.

Calabresi, Guido, and A. Douglas Melamed. 1972. "Property Rules, Liability Rules, and Inalienability: One View of the Cathedral." *Harvard Law Review* 85: 1089–1128.

Christie, George C. 1986. "An Essay on Discretion." *Duke Law Journal*, 747–78.

Coons, John E. 1987. "Consistency." *California Law Review* 75: 59–113.

Council of Europe. 1950. "European Convention for the Protection of Human Rights and Fundamental Freedoms." In Zaim M. Nedjati, *Human Rights under the European Convention*. Amsterdam: North-Holland Publishing Co., 1978.

Damaška, Mirjan. 1979. "Structures of Authority and Comparative Criminal Procedure." In *The Structure of Procedure*, edited by Robert M. Cover and Owen M. Fiss, 292–306. Mineola, N.Y.: The Foundation Press.

Davis, Kenneth Culp. 1969. *Discretionary Justice: A Preliminary Inquiry*. Urbana: University of Illinois Press, 1971 Illinois Books Edition.

_____. 1972. *Administrative Law Text*. 3rd edn. St. Paul, Minn.: West Publishing Co.

_____. 1977. *Administrative Law: Cases—Text—Problems*. 6th edn. St. Paul, Minn.: West Publishing Co.

Davis, Michael. 1982. "Sentencing: Must Justice be Even-Handed?" *Law and Philosophy* 1: 77–117.

de Smith, S. A. 1980. *Judicial Review of Administrative Action*. 4th ed. by J. M. Evans. London: Stevens & Sons.

Dworkin, Ronald. 1977. *Taking Rights Seriously*. Cambridge: Harvard University Press.

_____. 1985. *A Matter of Principle*. Cambridge: Harvard University Press.

_____. 1986. *Law's Empire*. Cambridge: Belknap Press, Harvard University Press.

Eisenberg, Melvin A. 1979. "Private Ordering Through Negotiation." In *The Structure of Procedure*, edited by Robert M. Cover and Owen Fiss, 115–32. Mineola, N.Y.: Foundation Press.

Ely, John Hart. 1980. *Democracy and Distrust: A Theory of Judicial Review*. Cambridge: Harvard University Press.

"Employment-at-Will Clauses." 1988. *Tallahassee Democrat*, 31 July, p. 1E.

Evans, Frederick D. 1983. "Fairness in Federal Administrative Disciplinary Proceedings: The Call for Disclosure under the *Brady* Doctrine." *University of Florida Law Review* 35: 471–91.

Feinberg, Joel. 1984. *Harm to Others. The Moral Limits of the Criminal Law*, Vol. 1. New York: Oxford University Press.

Fiss, Owen M. 1984. "Against Settlement." *Yale Law Journal* 93: 1073–90.

Fletcher, George P. 1984. "Some Unwise Reflections About Discretion." *Law and Contemporary Problems* 47: 269–86.

Flick, Geoffrey A. 1984. *Natural Justice: Principles and Practical Application*. 2d ed. Sydney: Butterworths.

Frankel, Marvin E. 1980. *Partisan Justice*. New York: Hill and Wang.

Friendly, Henry J. 1975. "Some Kind of Hearing." *University of Pennsylvania Law Review* 123: 1267–1317.

Fuller, Lon L. 1969. *The Morality of Law*. Revised edn. New Haven: Yale University Press.

_____. 1971. "Human Interaction and the Law." In *The Rule of Law*, edited by Robert Paul Wolff, 171–217. New York: Touchstone Books, Simon and Schuster.

_____. 1978. "The Forms and Limits of Adjudication." *Harvard Law Review* 92: 353–409.

_____, and Melvin Aron Eisenberg. 1972. *Contract Law*. 3rd edn. St. Paul, Minn.: West Publishing Co.

Galanter, Marc. 1979. "Why the 'Haves' Come Out Ahead: Speculations on the Limits of Legal Change." In *The Structure of Procedure*, edited by Robert M. Cover and Owen M. Fiss, 199–211. Mineola, N.Y.: The Foundation Press.

Galligan, D. J. 1986. *Discretionary Powers: A Legal Study of Official Discretion*. Oxford: Clarendon Press.

Gellhorn, Walter. 1976. "The Abuse of Occupational Licensing." *University of Chicago Law Review* 44: 6–27.

_____, Clark Byse, and Peter L. Strauss. 1979. *Administrative Law: Cases and Comments*. 7th edn. Mineola, N.Y.: Foundation Press.

Golding, Martin P. 1975. *Philosophy of Law*. Englewood Cliffs, N.J.: Prentice-Hall.

_____. 1978. "On the Adversary System and Justice." In *Philosophical Law*, edited by Richard N. Bronaugh, 98–121. Westport, Conn.: Greenwood Press.

_____. 1984. *Legal Reasoning*. New York: Borzoi Books, Alfred A. Knopf.

Goodin, Robert E. 1988. *Reasons for Welfare: The Political Theory of the Welfare State*. Princeton, N.J.: Princeton University Press.

Graglia, Lino A. 1985. "Would the Court Get 'Procedural Due Process' Cases Right If It Knew What 'Liberty' Really Means?" *Notre Dame Journal of Law, Ethics & Public Policy* 1: 813–28.

Hart, H. L. A. 1961. *The Concept of Law*. Oxford: Clarendon Press.

_____. 1983. *Essays in Jurisprudence and Philosophy*. Oxford: Clarendon Press.

Heine, William. 1981. "Ethical Problems of News Reporting." *Westminster Institute Review* 1, 1: 11.

Hewitt, D. J. 1972. *Natural Justice*. Sydney: Butterworths.

Hirshman, Linda R. 1988. "Postmodern Jurisprudence and the Problem of Administrative Discretion." *Northwestern University Law Review* 82: 646–704.

Institute for Electrical & Electronics Engineers. 1980. "Excerpts from the 'IEEE Bylaws' January 1980." In *AAAS Professional Ethics Project*, edited by Rosemary Chalk, Mark S. Frankel, and Sallie B. Chafer, 204–06. Washington, D.C.: American Association Advancement of Science.

Jones, David A. 1981. *The Law of Criminal Procedure*. Boston: Little, Brown and Co.

Latourette, Audrey Wolfson, and Robert D. King. 1988. "Judicial Intervention in the Student-University Relationship: Due Process and Contract Theories." *University of Detroit Law Review* 65: 199–258.

Law Reform Commission of Canada. 1979. *Our Criminal Law*. Ottawa: Law Reform Commission of Canada.

_____. 1982. *Criminal Law, the General Part: Liability and Defences*. Working Paper 29. Ottawa: Law Reform Commission of Canada.

_____. 1985. *Report on Independent Administrative Agencies*. Report 26. Ottawa: Law Reform Commission of Canada.

Lefas, Aubert. 1978. "A Comparison of the Concept of Natural Justice in English Administrative Law with the Corresponding General Principles of

Law and Rules of Procedure in French Administrative Law." *Queen's Law Journal* 4: 197–229.

Lorch, Robert S. 1980. *Democratic Process and Administrative Law*. Revised edn. Detroit: Wayne State University Press.

Lyons, David. 1973. "On Formal Justice." *Cornell Law Review* 58: 833–61.

_____. 1984. "Formal Justice, Moral Commitment, and Judicial Precedent." *Journal of Philosophy* 81: 580–87.

_____. 1985. "Formal Justice and Judicial Precedent." *Vanderbilt Law Review* 38: 495–512.

MacCormick, Neil. 1981. *H.L.A. Hart*. Stanford, Calif.: Stanford University Press.

Macdonald, R. A. 1980. "Judicial Review and Procedural Fairness in Administrative Law: 1." *McGill Law Journal* 25: 520–64.

_____. 1981. "A Theory of Procedural Fairness." *Windsor Yearbook of Access to Justice* 1: 3–34.

_____. 1987. "Procedural Due Process in Canadian Constitutional Law: Natural Justice and Fundamental Justice." *University of Florida Law Review* 39: 217–67.

Mashaw, Jerry. 1981a. "Administrative Due Process: The Quest for a Dignitary Theory." *Boston University Law Review* 61: 885–931.

_____. 1981b. "Conflict and Compromise Among Models of Administrative Justice." *Duke Law Journal*, 181–212.

_____. 1983. *Bureaucratic Justice: Managing Social Security Disability Claims*. New Haven: Yale University Press.

_____. 1985. *Due Process in the Administrative State*. New Haven: Yale University Press.

_____. 1987. "Dignitary Process: A Political Psychology of Liberal Democratic Citizenship." *University of Florida Law Review* 39: 433–43.

Michelman, Frank I. 1977. "Formal and Associational Aims in Procedural Due Process." In *Due Process: Nomos XVIII*, edited by J. Roland Pennock and John W. Chapman, 126–71. New York: New York University Press.

Miller, Charles A. 1977. "The Forest of Due Process of Law: The American Constitutional Tradition." In *Due Process: Nomos XVIII*, edited by J. Roland Pennock and John W. Chapman, 3–68. New York: New York University Press.

Monaghan, Henry Paul. 1977. "Of 'Liberty' and 'Property'." *Cornell Law Review* 62: 405–444.

Morris, William Otis. 1984. *Revocation of Professional Licenses by Governmental Agencies*. Charlottesville, Va.: Michie Co.

_____. 1986. "Revocation of Professional Licenses." *Mercer Law Review* 37: 789–815.

Nelson, William. 1980. "The Very Idea of Procedural Justice." *Ethics* 90: 502–11.

Organization of American States. 1969. "American Convention on Human Rights." In *The Human Rights Reader*, edited by Walter Laqueur and Barry Rubin. Philadelphia: Temple University Press, 1979.

Pierce, Richard J., Jr., Sidney A. Shapiro, and Paul R. Verkuil. 1985. *Administrative Law and Process*. Mineola, N.Y.: Foundation Press.

Posner, Richard A. 1973. "An Economic Approach to Legal Procedure and Judicial Administration." *Journal of Legal Studies* 2: 399–458.

_____. 1977. *Economic Analysis of Law*. 2d edn. Boston: Little, Brown and Co.

Radin, Margaret Jane. 1987. "Market-Inalienability." *Harvard Law Review* 100: 1849–1937.

Rawls, John. 1971. *A Theory of Justice*. Cambridge: Belknap Press, Harvard University Press.

Raz, Joseph. 1972. "Legal Principles and the Limits of Law." *Yale Law Journal* 81: 823–54.

Redish, Martin H., and Lawrence C. Marshall. 1986. "Adjudicatory Independence and the Values of Procedural Due Process." *Yale Law Journal* 95: 455–505.

"RKO License Renewals Denied." 1987. *Tallahassee Democrat*, 12 August, p. D7.

Rose-Ackerman, Susan. 1985. "Inalienability and the Theory of Property Rights." *Columbia Law Review* 85: 931–69.

Rosenblum, Victor G. 1974. "On Davis on Confining, Structuring, and Checking Administrative Discretion." In *Administrative Discretion: Problems of Decision-Making by Governmental Agencies*, edited by Clark C. Havighurst, 49–62. Dobbs Ferry, N.Y.: Oceana Publications.

_____. 1984. "Contexts and Contents of 'For Good Cause' as Criterion for Removal of Administrative Law Judges: Legal and Policy Factors." *Western New England Law Review* 6: 593–642.

Rubin, Edward L. 1984. "Due Process and the Administrative State." *California Law Review* 72: 1044–1179.

Saphire, Richard B. 1978. "Specifying Due Process Values: Toward a More Responsive Approach to Procedural Protection." *University of Pennsylvania Law Review* 127: 111–95.

Scanlon, T. M. 1977. "Due Process." In *Due Process: Nomos XVIII*, edited by J. Roland Pennock and John W. Chapman, 93–125. New York: New York University Press.

Schauer, Frederick F. 1976. "English Natural Justice and American Due Process: An Analytical Comparison." *William and Mary Law Review* 18: 47–72.

_____. 1987. "Precedent." *Stanford Law Review* 39: 571–605.

Schwartz. Bernard. 1976. *Administrative Law*. Boston: Little, Brown and Co.

Simon, Peter N. 1986. "Economic Analysis of Liberty and Property: A Critique." *University of Colorado Law Review* 57: 747–57.

Simon, William H. 1978. "The Ideology of Advocacy: Procedural Justice and Professional Ethics." *Wisconsin Law Review*, 29–144.

_____. 1983. "Legality, Bureaucracy, and Class in the Welfare System." *Yale Law Journal* 92: 1198–1269.

Smart, J. J. C. 1968. "Extreme and Restricted Utilitarianism." In *Contemporary Utilitarianism*, edited by Michael D. Bayles, 99–115. Garden City, N.Y.: Anchor Books, Doubleday & Co.

Smolla, Rodney A. 1984. "The Erosion of the Principle that the Government Must Follow Self-Imposed Rules." *Fordham Law Review* 52: 472–506.

Snoeyenbos, Milton, and John Wesley Roberts. 1983. "Ethics and the Termination of Employees." In *Business Ethics*, edited by Milton Snoeyenbos, Robert Almeder, and James Humber, 248–57. Buffalo: Prometheus Books.

Snoeyenbos, Milton, and Robert Almeder. 1983. "Ethical Hiring Practices." In *Business Ethics*, edited by Milton Snoeyenbos, Robert Almeder, and James Humber, 194–207. Buffalo: Prometheus Books.

Stevenson, Charles L. 1963. *Facts and Values: Studies in Ethical Analysis*. New Haven: Yale University Press.

Summers, Robert S. 1974. "Evaluating and Improving Legal Processes—A Plea for 'Process Values'." *Cornell Law Review* 60: 1–52.

_____. 1978. "Comment: 'On the Adversary System and Justice'." In *Philosophical Law*, edited by Richard N. Bronaugh, 122–26. Westport, Conn.: Greenwood Press.

Symposium on Administrative Law. 1987. "The Uneasy Constitutional Status of the Administrative Agencies." *American University Law Review* 36: 277–601.

Terrell, Timothy P. 1982. "'Property', 'Due Process', and the Distinction Between Definition and Theory in Legal Analysis." *Georgetown Law Review* 70: 861–941.

_____. 1985 "Liberty: The Concept and Its Constitutional Context." *Notre Dame Journal of Law, Ethics & Public Policy* 1: 545–93.

_____. 1987a. "Liberty and Responsibility in the Land of 'New Property': Exploring the Limits of Procedural Due Process." *University of Florida Law Review* 39: 351–86.

_____. 1987b. "Rights and Wrongs in the Rush to Repose: On the Jurisprudential Dangers of Alternative Dispute Resolution." *Emory Law Journal* 36: 541–56.

Thibaut, John, and Laurens Walker. 1975. *Procedural Justice: A Psychological Analysis*. Hillsdale, N.J.: Laurence Erlblaum Associates, Publishers.

_____. 1978. "A Theory of Procedure." *California Law Review* 66: 541–66.

Tullock, Gordon. 1980. *Trials on Trial*. New York: Columbia University Press.

United Nations. 1966. "International Covenant on Civil and Political Rights." In Zaim M. Nedjati, *Human Rights Under the European Convention*. Amsterdam: North-Holland Publishing Co., 1978.

Verkuil, Paul. R. 1986. "Crosscurrents in Anglo-American Administrative Law." *William and Mary Law Review* 27: 685–715.

Wade, H. W. R. 1982. *Administrative Law*. 5th ed. Oxford: Clarendon Press.

Werhane, Patricia. 1984. "Individual Rights in Business." In *Just Business*, edited by Tom Regan, 100–28. New York: Random House.

Westin, Alan F., and Alfred G. Feliu, eds. 1988. *Resolving Employment Disputes without Litigation*. Washington, D.C.: Bureau of National Affairs.

Whitebread, Charles H. 1980. *Criminal Procedure: An Analysis of Constitutional Cases and Concepts*. Mineola, N.Y.: Foundation Press.

Williams, Stephen F. 1983. "Liberty and Property: The Problem of Government Benefits." *Journal of Legal Studies* 12: 3–40.

Winston, Kenneth I. 1974. "On Treating Like Cases Alike." *California Law Review* 62: 1–39.

Wright, George R. 1987. "A Contractual Approach to Due Process." *Valparaiso University Law Review* 21: 527–62.

TABLE OF CASES

INDEX

Law and Philosophy Library

Publications:

1. E. Bulygin, J.-L. Gardies and I. Niiniluoto (eds.): *Man, Law and Modern Forms of Life.* With an Introduction by M. D. Bayles. 1985 ISBN 90-277-1869-5
2. W. Sadurski: *Giving Desert Its Due.* Social Justice and Legal Theory. 1985 ISBN 90-277-1941-1
3. N. MacCormick and O. Weinberger: *An Institutional Theory of Law.* New Approaches to Legal Positivism. 1986 ISBN 90-277-2079-7
4. A. Aarnio: *The Rational as Reasonable.* A Treatise on Legal Justification. 1987 ISBN 90-277-2276-5
5. M. D. Bayles: *Principles of Law.* A Normative Analysis. 1987 ISBN Hb: 90-277-2412-1; Pb: 90-277-2413-X
6. A. Soeteman: *Logic in Law.* Remarks on Logic and Rationality in Normative Reasoning, Especially in Law. 1989 ISBN 0-7923-0042-4
7. C. T. Sistare: *Responsibility and Criminal Liability.* 1989 ISBN 0-7923-0396-2
8. A. Peczenik: *On Law and Reason.* 1989 ISBN 0-7923-0444-6
9. W. Sadurski: *Moral Pluralism and Legal Neutrality.* 1990 ISBN 0-7923-0565-5
10. M. D. Bayles: *Procedural Justice.* Allocating to Individuals. 1990 ISBN 0-7923-0567-1
11. P. Nerhot (ed.): *Law, Interpretation and Reality.* Essays in Epistemology, Hermeneutics and Jurisprudence. 1990 ISBN 0-7923-0593-0

KLUWER ACADEMIC PUBLISHERS – DORDRECHT / BOSTON / LONDON